Green's book makes a major contribution to the sociology of popular music. Through introducing the term 'peak music experience' Green brings compelling new insights regarding the everyday meaning of popular music and its resonance with memory and emotion. Of equal importance is Green's consideration of how technological developments since the early 2000s also critically inform the way that people (re)experience music in their daily lives. Drawing on ethnographic research conducted in the city of Brisbane, the state capital of Queensland, Australia, Green also brings fresh perspectives to our understanding of the connections between local, trans-local and global scenes. This book will be essential reading for popular music scholars interested in music's significance as an everyday resource.

—*Andy Bennett (Griffith University)*

CW00684113

Peak Music Experiences

Peak music experiences are a recurring feature of popular music journalism, biography and fan culture, where they are often credited as pivotal in people's relationships with music and in their lives more generally. Ben Green investigates the phenomenon from a social and cultural perspective, including discussions of peak music experiences as sources of inspiration and influence; as a core motivation for ongoing musical and social activity; the significance of live music experiences; and the key role of peak music experiences in defining and perpetuating music scenes. The book draws from both global media analysis and situated ethnographic research in the dance, hip hop, indie and rock 'n' roll music scenes of Brisbane, Australia, including participant observation and in-depth interviews. These case studies demonstrate the methodological value of peak music experiences as a lens through which to understand individual and collective musical life. The theoretical analysis is interwoven with selected interview data, illuminating the profound and everyday ways that music informs people's lives. The book will therefore be of interest to the interdisciplinary field of popular music studies as well as sociology and cultural studies beyond the study of music.

Dr Ben Green is a cultural sociologist with interests in popular music and youth studies. He is a member of the Griffith Centre for Social and Cultural Research and teaches at Griffith University. Ben's work exploring musical experience in memory, identity and belonging has been published in journals including *Sociology*, *Popular Music* and *Journal of Sociology* and in edited books including *The Routledge Companion to Popular Music History and Heritage*.

Routledge Studies in Popular Music

For more information about this series, please visit: https://www.routledge.com/music/series/RSPM

Peak Music Experiences

A New Perspective on Popular Music, Identity and Scenes

Ben Green

Routledge
Taylor & Francis Group

LONDON AND NEW YORK

First published 2022
by Routledge
2 Park Square, Milton Park, Abingdon, Oxon OX14 4RN

and by Routledge
605 Third Avenue, New York, NY 10158

Routledge is an imprint of the Taylor & Francis Group, an informa business

British Library Cataloguing-in-Publication Data
A catalogue record for this book is available from the British Library

Library of Congress Cataloging-in-Publication Data
A catalog record has been requested for this book

ISBN: 978-0-367-55384-5 (hbk)
ISBN: 978-0-367-55385-2 (pbk)
ISBN: 978-1-003-09324-4 (ebk)

DOI: 10.4324/9781003093244

Typeset in Times New Roman
by codeMantra

For Christine

Contents

Acknowledgements

My sincere thanks to each person who participated in the research. Their stories are the heart of this book and I hope I have done justice to their generosity and passion. Thanks to Andy Bennett and Christine Feldman-Barrett for their mentorship and encouragement during my research and crucial feedback on early manuscripts. Thanks again to Andy for welcoming me so warmly into the academic world and nurturing the hopeful idea that reaches fruition here. I thank the Griffith Centre for Social and Cultural Research and the Griffith University School of Humanities, Languages and Social Science for institutional support. The International Association for the Study of Popular Music – Australia/New Zealand Branch and The Australian Sociological Association – Youth Thematic Group provided supportive environments for my ideas to be shared and developed, and I thank my colleagues and friends. Finally, thanks to Christine O'Neill for her endlessly inspiring belief and support, which made this book possible.

1 Introducing peak music experiences

Why do people engage with music, by listening to it, making it and in myriad other ways, often involving substantial investments of time, energy and money? To answer this, we are led first of all to ask what music can do, and how. This bundle of questions is fundamental to understanding popular music as a social, cultural and economic phenomenon. As it happens, they are questions that the fans, musicians and others who engage most intently with popular music are inclined to answer, more or less explicitly and sometimes spectacularly, when they talk about music and about themselves. This is epitomised by the tendency to single out experiences with music that are especially affecting, meaningful and memorable, which I call 'peak music experiences'.

Peak music experiences are remembered and described for a range of purposes. The evaluation of songs and artists in popular music, from personal favourites to widely recognised canons, is justified not only by their technical features and objective criteria but more often by reference to *that* time they induced *that* effect. The meanings that people attribute to songs depend in large part on specific encounters with them, subjectively linking music with people, events and inner states. In the same way, musical experiences are remembered as windows onto constellations of events, people, places and past selves. People narrate their biographical trajectories and turns through successive musical epiphanies, which chart processes like becoming a fan ('When I first heard…') and becoming a musician ('That's when I knew I wanted to…'), as well as broader developments like youthful identity and independence (first album, first concert, first dance, with these categories themselves tracing generational changes). Occasionally, a peak music experience is credited with profound importance as a pivotal moment that changed someone's life. More often, the transcendent, rewarding, healing or simply satisfying experiences associated with certain music and musical practices are cited as motivations for ongoing commitments: to performing, recording, attending and listening.

Underlying these various narratives about peak music experiences is a fundamental orientation towards music. It is the conscious belief and embodied knowledge that music has a unique capacity to create affecting and

DOI: 10.4324/9781003093244-1

meaningful experiences, which can affirm or renew our identities, our relationships to other people and our world. This is a major reason why people value music and a factor that guides their engagements with it. It is a key element of the ideology of popular music, reproduced partly by the narratives described above. The primary intention of this book is to take seriously the claims that are made about peak music experiences. This means paying attention and understanding them on their own terms, as well as critically analysing their causes and effects.

A popular concept

This book will present and consider many instances of people speaking about peak music experiences, drawing on original interviews and media sources. The sheer proliferation of these stories is a central theme. In selecting a first example that is especially clear in its claims about what music can do and why it matters, a reliable source is Bruce Springsteen, a rock musician known for addressing such themes in his performances and interviews. In 2016, he offered the following quote to an Australian journalist (Hann 2016):

> It's coming on stage with the idea: OK, well the stakes that are involved this evening are quite high. I don't know exactly who's in the crowd. But I know that my life was changed in an instant by something that people thought was purely junk – pop music records. And you can change someone's life in three minutes with the right song. I still believe that to this day. You can bend the course of their development, what they think is important, of how vital and alive they feel. You can contextualise very, very difficult experiences. Songs are pretty good at that. So all these are the stakes that are laid out on the table when you come out at night. And I still take those stakes seriously after all that time, if not more so now, as the light grows slightly dimmer. I come out believing there's no tomorrow night, there wasn't last night, there's just tonight. And I have built up the skills to be able to provide, under the right conditions, a certain transcendent evening, hopefully an evening you'll remember when you go home. Not that you'll just remember it was a good concert, but you'll remember the possibilities the evening laid out in front of you, as far as where you could take your life, or how you're thinking about your friends, or your wife or your girlfriend, or your best pal, or your job, your work, what you want to do with your life. These are all things, I believe, that music can accommodate and can provide service in. That's what we try to deliver.

Springsteen defines the 'stakes' of popular music in terms of what it can provide and accommodate, and on this he is clear: it can change someone's life. Popular music can affect how a person thinks and how they feel, generally or about certain experiences, people and problems. As to how music can do this, Springsteen is equally clear that it happens in an instant. The instant might last for a song or a whole evening, and indeed music can create a transcendent moment that is experienced as outside the rest of life and time, so there is no 'last night' nor 'tomorrow night' but only 'tonight'. However, such a moment lays out possibilities stretching into the future, and is remembered long after it has passed. In fact, moments like this are anticipated and worked for, by musicians and audiences. This points to the dual character of transcendent musical experiences: people can lose themselves 'in the moment', but through the search for and reflection on such moments, they can find themselves. According to the quote above, Springsteen draws his motivation as a career musician from the memory of what popular music has done for him in an instant, and he finds purpose in trying to provide the same for others.

It is reported that Springsteen made this speech 'without pause, without any errs or urrms, in a single perfect paragraph, that requires not one piece of tidying in the transcription' (Hann 2016). This presents the statement itself as a kind of performance, whether conscious or not; the words and sentiment were well worn if not rehearsed. Springsteen had in fact spoken of such instants in the past, beginning with his childhood memory of watching Elvis Presley perform 'Hound Dog' on television's *The Ed Sullivan Show*: 'When I heard it, it just shot straight through to my brain. And I realized, suddenly, that there was more to life than what I'd been living' (Kreps 2016). In any case, Bruce Springsteen was far from the first musician, or music fan, to say such things. In challenging the perception of 'pop music records' as 'junk', he is tracing narratives of their power and significance that must by now be familiar to many fans of popular music. Members of the Beatles, with whom Springsteen credits another life-defining experience watching *The Ed Sullivan Show* again in 1964, have been quoted numerous times about encounters with the music of Elvis Presley and his contemporaries that touched and changed their own lives (as discussed in Chapter 4). It is likely that Springsteen had heard his musical heroes speak in this way. His story about 'Hound Dog' was told on a BBC radio programme called *Desert Island Discs*, on which such anecdotes are frequently related by guests. However, the narrative is not restricted to famous musicians. Cultural anthropologist Daniel Cavicchi (1998) found the practice of talking about musical 'epiphanies' to be common among Springsteen's own fans in the 1990s. The proliferation of these stories in particular groups and media suggests a phenomenon of cultural practice as well as musical experience.

The currency of peak music experiences as a concept is demonstrated by its use in marketing. During the television broadcast of the Australian Football League Grand Final in 2012, soft drink manufacturer Coca-Cola debuted a commercial that 'follows a young girl at a music festival as she is lifted above the crowd to view the stage, experiencing a memorable moment that she will forever connect to the song being played', culminating in the tagline, 'every moment has a song' (Campaign Brief 2012). References to such transcendent experiences are used to promote live music events themselves. These events now form part of the 'experience economy', in which the business opportunities for music lie in facilitating and designing settings for certain kinds of experiential encounters as opposed to selling services or objects (Pearce 2013). This might explain why, even as music consumption is domesticated and individualised, live performance is an increasingly lucrative and important sector of the broader music industry (Frith 2007a). At the same time, music is also understood to have profound effects in private and intimate experiences. This was played upon by a 2015 poster campaign for digital music platform Pandora, in which public transport users were invited to share their personal 'music journey' using such social media hashtags as #firstsong, #firstgig and #firstkiss (Lowe 2015). As in the Coca-Cola advertisement, the implication is that every moment has a song and, likewise, every song has a moment.

These examples begin to illuminate two related ways in which music assumes importance for individuals and groups. First, music sometimes gives rise to singular experiences that stand out from other experience, as especially affecting or meaningful and occasionally transcendent in a holistic sense. People cherish these experiences and consciously seek them out, such that they structure ongoing activity as a teleological cause. Second, these experiences form the basis of stories that are shared by musicians and music fans who attribute autobiographical meaning and sometimes profound consequences to them. This is a popular way to remember and explain things about music and also about people's lives. It would therefore seem that peak music experiences play no small part in music's social and cultural importance. This book seeks to develop a sociological theory of peak music experiences, and it will be argued that this perspective offers new insight into the relationships between popular music, identity, memory and embodied practice, within the context of music scenes and in everyday life.

Defining peak music experiences

The term 'peak music experiences' captures the essential elements of the phenomenon. They are *peaks* because their defining characteristic is that they stand out – in perception, in memory and in description. While the term is reminiscent of Maslow's (1962) concept of 'peak experiences', it is not intended to import his psychological theories such as a hierarchy of needs. However, the similarity is apt, as both concepts (discussed further in Chapter 2) use the connotations of 'peaks' to distinguish especially affecting and meaningful experiences from general experience, while also recognising how they arise out of and influence the rest of life. As philosopher John Dewey (2004b: 269 [1934]) states, 'Mountain peaks do not float unsupported; they do not even just rest upon the earth. They *are* the earth in one of its manifest operations'. Meanwhile, the presence of peaks is not without consequences for the surrounding earth. Dewey's aesthetic philosophy is concerned with restoring continuity between 'the refined and intensified forms of experience that are works of art', and everyday experience (ibid.: 268). Likewise, this book will consider what makes peak music experiences distinct as well as how they relate to the rest of musical experience and social life. In Chapter 2, Dewey's pragmatist philosophy will help to frame this approach, including his relevant definition of 'an experience' as an aesthetically and emotionally unified arc of doing and undergoing. However, this is only a starting point for sociological inquiry into how those aesthetic and emotional parameters are constructed. In other words, this book will consider how peaks in musical experience are socially defined, as well as how they define the social.

In focusing on *experience*, this book will build on what have been termed 'post-cultural turn studies in the sociology of popular music' (Bennett 2008: 429). As it has been recognised that cultural meanings and social identities are produced through the continuing, complex interaction of various influences, in relation to which people exercise awareness and agency, the detail of subjective, lived experience has come to the fore. Study that is close to experience has proved especially important in relation to music, as the very malleability of music's meaning is key to its social significance. Accordingly, as detailed in Chapter 2, the focus of research has shifted from semiotic readings of what music signifies within structurally determined subcultures, to ethnographic explorations of locally articulated, subjective appropriations of music within more loosely bounded scenes and individualised lifestyles. Still, work in this area has been more concerned with general experience that is typical of particular genres, groups and perspectives, than with discrete and extraordinary experiences that might have unique significance. An understandable emphasis is placed on the study of existent meanings, established practices and objectified tastes. There has been a growing interest in how music forms part of 'everyday life' (DeNora 2000; Vroomen 2004; Bennett 2005) and this is associated with a focus on the 'mundane' aspects of experience. However, the now substantial body of work arguing that musical taste and practices are not pre-determined opens up questions about why and how people do commence, continue and alter their relationships with music. A burgeoning body of work considering social memory and social ageing in relation to music (Strong 2011; Bennett 2013) begins to address the relationship of popular music and biography, and the study of peak music experiences advances these understandings. Similarly, the broad abandonment of a simplistic account of unilateral, universal media effects leaves open the question of how music might actually affect people and, as DeNora (2004) asks, how music 'gets into' social reality. The study of peak music experiences responds directly to these questions. The focus on experience is a holistic approach, placing attention on the meeting between music and a person in a specific context, and taking into account perception and reaction, thought and feeling, doing and undergoing. Much emphasis will be placed on the contiguities, interactions and co-productive relationships between these dualisms, drawing on perspectives from pragmatist philosophy and from the sociology of music (DeNora 2004; Hennion 2010) and emotions (Ahmed 2004; Crossley 1998).

This book and the concept it names are concerned with *musical* experience, even though music itself is only one part of the cultural worlds that will be considered. Subcultures involve a range of stylistic practices, objects and symbols clustered around music consumption (see for example Hebdige 1979), and music scenes are understood to comprise both 'hard infrastructure' such as physical spaces and 'soft infrastructure' such as social networks (Stahl 2004). In terms of experiences, people might attribute profound feelings and meanings to a personal encounter with a favourite musician, an achievement in their own musical career, or a social interaction far away from the stage at a music festival, to use examples that arose in the ethnographic research for this book. However, I am most interested in experiences to which 'music's specifically *musical* properties' contribute (DeNora 2004: 36; emphasis in original). I do not suggest that it is useful or even possible to separate these musical properties entirely from other aspects of a peak music experience. In fact, a major benefit of considering music in terms of specific experiences is that it brings forward the multitude of internal and external factors that inform music's meaning and effects for a particular individual at a particular time. On one hand, this allows a degree of contingency, consistently with the popular belief in fateful encounters and people's reflexive attunement to settings and atmospheres around musical experience. By the same token, this perspective highlights people's conscious attempts to construct certain kinds of musical experience, employing both internal techniques and external technologies, perhaps most clearly apparent in the combination of music with recreational drugs (see Chapter 8). However, as suggested in its opening lines, this book will engage as much as possible with the question of what is so special about *music* that it might be said to define or change someone's life. In this regard, a useful framework is provided by DeNora (2000, 2004), who points out that music is a temporal medium that structures experience in time, with specific affordances that are both inherent and accrued. Additionally, Hennion's (2010) 'pragmatics of taste' provides a model of co-productive encounters between people and music, engaging listening techniques that are developed through use and to which music responds. While these micro-social perspectives have been thought to pose the risk of privileging aesthetic over social analysis (Prior 2011), their benefit here on the contrary is to enable consideration of how the listening or performing subject is not prior to experience, but constructed through it. Paradoxically, in the study of peak music experiences, a focus on discrete moments makes it possible to see beyond static texts and preformed listeners to consider instead how each is produced in encounters over time, within social and cultural contexts.

The interactional perspective described here challenges the fixity of musical texts and therefore problematises distinctions between popular and other kinds of music. Peak music experiences can easily be found in literature about classical music and folk music. For example, biographies of composer George Gershwin describe a 'flashing revelation' he experienced as a child in 1908, when by chance he overheard a fellow student's violin recitation of Dvořák's *Humoresque* (Ross 2009: 155). Sociologist Claudio Benzecry (2011: 66) observes that opera fans commonly describe an 'instant of revelation' among their first encounters with live performance, creating an intense attraction that they are then compelled to explore and organise. Researchers in psychology have collected a wealth of examples of 'strong experiences' and 'peak experiences' with classical music in particular, as well as diverse other forms (Gabrielsson 2011; Panzarella 1980; see Chapter 2). Ethnomusicologist Judith Becker (2004) casts a deliberately wide net in considering traditional, non-Western musical rituals (folk music in the strictest sense), as well as both religious and secular performance and consumption in post-industrial societies, as settings for trance states and strong emotional responses to music. Becker hypothesises that the worldwide linkage of music and religious ecstasy, as well as its parallels in some secular musical experiences, has a physiological human basis. Moving to the blurred boundary between folk and popular music, influential rock figure Bob Dylan (2004: 244) recalls an instant 'epiphany' when he first heard a recording of US folk singer Woody Guthrie in 1959. Like Frith (1998: 19), I prefer to begin from the principle that there is no difference between high and low culture and then to consider how such difference is produced as a social fact. However, in light of that social fact, this book is specifically concerned with peak music experiences in relation to *popular music*, referring to certain historical, cultural and material frameworks as well as a certain history of academic research. Popular music is notoriously difficult to define and some of its sociological interest lies in classificatory contests and tensions. Perhaps the most important distinctions are against art music, including and best known through classical music, and on the other hand folk music, although these are not purely external points of comparison but also represent tendencies within popular music (as the foregoing examples suggest). Popular music is partly a form of popular or folk culture with social functions, partly an art form that produces aesthetic experience and holds cultural value, and partly in tension with both as a mass commodity with economic ends (Frith 1998: 42–43; Gracyk 2001: 18–23; Shuker 2001: 7–9). In addition to the technological, historical and economic features of popular music, Frith (in Advisory Editors 2005: 134) adds 'music made for social and bodily pleasure', suggesting that it is partly defined by an emphasis on certain kinds of experience. Stratton (1983) observes that in accordance with its prevailing Romantic discourse, popular music can only be recognised by experience in a process that is non-analytical and magical. Instead of articulable criteria, one learns through direct involvement to 'know' popular music and to distinguish sub-categories such as rock music, as well as to judge 'good' popular music. This suggests an important role for peak music experiences as revelations and ideals, and this book will consider how they are grounded in and feed back into systems of classification and evaluation.

A problem with studying experience is that 'one can never truly move beyond one's own; another person's experience can be shared only through the artifice of expression' (Cavicchi 1998: 19). It is my intention to examine that artifice as an object of interest in itself. This is a study of peak music experiences as *stories* through which reality is remembered and explained. The aim is not to determine their objective truth or falsity, since people act on the basis of their understandings and if they define situations as real, those situations are real in their consequences (Minichiello et al. 2008: 130–131). The more productive questions are how the understandings reflected in stories about peak music experiences are constructed, and what is the effect of these stories and understandings. This inquiry will make use of Denzin's (2001) sociological formulation of 'epiphanies': interactional moments that leave marks on people's lives as turning points and manifestations of personal character. Epiphanies are narrative resources with which people interpret their lives for themselves and others, and they provide a focal point for studying lives in their social contexts. Considering peak music experiences as epiphanies is a way of recognising music's role in identity construction, building on previous work regarding musical memory (DeNora 2000; Strong 2011) and ageing music fans (Bennett 2013). As Denzin (2001) observes, the meaning of epiphanies is continually reconstructed and this is shaped by group contexts and cultural texts. Peak music experiences can be understood as collective productions, as well as a means by which cultural narratives are in turn reproduced and reshaped. For example, the quote from Bruce Springsteen presented earlier in this chapter implicitly constructs the musician as someone who both plays for high stakes and works hard to provide a service; the listener as someone with a job, a girlfriend or wife and a best pal; musical experience as a source of felt vitality and a resource for purposive reflection, and perhaps at a deeper level, life as a reflexive moral project. Peak music experiences are both shaped by and contribute to the discursive construction of ways of experiencing and, therefore, experiences and the subjects who have them.

In considering the structuring role of discourse, I will not seek to separate meaning and thought from feeling and sensation, but to consider how they are related, following the approaches of sociologists Nick Crossley (1998) and, in particular, Sara Ahmed (2004, 2014). Ahmed's cultural politics of emotion recognises that meaning is mediated by feelings, and those feelings rehearse and test associations developed over a lifetime of encounters, in which the most intense feelings 'stick'. Encounters and the feelings produced in them are shaped by discursive expectations, and feelings in turn are an important way that discourse acts on and constructs the self. It will be shown that this relationship between meaning and feeling is key to music's unique power and significance. The affective intensity and frequently ineffable qualities of peak music experiences are informed by, and contribute to, cumulative judgements of value and meaning. Peak music experiences thus leave lasting impressions, informing people's future attitudes to the objects (songs, artists, places) that they hold responsible for those feelings. Accordingly, these experiences offer insight into how encounters with music can affect or reorient people in enduring ways, a phenomenon to which music fans are reflexively, expectantly attuned. Peak music experiences may involve the loss or transcendence of the self in sensuous activity and collective affect, but the same experiences may also be rationalised within the narrative, purposive construction of the self. Exploring these two aspects of peak music experiences contributes to the reconciliation of two apparently competing macro-social theories of contemporary life, namely affective sociality (e.g. Maffesoli 1996) on the one hand and reflexive individualisation (e.g. Giddens 1991) on the other.

Scope and methods

Since peak music experiences are always grounded in social and cultural contexts, it is important to consider the phenomenon within specific settings. The settings considered in this book are four music scenes in Brisbane, Australia, which are local articulations of global genres: the dance music scene, the hip hop music scene, the indie music scene and the rock 'n' roll scene. As discussed in more detail below, although Brisbane may still be considered a 'second-tier' music city in comparison to the larger and more established cultural capitals of Sydney and Melbourne (Bennett and Rogers 2018), it is nevertheless a cosmopolitan metropolis with a firm place in trans-local cultural networks including live music touring circuits. Brisbane is therefore representative of global trends in contemporary music production and consumption, as much as any place can claim this. The case studies in this book will demonstrate the utility of peak music experiences as a conceptual lens with which to analyse music scenes, although some of the chapters will have a more individual and micro-social focus. Further, as a consequence of the case studies, this book presents an ethnographic study of the four chosen music scenes. The picture that emerges from the peak music experiences of scene participants will be shown to provide significant insight into the collective identities of the scenes, especially in terms of the affective aesthetic underlying the variety of activities and situations that comprise each one. This perspective is an important complement to the more objective study of a scene's infrastructure and history.

The scholarly concept of scene can be distinguished from community, place and genre, although each of these plays a role in scenes. According to Straw's (1991: 373) influential definition, a scene is a cultural space in which a range of musical practices may coexist and interact, within various processes of differentiation and according to varying trajectories of change. Consistently with this description, a substantial amount of research has identified local, trans-local and virtual dimensions to music scenes, which overlap and interact (Peterson and Bennett 2004). Thus, the concept can be applied to the dance, hip hop, indie and rock 'n' roll scenes of Brisbane, which are local articulations of trans-local scenes, while at the same time they all form part of an overall, local Brisbane scene. This also includes other sub-scenes that will not be covered in any detail here, such as the Brisbane metal and punk scenes, for example, although these and others will be mentioned in passing. Building on the tripartite model of local, trans-local and virtual scenes, Bennett (2013: 60) adds the concept of affective scene, which refers to a shared sense of sceneness between individuals who are not directly visible to each other, but knowingly consume the same music and related media and above all, make 'a similar sort of sense out of what they are hearing, reading and watching, based on their shared generational memories and cultural experience of that music'. Peak music experiences can be seen as a structured and structuring aspect of this shared sense-making, as collective ideals and frames for making sense of musical experience. I will therefore explore how peak music experiences anchor affective sceneness, specifically as an aspect of local and trans-local scene activity and identification. Bennett and Rogers (2016) develop the affective aspect of scenes by analysing how the 'predominant past-tense and memory-based nature' (ibid.: 34) of music scenes informs their ongoing articulation in the present. They argue that despite a lack of attention to this retrospective nature, the study of cultural memory is important to the understanding of music scenes. Peak music experiences, as culturally grounded productions of memory and identity, will be shown to contribute to this understanding.

Brisbane is the capital of the north-eastern state of Queensland and the third most populous city in Australia with a population of over 2 million. The city's indie music scene in particular has been the subject of previous research by Rogers (2008) and Bennett and Rogers (2016). Rogers (2008) observes that over the last three decades Brisbane has grown from a so-called 'large country town' to a rapidly developing metropolitan centre. Consistently with this history, the local music scene has progressed from notions of 'insularity, punk, isolation and persecution' within a highly conservative political and cultural setting, to a more global, ambitious and professional image with broader public acceptance, peaking with the recognition of Brisbane as a music industry 'global hotspot' by *Billboard Magazine* in 2007 (ibid.: 642). This narrative is reflected in a popular book (reprinted twice to date) about Brisbane's music history from the 1970s to the turn of the millennium, entitled *Pig City: From The Saints to Savage Garden* (Stafford 2004), along with other recent cultural texts including a State Library of Queensland exhibition entitled *Live!: Queensland Band Culture* (2012) and an Australian Broadcasting Corporation documentary entitled *Stranded: The Saints & The Birth of Punk in Joh Bjelke-Peterson's Brisbane* (Ou 2015), referring to the conservative State Premier who served from 1968 to 1987. Despite this narrative, Brisbane continues to demonstrate qualities that Bennett and Rogers (2016: 96, 113) attribute to peripheral cities with smaller population density, including a fluctuating live music infrastructure that is highly responsive to policy changes and 'architectural churn', as well as relatively porous boundaries between the audiences for given styles. The overlapping local music scenes are oriented around live performance venues ranging from houses and other repurposed spaces, through small bars and larger clubs to major entertainment venues and festivals.

Brisbane's dance, hip hop, indie and rock 'n' roll music scenes are local articulations of global, mass-mediated genres and trans-local scenes that are documented to varying degrees in academic literature. Dance music refers here to what is increasingly called 'electronic dance music' or 'EDM', typically produced using synthesised and sampled musical elements with an emphasis on continuous beats, and usually reproduced in clubs by DJs and live 'P.A.' or personal appearances by producers, in contexts of collective dancing (see for example Thornton 1995; Bennett 1999a; Malbon 1999; Riley et al. 2010). Hip hop is a multi-dimensional cultural system encompassing dance, visual art and postural/style elements as well as music, originating in African American urban culture in the 1970s (Tate 2003). The primary musical elements of 'rapping' (rhythmically spoken and often rhyming vocals) over characteristic beats and the associated techniques of deejaying and sampling (methods of appropriating and repeating parts of existing recordings) have been globally influential and adapted to various local contexts (see for example Bennett 1999b, c; Mitchell 2003; Schloss 2004). Indie is less defined by specific musical elements and is instead positioned at the intersection of various aesthetic, social and commercial phenomena (Hibbett 2005), encompassing a mixed bag of practical, historical and aesthetic ideologies (Rogers 2008). As the name derived from 'independent' suggests, it is self-defined in opposition to the economic, political and aesthetic values of a perceived mainstream. Like punk, the term has been associated with specific stylistic choices such as 'jangly' guitars and overtly amateur production values (Bennett 2001; Bannister 2006), but especially in this century it has been defined partly by conscious eclecticism (Rogers 2008). By contrast, rock 'n' roll involves relatively clear musical dimensions as well as attitudinal and visual style. The term rock 'n' roll is typically used in popular music literature to refer to a classic style developed from the late 1940s to the early 1960s, typified in its influential guitar-centred form by Chuck Berry (see for example Bradley 1992). However, I will be using the term in accordance with the emphatic self-description of participants in a local Brisbane scene, within a trans-local scene in at least Australia, parts of Europe and the United States. For them, the term refers to an overtly hedonistic culture involving a guitar-centred musical mix of garage rock, punk and hard rock, with accompanying stylistic elements such as denim, leather jackets and tattoos.

My ethnographic fieldwork in the Brisbane dance, hip hop, indie and rock 'n' roll music scenes was conducted between February and November 2015, building on a small pilot study in 2012, and involved three methods.

These were participant observation in activities of music consumption and production, such as attending gigs (live performances) and club events as well as performing as a musician in those contexts; reviews of secondary data sources in local and global media relevant to the scenes in question; and, most importantly in light of the research questions set out in this chapter, in-depth interviews with 44 people who participated in the respective scenes by variously listening to, performing and working in the production or promotion of live and recorded music. To an extent this was 'insider research', as I was interested in the topic of peak music experiences partly because of my own memories of powerful experiences with music that I feel have affected the course of my life. In this regard, I had probably been influenced by my eager and sustained consumption of such narratives in the music press, popular literature, peer group discussions and so on. Prior to this research, I had participated in the Brisbane indie music scene in various capacities for more than 15 years and during the fieldwork I performed regularly as a member of an indie rock band. This involvement was helpful in designing the research and recruiting some participants, but it also threw into stark relief the limitations of my knowledge and access in other cultural spaces, such as the hip hop scene. I began by recruiting less than ten participants with whom I was already acquainted or who I met at events, then used chain or 'snowball' sampling (Minichiello et al. 2008: 172–173), which enabled access to people with whom I had no prior relationship and avoided the prejudice of a researcher-selected sample, in which I would have decided who belonged to particular scenes. The total sample comprised 20 women and 24 men between the ages of 23 and 58, who participated in the various scenes as music listeners, musicians, event organisers, venue workers, media workers and in other capacities, which were often multiple (see Appendix 1 for more information). Pursuant to the conditions of ethical approval from Griffith University, pseudonyms have been used in this book to preserve the anonymity of interview participants. As to participant observation, during the research period I attended 68 music events in Brisbane, usually comprising multiple live performances or DJ sets. Many of these events involved interview participants in various roles and I included my own performances in the study. I recorded my observations of all events in a fieldwork diary running to just under 10,000 words. Prior to and during the participant observation and interview period, I reviewed secondary data sources such as advertising, event promotion, music press, biographies and documentaries, so as to examine the cultural texts relevant to peak music experiences and the scenes in question.

In studying the subjective phenomenon of peak music experiences, in-depth interviews were the primary source of data. In-depth interviews are a means to elicit information about individuals' perceptions and constructions of reality (Sarantakos 2005: 134; Minichiello et al. 2008: 63). The interview questions were open-ended, giving participants the opportunity to elaborate on their responses to my questions and, in so doing, to open new areas of discussion. However, in order to study a particular phenomenon, interviews were semi-structured through the use of funnelling questions to ensure key aspects of the research topic were addressed (Minichiello et al. 2008: 51–52). The interviews were broadly biographical in shape and the basic topics included personal background and context; the development of the informant's interest, involvement and preferences in relation to music; direct questions about peak music experiences, including where relevant in specific roles, such as performer or listener; and current interests and practices with music. One aim of the interviews was to see whether and how people would draw upon their peak music experiences in discussing musical practices, contexts and developments, before being asked specifically about such experiences. This did turn out to be a common way of answering the more general questions, so perhaps the broadest and most fundamental finding from this research was that these music scene participants did indeed tend to discuss music, and themselves, by reference to peak music experiences. Numerous examples are provided throughout the following chapters and where relevant, these are placed alongside examples from popular media, to illustrate particular ways of speaking about music.

Outline of this book

Since this book is the first study of peak music experiences from a social and cultural perspective, Chapter 2 will consider why sociology and cultural studies have not mirrored the popular fascination with singular, extraordinary experiences. The absence is explained in part by a historical suspicion of subjective experience as an object of study, although such experience has increasingly come to the fore with the cultural turn summarised earlier. The study of peak music experiences builds on and advances particular disciplinary directions in relation to popular music, and particular theoretical approaches from sociology more broadly, including interpretive biography and the sociology of emotion and of memory. These approaches are united in John Dewey's pragmatist philosophy of experience.

The next three chapters consider the main ways in which peak music experiences are situated at the nexus of music and identity and exemplify their interaction. Chapter 3 considers how peak music experiences are used narratively to map a person's history of listening, through which music and biography are linked and take meaning from each other. With reference to examples from popular and academic literature and research interviews, the chapter considers three prominent tropes through which peak music experiences are woven into such histories. These are first encounters, referring to a person's first experience of a particular musical object such as a song, artist or genre; gateway experiences, in which possible directions of music listening are revealed or made appealing; and conversion experiences, which are credited with a change in the listener's taste and consequent identity, for example in becoming a fan. These tropes are common across popular music genres and therefore reveal both similarities and differences in the priorities of listeners. By describing their first encounters, gateway experiences and conversion experiences, people situate themselves in relation to collective orientations to music and the values underlying them, while also emphasising their own uniqueness and agency. These narratives all privilege responses to music which are surprising, emotional and physical, thus promoting notions of natural affinity and of music acting on people. They enable and to an extent require people to present their relationships to popular music as personal and authentic according to specific collective values.

Chapter 4 engages with the idea that music changes people's lives. This popular notion has been treated with understandable suspicion in social and cultural studies, but invites serious attention. People credit peak music experiences with significant effects, as a source of inspiration to engage in certain activities and thus to become a musician, a fan and so on, and as an enduring influence on ways of seeing and acting in both musical practice and other aspects of life. This draws focus to the situated, embodied experiences from which music's meaning and effects derive, highlighting in particular the crucial role of affect in music's social agency. The feelings produced in musical experience are inseparable from subsequent interpretations, judgements and dispositions. The converse of this is that music's affective power is itself shaped by narrative meaning and underlying discourse. The practice of identifying peak music experiences as sources of inspiration and influence forms part of the discourse of popular music, promoting particular ways of relating to music and emphasising the agency of both music and individuals over more mundane social and cultural factors. I do not seek to disentangle these discursive constructions from music's 'real' effects but rather to consider the real effects that flow from them. Put simply, what music does depends on what people believe it does, and peak music experiences are an important way of believing in what music can do.

Chapter 5 turns directly to the question of what motivates people to invest their time and resources in musical activity, often basing their social lives around it and defining themselves in relation to it as musicians, fans or otherwise. Theories of escape, rebellion and distinction help to explain this but largely fall short of identifying what is specific to music that might attract such devotion. It will be shown that peak music experiences are an important source of motivation for continuing musical practice and scene participation. As embodied experiences they provide an intrinsic reward that is often described as both therapeutic and addictive. As memories and sought-after ideals they represent what people hold important and why, acting as affirmations of identity. In the scene-related careers of musicians, organisers and others, peak music experiences anchor narratives of fulfilment, vindication and success, as well as a contrasting narrative of authenticity in which the direct pleasures of musical experience are prioritised over other, extrinsic motivations for musical practice. It will be seen that peak music experiences, as manifestations of both symbolic capital and internal goods, work to motivate and direct participation in music scenes.

Chapter 6 examines the role of peak music experiences in interpersonal relationships, including between family, friends and romantic partners.

This builds on previous theorisations of music as a resource for the identification and articulation of emotions in the context of 'courtship', romance and other interpersonal relationships (Horton 1957; Frith 1989), but replaces their focus on lyrics and textual meaning with the experiential approach developed in this book. It will be shown that music can heighten and define the experience of certain micro-social events and situations, for individuals but also at an intersubjective level. Music can create a common affective space in which extraordinary kinds of expression and interaction are possible. People may consciously plan or seize upon shared experiences of music as a way to acknowledge, explore and celebrate aspects of their relationships. These are ways in which musical experiences can be imbued with highly personal significance and emotional resonance, creating peak music experiences through which people and relationships are remembered and narrated.

Live music events are the setting for the greatest number of peak music experiences reported by the research participants. This reflects the valourisation of the live setting in popular music culture, as acknowledged in a range of scholarly work (e.g. Cohen 1991, 2012; Cavicchi 1998). In Chapter 7, analysis of these experiences reveals what people value most in the live context and provides insight into what it is that marks out live music as special. Common factors include the role of venues, sound, physicality, performance, presence and collective affect, each of which involves expectations that differ between particular music cultures. Together these elements create a space for the exploration and celebration of individual and collective identity, including uncommon performances of self and belonging. By enabling extraordinary feelings and behaviour, live music creates especially affecting, memorable and meaningful experiences, which help to account for its special status.

Chapter 8 develops the study of peak music experiences as a new contribution to the understanding of music scenes. It is shown that the peak music experiences described by participants in dance, hip hop, indie and rock 'n' roll scenes reveal shared clusters of priorities. While these are consistent with existing literature regarding each of the genres in question, this approach provides new insight into how scene participants identify with and reproduce such collective values as an aspect of scene belonging. While the findings show the synchronisation of various elements including musical style, thematic content, physical activity, preferred settings and substance use, these preferences are not attributed directly to structural causes as in subcultural theories of homology (e.g. Willis 1978; Hebdige 1979), but to a shared aesthetic that idealises particular kinds of experience. Beyond the content or objects of taste, such as musical and visual styles, the scenes favour ways of experiencing music and, in turn, the self and its relationship to others. Accordingly, they are bound by an 'ethic of the aesthetic' (Maffesoli 1991), offering new insight into 'affective scene' belonging (Bennett 2013). It is shown that these ideals are expressed and reproduced through the peak music experiences described by participants. As shared frames through which personal experience is remembered and understood, peak music experiences are an aspect of collective memory in music scenes, contributing to the burgeoning study of this dimension of scene identity (e.g. Bennett and Rogers 2016).

Chapter 9 reviews the research findings and theoretical arguments presented throughout the book and distils three major themes that run through the preceding chapters. First, I consider how the findings respond to the opening questions: what can music do, how can it do so, and what does this tell us about why people invest in music and the scenes oriented around it? Second, I sum up how peak music experiences play a role in both affective sociality and reflexive individualisation, demonstrating the co-existence and interaction of these ostensibly opposed, macro-level theories of late- or post-modern social being (Giddens 1991; Maffesoli 1996). Third, I underline the ways that peak music experiences are shown to be collective productions, demonstrating the role of collective memory and shared aesthetics in structuring both narrative and affective aspects of individual identity and practice, especially in the context of music scenes. The chapter also suggests further applications and extensions of the study of peak music experiences. These include the empirical investigation of the concept among people who do not so closely participate in local music scenes. I also argue for the value of peak music experiences in considering how broader social factors such as class, gender and race shape people's engagements with music. Finally, I comment on the relevance of peak music experiences to questions of music's value, with a bearing on cultural policy concerning live music in particular as well as analyses of technological change.

Conclusion

This introductory chapter has established what is meant by peak music experiences and provided an outline of what the concept offers to music sociology and popular music studies. Over the course of this book, I will develop a theory of peak music experiences that takes account of this way in which people relate to music, as an important aspect of its social and cultural being. It will be shown that peak music experiences are used to map individual histories of listening, in which they explain the construction of musical meaning as well as crucial matters of inspiration, influence and motivation. Peak music experiences provide insight into music's role in interpersonal relationships and in far broader forms of collective belonging. They offer a new perspective on what makes live music special and on the structuring of affect and memory as an aspect of music scene identity. The theoretical background and framework for this analysis will be detailed in Chapter 2.

2 Theorising peak music experiences

In developing a theoretical approach to peak music experiences, the philosophy of 19th and 20th century pragmatist John Dewey provides a useful starting point. Dewey (2004a [1929]: 251) notes the ancient Greek sense of experience, as a store of practical wisdom distilled from sensation and perception. From Plato to the enlightenment, experience was regarded as separate and inferior to reason and science, which by contrast offered access to universal and eternal truth. This basic dualism, which remains deeply influential, is rejected in Dewey's pragmatist philosophy that regards knowledge, value and fundamental reality as the contingent, evolving product of living humans interacting with their environment. On this view, there can be no sharp division of practice and experience on the one hand from reason and knowledge on the other, nor of mind from body, nor of fact from meaning. In challenging these dualisms, Dewey's theory anticipates the more recent corporeal, affective and mnemonic turns in sociology and popular music studies that will be important for present purposes. In setting aside the search for objective truth and focusing instead on the consequences of believing certain things to be true, the pragmatist philosophy turns from abstract universals to the specificities of lived experience, which must always be socially, historically and otherwise contextualised.

Most relevantly, Dewey (2004b [1934]: 274) considers what defines 'an experience'. Experience, in its modern sense of conscious undergoing, is often inchoate, appearing as a loose succession of elements that lack either distinction from or connection to each other. In contrast, we have *an* experience when what is experienced runs its course to fulfilment, with a self-sufficient, individualising quality that demarcates it from the general stream. While philosophy has tended to speak of experience at large, idiomatic speech refers to these singular experiences. They include tremendously important experiences like a quarrel with a loved one or a narrowly averted catastrophe, as well as slighter experiences like a meal that stands out as an enduring memorial of what food may be, or the passage through a storm. Each has a unity – *that* meal, *that* storm – constituted by a single quality that pervades the experience, in spite of its various constituent parts. An experience has pattern and structure because it consists of doing and undergoing not

DOI: 10.4324/9781003093244-2

just in alternation, but in relationship to each other. According to Dewey, the unity of an experience is neither solely emotional, practical nor intellectual, although these internal distinctions can be made. What defines it more fundamentally as an experience is the integration of elements in a coherent whole: an aesthetic quality, in which emotion plays an important role (ibid.: 277). Pursuant to the pragmatist philosophy, emotions are not reified, private entities, but are attached to events and objects as they move towards outcomes that the individual desires or dislikes. Emotion is the force that selects experiential materials as congruous and dyes them with its colour, providing qualitative unity to an experience. Consequently, it is through their emotions that people see the shape and character of events and objects. In Dewey's example, a prospective employer sees by his own emotional reactions whether an applicant's presence and behaviour harmonise with his own attitudes, leading the varied elements of the interview to a decisive end. The aesthetic quality of every complete experience takes on further significance in Dewey's philosophy of art. Art is defined by experience that is distinctively aesthetic, placing emphasis on the integration of the parts over their conclusion. For example, the point of a novel or a play is not its closing line (Dewey 2004b: 268) and the same could be said of a harmonic or lyrical resolution in a piece of music. It is most significant for present purposes that Dewey does not locate the work of art in an independent object, but in what that object does with and in *experience*. This is so for both the producer and the consumer, as it is in the experience of each that the work of art is perceived as such and has particular qualities. Further, Dewey's conception of an experience as a *perceived* relationship between doing and undergoing posits an active and creative role for the consumer of art. To perceive a work of art is not merely to take what is there in finished form, which Dewey calls bare recognition, but to organise the elements through a process that is analogous to the artist's creative process. Adequate yielding of the self to an aesthetic experience is made possible through controlled, possibly intense activity. In keeping with the pragmatist, anti-dualistic underpinning of Dewey's philosophy, an aesthetic experience involves close relations between sensory perception, knowledge and activity, guided by purpose and permeated by emotion.

Dewey's philosophy of experience as described here draws together the major theoretical underpinnings of this book, which in the following sections of this chapter will be situated more specifically within recent branches of sociology and popular music studies. The concept of 'an experience' is fundamental to this investigation of peak music experiences, which are defined by their being perceived distinctly from the general experience out of which they arise. More broadly, this book follows the pragmatist insistence that meaning, truth and indeed reality are produced in experience that is subjectively embodied within time, place and social interaction. That philosophy, especially as developed in more social terms by Dewey's colleague and mentee George Herbert Mead, was directly influential on the symbolic interactionist perspective within sociology (Ward and Throop 1989; Denzin 1992: xiv), which is reflected in the qualitative, interpretive approaches this book employs (Denzin 2001; Minichiello et al. 2008: 130). Dewey's rejection of strict divisions between thought and emotion, mind and body, fact and meaning, and person and context is also echoed in the recent sociological theory on which this book will build. In particular, I will follow Dewey in locating the work of art not in an object but in the experience, which the consumer has an active but incomplete role in creating. The concept of peak music experiences recognises that the meanings and effects of music are based in the experiences in which it is encountered. Where this book will most clearly go beyond Dewey's model of aesthetic experience, apart from applying it to the specific case of popular music, is in considering the social construction of peak music experiences along with their role in constituting the social.

Mirroring Dewey's critique of philosophy, the study of popular music has tended to speak of experience at large, in contrast with the idiomatic discussion of singular experiences. This historical tendency will now be considered, before introducing more specific literature on which this book will build.

Experience in popular music studies

Mass culture and subcultures

The academic field of popular music studies has developed from foundations in the 1960s and 1970s and employs multi-disciplinary perspectives, spanning musicology, ethnomusicology, media and cultural studies, anthropology and sociology (Bennett and Waksman 2015). According to Dowd (2007), the recent vitality of music sociology contrasts with the near dormancy of its past, which for the first half of the 20th century was marked by scattered works that did not generate sustained scholarly interest. This is not to suggest that the early work lacks contemporary relevance, as demonstrated in the discussion of Horton (1957) in Chapter 6. In any case, a notable exception is the famous mid-century work of critical sociologist Theodor Adorno, which continues to be referenced and debated (see for example DeNora 2003 as discussed in Chapter 4). While Adorno (1976: 4), unlike Dewey, locates the aesthetic quality and meaning of music in its internal compositional structure, he is also interested in experiential factors that affect the listener's access to that meaning. These include the delivery of the music, such as his criticism of radio as a medium for symphonies (Adorno 1941), as well as the listener's knowledge and effort, in which regard Adorno proposes a typology of listeners ranging from the expert through the entertainment listener to the indifferent (Adorno 1976). Most significantly, however, Adorno (1990) denigrates popular music as a whole in comparison to what he calls 'serious' music, and more specifically 'good' serious music. The key distinction is in popular music's standardised form and content which, unlike the aesthetic totality of serious musical works, does not require or reward effort but effectively hears for the listener. Concrete musical details and differences are contained within the predictable abstract structure of popular songs, ultimately resulting in a familiar experience. Based on this analysis, there is no reason to consider particular experiences with popular music, as their social significance lies in their uniformity.

Musical experience is also restricted largely to typological analysis in the subcultural studies of the 1970s that, according to Dowd (2007), presaged the proliferation of sociological perspectives on the reception of music. In contrast to Adorno's critique of oppressive mass culture, the work of scholars associated with the Birmingham Centre for Contemporary Cultural Studies (CCCS) generally holds that popular music, along with other mass commodities such as clothes and consumer technology, can be re-interpreted and re-purposed for a cultural form of resistance: 'The trivia which trap us can be turned against what lies behind them' (Willis 1978: 166). This suggests a role for the consumer of music in creating meaning and, consequently, the potential for differing and conflicting meanings for the same music: 'objects, artifacts and institutions do not, as it were, have a single valency', and the act of social engagement brings out particular meanings (ibid.: 193). However, music is but one element considered in the study of youth subcultures, as noted by Laing (1985: 4) when comparing his semiotic analysis of punk as a musical genre with Hebdige's (1979) influential study of punk's broader stylistic ensemble, which favoured its visual aspects. Further, consistently with the focus on subcultures as expressive resistance, there is a preponderance of historical and semiotic analysis over phenomenological analysis, even though all three levels are identified by CCCS affiliate Phil Cohen (2005 [1972]: 90) as necessary for any complete subcultural analysis. In other words, the influential work on subcultures is more concerned with public expression than private experience, as noted in McRobbie's (1980: 69) criticism that in the 1970s studies, '[o]nly what happened out there on the streets mattered'.

A further issue rooted more deeply in theory is that in the original subcultural studies, music consumption and experience are assumed to be products of structural determination. Drawing on uncommonly ethnographic research among English hippies and 'motor bike boys' in 1969, Willis (1978) presents detailed accounts of the particular kinds of musical experience preferred by members of these groups. For example, the motor bike boys favoured rock 'n' roll with a strong beat for dancing, while the hippies preferred more complex progressive rock which demanded intellectual attention, enhanced by the use of psychedelic drugs. Willis provides a concept of 'objective possibilities' to describe how the unique material features of cultural items like music enable and limit a range of potential meanings, feelings and uses (ibid.: 200–201). However, the ensuing analysis then restricts these possibilities by abstracting subjective experiences into types, using the concept of homology. Pursuant to this theory, the continuous play between a social group and its preferred items is determined largely by structural factors like class and generation (ibid.: 91); the bike boys' enjoyment of brash and basic rock 'n' roll reflects their working class physicality, lacking the educated hippies' capacity and desire to engage with the political and psychedelic possibilities of progressive rock. Accordingly, what on the surface appear to be subjective musical experiences are only examples of general, structurally determined tendencies. As with Adorno's approach, this theoretical assumption means there is little point in looking at the specifics of individual experiences.

Such a view of music consumption has been challenged in subsequent ethnographic work. One example is Jones's (1988) study of how Jamaican reggae and related styles had a collective 'impact' on black and white youth and communities in the United Kingdom, with a focus on the city of Birmingham. While considering broad formations of race and class, Jones argues that people's reasons for liking reggae, and the precise kinds of subjectivity the music might express and produce, may be 'as diverse as the infinite variety of contexts in which they hear and experience the music' (ibid.: 117). Accordingly, Jones's study is concerned with the situated, embodied practices through which reggae music was incorporated into local and personal lives. This sensitivity to context and practice allows for varied and unique musical experiences, without downplaying their potential significance in cultural change: 'For reggae did not produce ready-made forms of political consciousness, but worked through the pleasures of its consumption to propagate values, sensibilities and fundamental perspectives on life' (ibid.: 160). This book aims to strike a similar balance between recognising the diversity of musical experiences and tracing their relationships with social processes.

Scenes and fan cultures

Some of the more recent work on music in subcultures has explicitly moved beyond CCCS-style semiotic analysis and structural explanation to bring increased attention to lived points of view, as exemplified in Feldman's (2009) ethnographic study of Mod culture's articulation in various global contexts. This methodology is also central in what has been described as 'post-subcultural' research on youth culture and popular music, which has developed since the 1990s (Bennett 2011). A substantial amount of this research has been oriented around scenes, a concept describing cultural spaces in which a range of musical practices may coexist and interact (Straw 1991) at various levels including local, trans-local and virtual (Peterson and Bennett 2004). The study of local scenes, which an audit by Bennett and Rogers (2016: 25) found to comprise a large proportion of scene research, is attentive to how specificities of place and microsocial interactions inform musical practice and meaning. This framework and the typically ethnographic approach it entails bring attention to lived experience. Understandably, this is directed towards the elaboration of typical experiences within particular scenes and sub-groups, instead of singular experiences in their own right and, more specifically, singular experiences of music.

However, instances of what I call peak music experiences are apparent in some of the work on scenes. In London dance club culture, Malbon (1999) observes that 'ecstatic' and 'oceanic' experiences are sought and occasionally undergone by clubbers while dancing to music in a crowd, with those terms referring respectively to experiences with and without drugs. These experiences have an 'afterglow' and can provide motivation for the days, weeks or even years to come, informing everyday identity (ibid.: 187). This illustrates how particular, extraordinary experiences can be an important and even defining feature of music scene participation. The centrality of ecstatic and 'peak' experiences in clubbing is also discussed by Pini (2001), based on her interviews with women who attended London-based dance events, who would carefully plan and work for their desired experiences of freedom and transcendence on the dance floor. Kahn-Harris (2004: 111) reports on the significance in extreme metal culture of a person's shocking first encounter with the genre, which can be 'a musical experience separate from previous musical experience' and may inspire a frantic search for more of the same. Although this initially shocking music might provide diminishing returns, long-standing scene members can be rejuvenated from time to time by 'the experience of music through the body' (ibid.: 116). Similarly, Tsitsos (2012) finds that for ageing punks, occasionally 'returning to the pit' to slamdance is a way to reconnect emotionally to their scene. These diverse examples demonstrate that singular musical experiences can have significance for individuals, including as part of their connection to a scene, and I will map their common ground (see Chapter 3) in the course of developing a general theory of peak music experiences. However, while these studies recognise the status of particular types of musical experience within music cultures, they do not engage critically with the origin and reproduction of this status.

Precedents for analysing the narratives of peak music experiences as a discursive practice can be found in two studies of popular music fan culture. Cavicchi's (1998) 'experience-near anthropology' of Bruce Springsteen fans reveals the way they talk about their relationship to his music, in online forums and fanzines, by way of 'Bruce stories'. These follow common patterns, marked by quasi-religious tropes of epiphany and conversion that emphasise the dramatic impact of specific experiences that arise when listening to recordings or attending concerts. One fan is found to have reshaped his story of becoming-a-fan to fit the prevailing 'Bruce story' formula for an online discussion, by describing a more specific listening setting and a more sudden epiphany than he did in a previous setting. It is not suggested that the story is false and the experience is invented; rather, Cavicchi argues that Bruce stories work to order fans' personal experiences according to socially derived categories, enabling them to understand their experiences as shared. The story formula also shapes expectations of group behaviour, by promoting values and serving as a model for reacting in certain situations. Similar observations are made in Bailey's (2005) study of fans of the rock band KISS, which makes use of media and cultural theory as well as aspects of pragmatist philosophy. Bailey finds that the 'Kisstories' told by fans about their musical salvation emphasise self-realisation and individual uniqueness, marked by religious intensity, which he theorises as a response to the contradictions between these values and the music's artificial, commercial aspects. Thus, the circulation of peak music experience stories can be seen as a discursive practice that helps define who belongs to a group and enables them to feel that they belong. This suggests peak music experiences may be a window for studying the values of a group and how those values are reproduced. The narrative patterns of peak music experiences will be considered in Chapter 3, while the collective scene values revealed by those narratives will be discussed in Chapter 8.

Technologies of the self

Dowd (2007) observes that scholarship on the *reception* of music has contributed greatly to the vitality of music sociology since the 1990s, becoming a leading area of theory and research following previous work on context and production. This has entailed a closer focus on the subjective experience and use of music, with authors like Tia DeNora (2000, 2003) and Antoine Hennion (2001, 2007, 2010) conceiving an active role for both musical content and individual listeners within particular contexts. This is consistent with some earlier work recognising music's contextual polysemy and the active role of audiences in constructing meaning. Interactionist sociologist Norman Denzin (1970) criticises an earlier tradition that regarded artistic productions as social facts independent of the interpretations people brought to them, arguing instead that artistic productions must be seen as interactional creations of artists and audiences. Popular music scholar Dave Laing (1985) observes that music comprises a combination of signs that may be written, spoken, sung, played and gestured, which are not always in the service of communication and to which audiences may direct varying levels of attention. For example, some listeners might be concerned with a song's lyrics while others respond more to its rhythm. Music's semiotic openness and abstractness increase the importance of the context of reception. Simon Frith (1998), who was influential in bringing sociological attention to popular music, notes that music is never heard outside a situation and, further, that different situations produce different aesthetic objects. This view, reminiscent of Dewey's pragmatist theory, suggests the potential significance of specific musical experiences. Similarly, DeNora (2003: 154–156) notes that music may afford different actors different things at different times, as it only acts in concert with the material, cultural and social environments in which it is located. She therefore proposes the study of 'Musical Events' (capitals in original), referring to instances of musical engagement, in order to pay equal attention to both musical materials and the circumstances in which they are heard and integrated into social experience.

While the reception of music is shaped by subjective experience, the reverse is also true. Critically, DeNora (2000) observes that music is a temporal medium that structures experience as it unfurls, not only reflecting and expressing feelings but providing them with the aesthetic form through which they are recognised and shared. Music's properties in this regard can be inherent (such as tempo), by common association (such as key) and by personal association (such as memories), so that a song accrues subjective affordances as it is re-experienced over time in recorded form or, as discussed in Chapter 7, when it is performed. DeNora's theory of affordances can be seen as an expansion of Willis's (1978) theory of objective possibilities, allowing greater scope for highly individual interpretations and uses as compared to a deterministic homology. DeNora (2000) calls music a technology of the self, referring to its capacities for ordering experience and for enabling past experiences, along with the self that experienced them, to be relived and re-evaluated in the present. This is demonstrated through ethnographic analyses of music being used to manage activity, emotion and memory in 'everyday' situations, such as people playing a certain song when getting ready to go out, responding to a song on the radio by reflecting on deceased family members, or using particular music to control the atmosphere in a clothes shop. While the focus of DeNora's empirical work is therefore on common and habitual practices rather than singular or especially memorable Musical Events, this theoretical approach provides a useful framework for the study of peak music experiences, as a specific way that music is involved in individual identity.

The importance of context does not mean that every experience of music begins with a clean slate or produces an entirely new aesthetic object. Music's lack of fixed, inherent meaning allows it to be invested with contextual, personal meanings that are strongly adherent. The highly subjective interpretations of music demonstrated in DeNora's work are observed by Bennett (2013) to create strong feelings of textual ownership, bound up with people's sense of themselves. This is demonstrated in media scholar José van Dijck's (2006: 361) analysis of written responses to a Dutch popular music poll, including the following examples:

> It was 1971, I was waiting on a boat someplace in Norway when I heard this song ['Imagine' by John Lennon] for the first time. It was such a perfect day, everything was right: the weather, the blue sky, the peaceful tidal waves in the fjord matching the melodious waves of music. There are moments in life that you feel thoroughly, profoundly happy. This was such moment [sic], believe me.
>
> (posted by Jan from Eindhoven)

My father died suddenly in November of 1986. That night we all stayed awake. I isolated myself from my family by putting on the head-phones and listening to this song ['With or Without You' by U2]. The intense sorrow I felt that night was expressed in Bono's intense screams. I will never forget this experience, and each time I hear this song I get tears in my eyes.

(posted by Jelle van Netten from Woudsend)

These examples show how people's favourite songs can be bound up with their memory of specific experiences, as well as how those songs may have contributed to the shape and meaning of those experiences in the first place. This demonstrates how DeNora's theorisation of the two-way link between music and experience may be applied to peak music experiences, which will be explored with reference to interpersonal relationships in Chapter 6. Additionally, as van Dijck notes, the personal emotions attached to musical experience are articulated in explicit memory narratives that people like to exchange, as in the Dutch poll she analyses. This highlights the social context of musical memories, which I will explore in terms of narrative forms (Chapter 3) and the role of collective memory (Chapter 8).

The importance of subjective experience(s) in the construction of music's meaning suggests the possibility of a similarly nuanced approach to the sociological question of taste, beyond quantitative and indexical analysis. Such an approach is presented by Hennion's (2010) 'pragmatics of taste', in which taste is not a static, passive disposition but an evolving and active technique, to which an object reciprocates with feedback, so that the taster and the object being tasted produce each other in the encounter. Thus, music's effects are uncertain, variable and participatory: 'the means we give ourselves to grasp the object – to be able to listen to it, in the case of music – are part of the effects it can produce' (ibid.: 140). This clearly resonates with Dewey's pragmatist aesthetic philosophy outlined at the start of this chapter, and Hennion (2015, 2017) engages explicitly with the sociological relevance of pragmatism as conceived by Dewey's forebear William James. Hennion's (2007, 2010) empirical work on this topic focuses in detail on personal engagements with music, describing people's elaborate, personalised routines of listening which they have developed over time and consciously employ in search of desired results. Importantly, despite this active and conscious listening, there is always an element of uncertainty concerning the outcome. As in Dewey's model the controlled and intense activity of the listener does not on its own create the aesthetic experience, but adequately yields to it. It would seem that we should not locate agency solely in the music or the individual, but in their collaborative meeting. While the focus of Hennion's research is on established practices more than their development, let alone disruption, his pragmatics of taste offers concepts for understanding peak music experiences. It accounts for how specific encounters with even the same music can be unique and even revelatory, while recognising that they are informed by and contribute to an ongoing history of encounters, of which the listener is reflexively aware.

The main risk associated with the approaches outlined here is that an insufficiently critical focus on people's subjective accounts of musical experience may lead to mere 'microaestheticism' (Prior 2011: 134), which would simply adopt the language being studied at the expense of sociological query or explanation. Varriale (2016) argues that both DeNora and Hennion neglect the social histories and differences that inform the ways people engage with cultural materials. However, as Prior (2011) notes, their works discussed above are explicitly concerned with addressing what had been oversimplified or simply overlooked in previous sociological orthodoxies, by taking seriously the aesthetic and everyday concerns that motivate music listeners and the substantial thought and effort they invest in those concerns. The theoretical tools developed in that process are not inconsistent with the sociological analysis of ideology, power and distinction. In fact, I want to show that subjective experiences and personal narratives are fruitful sites for such critical analysis with regard to popular music. Accordingly, this thesis will take up DeNora's concern with the role of specifically musical experience in constructing the self, and will then connect this to broader processes of social memory and identity. Similarly, Hennion's model of co-productive encounters between listeners and music will be situated in relation to the discursive frameworks of popular music culture and scenes. As Hennion (2001: 14) observes of the sublime moments cherished by both rock and classical concert-goers: 'Immediacy is the paradoxical result of a lengthy sequence of mediations'. While he refers mostly to embodied techniques and practices, these mediations also include the discourse by which musical experience is anticipated, remembered and presented in different contexts. In making these links, this analysis will bring to popular music studies the sociological concepts considered in the next section of this chapter.

Sociological perspectives on experience

Epiphanies

Perhaps the closest analogue to the Deweyan idea of 'an experience' in sociology is Norman Denzin's (1989, 2001) concept of an epiphany. Epiphanies are interactional moments that leave marks on people's lives and in which personal character is manifested and made apparent. They arise out of everyday, lived experience but are distinguished from it by their form, as dramatic events with beginnings, middles and endings, and by the rupture that they represent as liminal experiences. Denzin identifies four kinds of epiphany: the major epiphany, which touches and changes every aspect of a person's life; the cumulative epiphany, which represents the culmination of a series of events; the minor or illuminative epiphany, which reveals underlying aspects of a situation or relationship; and the relived epiphany, in which an individual relives a major turning point in their life. These experiences become narrative resources with which people interpret their lives for themselves and others. Importantly, Denzin notes that the meaning of experiences is given retrospectively and is never definitive; like the selves they inform, epiphanies are always unfinished productions. Further, stories of personal experience are never individual productions but are produced in and for group contexts that include cultural texts, shared histories, and criteria of truth and form.

Epiphanies are central to the sociological approach that Denzin calls interpretive interactionism, which through a focus on the particulars of lived experience seeks to uncover the social and cultural forces that shape it. This is based on the understanding that the self is a narrative production shaped by material social conditions, discourses and narrative practices. Experience is remembered and represented in stories and we can study it only through such representations. The sociologist's task is neither to accept these stories on their face value nor to determine which are false, but to study how people produce, and learn to produce, stories of personal experience which accord with group standards of truth and storytelling. The stories told within groups are reflective of the larger system of cultural understandings, containing conceptions of lives and meaningful experience.

Denzin's focus is on personal experiences that are problematic and related to traditional social themes, such as addiction and domestic violence. However, he does conceive of both positive and negative epiphanies and is attentive to historical context and the shaping role of cultural texts such as films. Theorists like Giddens (1991) and Chaney (1994) observe that the project of the self is increasingly informed by and constructed from mass media and commodified leisure culture. Thus, Woodward (2001), citing Denzin, coins the term 'taste epiphanies' for the stories that the participants in his study tell about significant domestic objects, as a way of presenting effective self-narratives. Woodward's study reveals the fusion of aesthetic taste with ethical values, as well as the significance of taste to broader social and cultural identifications, inviting biographical approaches to the study of popular culture to complement the more established study of objectified taste. With work like DeNora's (2000) as discussed above, and Bennett's (2013) work on music and ageing demonstrating that music consumption features significantly in people's long-term self-identity, it follows that people might have epiphanies arising out of their interactions with music. The previously discussed examples of memorable musical experiences in the work of Cavicchi (1998), Malbon (1999), Kahn-Harris (2004), Bailey (2005) and Tsitsos (2012) can be seen as epiphanies, as they are experiences that are remembered by people as having marked their lives, and stories that are told to explain identity. Indeed, Cavicchi (1998) uses the term 'epiphany' in its broader sense, without reference to Denzin, to emphasise similarities between the narratives of Springsteen fans and those of 'born-again' Christians. This analogy highlights the deep importance with which musical experience can be invested. Likewise, Cavicchi's case of the fan who reshaped his story to fit the expectations of the online Springsteen community illustrates the provisional, collective construction of epiphanies and their consequent value for illuminating social processes and cultural systems.

The possible application of Denzin's theory of epiphanies to popular music can be further illustrated by comparing one of his prominent examples of an epiphany, involving religious and political conviction, to a specifically musical experience. In suggesting that there may be positive epiphanies as well as troubling ones, Denzin (2001: 35) makes reference to an experience recounted on numerous occasions by African American civil rights activist Martin Luther King, Jr. The story is that during a sleepless night of intense doubt and fear in 1956, King sat at his kitchen table and heard a voice that he took to be Jesus Christ, urging him to fight on and promising eternal support. According to primary quotes and biographies, this was a transformative experience that King would reflect on for motivation and recount to inspire various audiences throughout his life. This demonstrates the revelatory and motivational effects of an epiphany for the person who experiences it, as well as the exemplary and normative potential of sharing the story with others. We can find parallels to this story in a secular, musical epiphany described by civil rights lawyer Charles Black, who played a prominent role in the *Brown v Board of Education* case in which the US Supreme Court ruled that segregated state schools were unconstitutional. In an article written for the *Yale Review*, Black (1986: 1596–1597) claims to have felt for many years that he 'started walking toward the Brown case, where [he] belonged', when as a teenager in 1931 he saw the jazz trumpeter Louis Armstrong perform in Austin, Texas. Black writes in poetic detail of the music's '[s]team-whistle power, lyric grace, alternated at will, even blended', characterising it as his first experience of genius:

> The moment of first being, and knowing oneself to be, in the presence of genius, is a solemn moment; it is perhaps the moment of final and indelible perception of man's utter transcendence of all else created. It is impossible to overstate the significance of a sixteen-year-old Southern boy's seeing genius, for the first time, in a black.

Charles Black (ibid.: 1600) claims that from that evening on, Armstrong was a continuing presence in his life, both as a musical passion and as an artist who instructed him 'as only high art can instruct' on ethical matters. As in Martin Luther King Jr's relationship to Christ, this lifelong presence was anchored in the memory of an epiphany. Both stories are powerful illustrations of how a highly subjective, private experience can motivate distinctly social attitudes and action. At the same time, both experiences invite exploration of the historical, social and cultural factors behind them, such as the influence of particular religious traditions on King and the civil rights movement, and the narratives of race and artistic value that informed Black's youth as a Southern university student.

As this comparison shows, Denzin's interpretive approach provides conceptual tools for taking seriously the subjective experiences of individuals with music, not for their objective truth but for their real effects, and not as separate from social structures but as an interface through which those structures are known and navigated. As feminist historian Joan Scott (1992) argues, it is not individuals who have experience, but subjects who are constructed through experience, which does not happen outside established meanings but occurs within discursively constructed ways of experiencing. Experience is therefore 'not the origin of our explanation, but that which we want to explain' (ibid.: 38). It has been observed that the very definition of music is a discursive production that takes effect in subjective experience. Frith (1987: 139) notes that we 'hear things as music' because they obey a particular, familiar logic. Similarly, social anthropologist Ruth Finnegan (1989: 7) states that what is 'heard as' music is characterised not by its formal properties but 'by people's view of it, by the special frame drawn round particular forms of sound and their overt social enactment'. Consequently, to understand the social significance of music it is necessary to pay close regard to the subjective experience in which music and its significance are made real, and then to treat this as a starting point for inquiry. The study of peak music experiences is specifically attentive to the narratives involved in constructing and reconstructing music, the people who create and listen to it, and the experiences in which they interact. In this book, the perception, meaning and commemoration of peak music experiences will be situated within particular discourses, including consideration of how those experiences shape future subjectivities by reproducing and disrupting such discourses.

Affective encounters

One prominent aspect of peak music experiences is what can be called the affective realm: the role of emotions, feelings and bodily responses. I will use the words affect and affective in this broad sense rather than in the narrow sense associated with debates in affect studies, in which some theorists like Brian Massumi position affect as pre-personal, pre-intentional, unmediated and outside signification while emotion is on the other side of each of those dichotomies (as discussed and critiqued in Ahmed 2014: 207; see also Leys 2011). On the contrary, this book is concerned with emotions, feelings and sensations primarily to the extent that they are social, in the sense of informing and being informed by social processes. This will include attention to how these aspects of experience are involved in judgement and meaning-making about music, as well as how the feelings themselves are shaped by narratives that promote particular ways of experiencing music. There will also be some consideration of apparently pre-personal or shared affect, especially in Chapter 7 regarding live music. In these regards, this book builds on work in the sociology of emotions.

Crossley (1998) brings emotions into interactionist theory and specifically the communicative model of Jürgen Habermas, arguing that emotions form part of a mutually meaningful, intersubjective interworld and they are 'accountable', which is to say they can be judged as appropriate or inappropriate, rational or irrational. Indeed, while emotions are part of the pre-reflective structure of consciousness, they are also thought about, talked about and given value in the reflexive projects and accounts of social agents. The discussion and rationalisation of emotions will be a recurring motif within this book, as it is shown that people remember but also anticipate and even try to engineer peak music experiences. The partly performative significance of emotions in popular narratives of peak music experiences will be considered in Chapter 3, while the ordering of emotions themselves as part of the shared aesthetic of music scenes is the subject of Chapter 8. However, drawing on the philosophies of Maurice Merleau-Ponty and Jean-Paul Sartre, Crossley recognises that emotions are more than consciously managed behavioural masks; they are an embodied manner of intending, apprehending and understanding the world. Emotions bestow value or significance on things and a change in one's emotions brings about a change in one's conscious apprehension of the world. Here, again, there are parallels to Dewey's pragmatist, anti-dualist model of experience and judgement, which also emphasises the intentionality of emotions. Further, emotions are a part of individual personality; one's 'emotional habitus' is the result of repeated responses and interpretations becoming sedimented into stable preferences over time, not in individual isolation but within a shared history of communicative action. The relevant implications for present purposes are that any emotional response is not reducible to the particularity of the individual's current situation, but also points backwards to their history, while by the same token communicative situations and actions can have a relatively permanent effect on emotional ways of being (ibid.: 33). This offers a means for understanding how the emotional power of a peak music experience can have a lasting influence on an individual as both perceiving subject and social actor, without romanticising or dismissing this affective dimension as outside social structures.

The idea of emotions mediating our perception of the world through a history of encounters is developed in the work of sociologist Sara Ahmed (2014). Ahmed is not concerned with emotionality as a characteristic of individual and collective bodies, but with how emotions make and shape those bodies as they interact. Drawing explicitly on the philosophy of René Descartes but also echoing Dewey, she observes that our feelings about objects do not derive from the nature of those objects but from how we are affected by them, although we then come to read those feelings as being 'in' those objects. It is through intensifications of feeling that people recognise surfaces and make judgements, constructing subjects and objects, inside and outside, individual and collective. As in Scott's (1992) notion of subjects produced through experience, Ahmed argues that both the subject and the object are shaped in their affective encounter, as the object is attributed with characteristics while the subject is reoriented in relation to it. Like Dewey, Ahmed avoids analytical distinctions between bodily sensation, emotion and thought as if they could be experienced distinctly, utilising instead the multiple meanings of 'impression' to highlight the contiguity between felt contact and judgement. Importantly, impressions are not created anew or individually in each encounter. Feelings rehearse and test associations developed over a lifetime of encounters in which the most intense feelings 'stick'. These associations are also based on social expectations, such as the anticipation of happiness on one's wedding day (or by extension, at a concert). As to collective feelings and affective atmospheres, Ahmed avoids the suggestion that it is emotion itself that circulates, either from individuals outwards or from the collective inwards, as shared feelings are not necessarily about feeling the same and are often subject to miscommunication. Instead, Ahmed proposes that what circulates are the objects of emotion, which are saturated with affect as sites of personal and social tension.

Ahmed's cultural politics of emotion, as she calls it, suggests a means for understanding how peak music experiences can leave lasting impressions, informing people's future attitudes to the objects (songs, artists, places) that they hold responsible for those feelings. As meanings are mediated by feelings, the meanings mediated by the strongest feelings may be the ones that persist. Peak music experiences therefore provide concrete insight into the question of how encounters with music can affect or reorient people in enduring ways. Importantly, this theoretical framework is attentive to how those feelings are shaped by discourse, inviting attention to how dominant narratives, including narratives of peak music experiences, influence the anticipation, experience and memory of emotional responses to music and in turn the experiencing self. Peak music experiences depend on orientations shaped by personal and social histories, but also contribute to their future shape. The narrative construction of biographies around peak music experiences will be considered in Chapter 4, while the influential power of peak music experiences will be investigated in Chapter 5. Ahmed's model of an affective economy, in which the objects of emotion circulate, is useful in considering music as the object of collective feelings, including identification with others based on their apparent feelings towards that music. Building on this approach, peak music experiences will be considered as an aspect of interpersonal relationships in Chapter 6, as a function of 'affective scenes' (Bennett 2013) in Chapter 8, and as a means for understanding the commonly reported type of experience in which people at live concerts and other collective musical events feel as one with a crowd, which will be explored in Chapter 7.

Psychology and cognitive science

Strong experiences with music

The closest precursor to the concept of peak music experiences is the work of psychologist Alf Gabrielsson and colleagues on 'strong experiences with music' (Gabrielsson 2011). It is therefore necessary to distinguish that concept and its treatment, as well as to acknowledge their relevance. In Gabrielsson's project between the late 1980s and early 2000s, 965 participants responded to a request to describe in detail 'the strongest, most intense experience of music that [they] have ever had', with some multiple responses resulting in about 1,350 examples, spanning almost a century and incorporating multiple kinds of music encountered in varied circumstances, though most involved live music (ibid.: 449) and classical and religious music far outweighed the other 14 categories with almost half the responses combined (ibid.: 406).

Some 488 participants estimated how often they have an especially strong experience with music, with answers ranging between every day (1%) and once in a lifetime (8%), but a great majority answering once a year (44%) or a few times in a lifetime (32%) (ibid.: 401). This range may reflect the lack of a precise definition, which was presumably deliberate for exploratory purposes, and the subtle variance in terminology between 'strongest', 'especially strong' and 'strong'. By contrast, peak music experiences are those which simply stand out from general experience, a distinction best explained in John Dewey's discussion of 'an experience' as detailed earlier. This is a broader category that certainly includes all of the strong experiences considered by Gabrielsson, but also many others that may be demarcated by any number of features besides strength or intensity. Those descriptors imply a focus on feeling, which points to a fundamental difference concerning 'experience'. Gabrielsson (ibid.: 5–6) explicitly distinguishes the *perception* of music, as a matter of its objective form and expression about which a person can be completely 'neutral', from the *experience* of music that concerns how a person reacts to it, and which is where neutrality ends. He acknowledges these are simplified poles and that both may often be present, but aims to focus on the latter. By comparison, this book will insist that perception and reaction are inseparable, recognising that 'neutral' perception of a musical (or any other) object is impossible. Here, the term 'experience' covers all aspects of doing and undergoing, including perception and reaction, in accordance once again with both the pragmatist philosophy and the sociology of emotions outlined earlier. It should be noted that this discussion is based on an English translation of Gabrielsson's Swedish writing, though the distinctions seem rooted beneath mere semantics in epistemological and ontological difference. The focus on emotion in Gabrielsson's and many other psychological studies of musical experience is critiqued by Clarke (2014), who seeks to join this dimension with perceptual and embodied aspects in musical consciousness.

As to the method by which strong experiences with music are analysed, Gabrielsson's investigation is of a 'descriptive character', mapping and ty-pologising strong reactions to music and their self-identified causes and consequences without venturing a theoretical explanation (ibid.: 458). The mapping does include ample recognition of personal and social factors in a strong reactions to music (for example, the company of others) and in its consequences (for example, a sense of belonging). However, participants' stories function solely as evidence of what is described, where this book instead takes those stories as starting points for inquiry into the social con-struction and purpose of both stories and experiences. Nevertheless, to this end, the work on strong experiences with music is directly relevant both as a corroboration of a widespread phenomenon of self-reported, extraordinary musical experiences, and as a comparative set of data. A recent addition to this is an Australian study of people's self-reported favourite musical expe-riences, which were found to map well onto Gabrielsson's system (Krause et al. 2020).

Peak and flow experiences and bright moments

There is an apt similarity in terminology between peak music experi-ences and psychologist Abraham Maslow's (1962) concept of 'peak ex-periences'. Both use the word 'peak' to distinguish especially important experiences from the general experience out of which they arise, as illus-trated by Maslow in the following provocation (1962: 67):

> I would like you to think of the most wonderful experience or expe-riences of your life; happiest moments, ecstatic moments, moments of rapture, perhaps from being in love, or from listening to music or sud-denly 'being hit' by a book or a painting, or from some great creative moment.

The defining features of Maslow's peak experiences include feelings of in-ternal and external wholeness and harmony, timelessness and spacelessness, complete mindfulness of the present and full use of one's capacities. These experiences are felt as valuable and lead the individual to see themselves and the world as worthwhile and meaningful, as well as to seek more peak expe-riences, although they cannot be commanded. They are associated with the self-actualisation that represents the apogee of a hierarchy of human needs (often popularised as a pyramid). Maslow regards as healthy the ability to 'religionise' any part of life, including aesthetic experience, and he considers aesthetic peak experiences to be a central aspect of human life with long-term consequences for people's identities and perspectives. As the earlier quote makes clear, Maslow attributes peak experiences to music and in later work he cites music and sex as, statistically, the 'two easiest ways of getting peak experiences' (Maslow 1993 [1971]: 169). Panzarella's (1980) subsequent study of people's 'intense joyous experience of listening to music', influenced by Maslow's ideas, found that these affected people's views of themselves, other people, life and the world, in addition to their appreciation of music. As observed by Dennis and Powers (1974), there are similarities between the theories of Maslow and John Dewey. These include a dynamic view of the world in which meaning is produced through lived experience, a lack of division between intelligence and emotion, a concern with the quasi-religious and aesthetic qualities of everyday life, and the desire to bring subjective experience into scientific study. These similarities also apply to the theory of peak music experiences expounded in this book.

A closely related concept is that of flow experiences, as described by psychologist Mihaly Csikszentmihalyi (1975). Flow refers to 'the holistic sensation that people feel when they act with total involvement' (ibid.: 36), featuring a merging of action and awareness; a narrowing of attention; a loss or transcendence of self-consciousness in fusion with the world; a sense of control without concern; uncontradictory demands and feedback for action; and intrinsic reward, although flow goes beyond the simpler concept of 'pleasure' as it is often produced in physically and mentally demanding activities, such as rock climbing or writing. As Csikszentmihalyi observes, flow shares many distinctive features with Maslow's peak experience. In considering circumstances where flow often arises, Csikszentmihalyi includes 'rock dancing' (ibid.: 11), and Malbon (1999) uses the concept in his sociological study of clubbing to explain the experience prized by dancers, noting how music allows them to focus their awareness on a narrow set of mentally and physically absorbing stimuli. This book will further explore how people seek out and value the involving qualities of musical experience and the flow states associated with it.

From the perspective of cognitive science, William Benzon (2001) uses the term 'bright moments' for musical experiences that resemble peak and flow experiences in terms of effortless engagement and altered body sense, but are characterised more specifically by a sense of heightened, non-verbal communication with other musicians and listeners. Benzon's starting point is the prevalence with which such altered states of consciousness are reported. He credits the term to jazz musician Rahsaan Roland Kirk (ibid.: 143) and provides the following exemplary quote from Ringo Starr of the Beatles (ibid.: 147):

> It feels great; it's just a knowing. It's magic actually; it is pure magic. Everyone who is playing at that time knows where everybody's going. We all feel like one; wherever you go, everyone feels that's where we should go. I would know if Paul was going to do something, or if George was going to raise it up a bit, or John would double, or we'd bring it down. I usually play with my eyes closed, so you would know when things like that were happening … you've got to trust each other.

Benzon notes that this magic is often said to extend to listeners, with the sense of energy flowing between performers and audience. His argument is that while the literature on altered states of consciousness is primarily about individual brains, we should think of bright moments in music as arising from coupled interaction between brains (ibid.: 148). Music is a vehicle for collective intentionality and the sharing of otherwise private experiences, with shared time and rhythm playing a substantial role. In this focus on temporal integration between physically separate individuals, Benzon's analysis is similar to that of DeNora (2000) in sociology, and the concept of music as a vehicle for shared intentionality coincides with Ahmed's (2014) theory of objects as vehicles for the circulation of directed emotion.

A number of the exemplary peak music experiences described and analysed in this book will show elements of peak experiences, flow experiences and bright moments, and this will be observed where relevant. These concepts are not introduced in order to explain peak music experiences by selective appropriation of psychological and cognitive theory, but instead to observe how these approaches complement each other and to corroborate the basic phenomenon being considered. As Benzon (2001: 165) observes, 'there is no doubt that music affords us deep and powerful experiences, experiences that challenge our ordinary sense of reality'. These experiences have been taken seriously and examined fruitfully in psychology and in cognitive science, and my claim is that such examination can also enrich the sociological understanding of music.

Conclusion

In this chapter, I have situated the study of peak music experiences in relation to existing studies of popular music, and outlined the theoretical framework to be applied throughout this book. Dewey's definition of 'an experience' provides a model for understanding how the more specific concept of a peak music experience relates to general experience, and his aesthetic philosophy resonates through the relevant sociological perspectives. The through line is an insistence on seeing human activity as a process of purposeful, responsive interaction with a perceived world of people and objects, drawing on and generating knowledge, meaning and feelings in close relation to each other. I have shown that while historically influential theories of mass culture and subcultures tended to overlook or dismiss subjective experience, this has increasingly become a major focus of music sociology and popular music studies. The sociological study of popular music has still tended not to focus on singular experiences, although examples have arisen and in some cases have been granted importance. However, the study of peak music experiences builds directly on particular developments in music reception studies, including in particular the work of DeNora (2000) and Hennion (2010). In advancing this work and especially in linking the personal and unique to the social and ongoing, Denzin's (2001) theory of epiphanies provides a useful framework. In this way, this study of peak music experiences advances the understanding of how people's interactions with popular culture and media can have deep and enduring significance for identity and sociality. In considering the specific qualities of musical experience in this regard, this book also builds on work in the sociology of emotion, especially Ahmed's (2014) model of how perception and meaning are mediated by feelings produced over a lifetime of encounters. This is a notably Deweyan approach to the construction and interpretation of reality, although Ahmed emphasises the ways in which this process is both socially shaped and gives shape to the social. Utilising this framework, I will explore how emotionality of peak music experiences is central to understanding the social causes and effects of the phenomenon and of musical activity more generally. More specific theoretical frameworks, within this overall approach, will be set out in each chapter as they become relevant.

3   Histories of listening

First encounters, gateways and conversion experiences

Discussions of popular music are replete with lists. Charts and countdowns have long been crucial in determining what is popular as well as distinguishing genres (Hakanen 1998), tasks that are now also achieved by digital playlists that look beyond genre to themes, moods and situations (Fleicher and Snickars 2017; Dhaenens and Burgess 2019). Media outlets conduct annual polls of fans and critics to rank the year's new releases (Strong 2010), ultimately contributing to the canon represented in lists like the '500 Greatest Albums' of *Rolling Stone* magazine (Schmutz 2005) and the annual 'Top 2000' song poll and countdown broadcast on Dutch national radio, known as the 'lijst der lijsten' or list of lists (Van Dijck 2006). Thus at the collective level, popular music is defined, classified and evaluated through lists. Similar processes take place at the individual level, as exemplified in the novel and film *High Fidelity* (Hornby 1995; Frears 2000), which depict fictional record collectors whose main conversation is comparing their 'all-time top five' songs in endless categories. More commonly, it is not surprising to be asked – and to be able – to name one's favourite songs or musical artists, and this list-making is a typical part of a search for bandmates, self-presentation in fan communities and social media, and everyday conversation.

However, these lists are not the full story of how people relate to popular music, but more like a table of contents. It is neither expected, nor sufficient to evaluate music in the abstract or at arm's length. Instead, popular music culture is substantially fuelled by people attributing subjective meaning and value to songs and artists based on personal relationships with them over time. When people explain and justify their tastes, interpretations and evaluations concerning popular music, it is often by narrating those relationships, presenting a dynamic temporal dimension of which the list of favoured objects (such as songs, albums or artists) at any given time is merely a cross-section. In the film adaptation of *High Fidelity*, the main character Rob is depicted sorting his personal record collection, neither alphabetically nor chronologically by release date, but autobiographically. Rob explains that if he wants to find the song 'Landslide' by Fleetwood Mac, he must remember that he bought it for someone in the Fall of 1983 but did not give it to them for personal reasons. This exaggerated undertaking mirrors

DOI: 10.4324/9781003093244-3

the film's emplotment around Rob's crisis-driven reflection on his all-time top five romantic relationships. However, the scene makes concrete the immaterial, everyday ways in which people do sort and understand music, by placing their experiences with it into autobiographical narratives. Empirically, Shuker's (2004) study of record collectors finds practices that partially embody the '*High Fidelity* stereotype', including a focus on collections as prompts for memory, analogous with souvenir collecting.

A person's narration of their relationship with popular music, while unique in its details, tends to follow a recognisable form with certain points of emphasis. Peak music experiences are key elements from which these narratives are constructed. This chapter will consider three narrative tropes of peak music experience that span genres and scenes: first encounters, gateway experiences and conversion experiences. First encounters celebrate the unique experience of hearing certain music for the first time. In a gateway experience, possible directions of musical practice are revealed or made appealing, while conversion experiences are credited with personal change in terms of taste and identity, such as becoming a fan. These shared narrative devices give shape to the identities that may be constructed around popular music, setting up expectations for how popular music might be engaged with over the course of a life and promoting certain values and attitudes. The common forms highlight substantive differences between cultures oriented around particular popular music genres, performers and scenes. However, at the same time, the forms themselves promote more fundamental, common ideals of listening and fandom. Significantly, in the face of popular music's mass-mediated, commercial circulation, these narratives enable and encourage people to present their relationships to popular music as personally meaningful and authentic in accordance with certain cultural values.

Common tropes

Prominent examples of first encounters, conversion experiences and gateway experiences help to demonstrate their core elements and uses. Discussing the impact of radio in the mid-20th century, sociologist Simon Frith offers a personal account:

> I can still remember the instant exhilaration of [US musician] Little Richard's 'Long Tall Sally', which I heard for the first time when I was about ten years old,[1] growing up in a small Yorkshire town, with no idea at all about who or what Little Richard was. That conversion to black music, similar to the experience of small town middle-class children before the war hearing Louis Armstrong for the first time, was being repeated, as a result of rock 'n' roll, for teenagers all across Europe, and can't be explained away in terms of commercial cultural imperialism.
>
> (1986: 270)

Frith's claim that his experience was generational is corroborated by John Lennon, who 'spoke several times of the occasion [of first hearing 'Long Tall Sally' at a friend's house], of how the record presented first a challenge and then a wedge that opened his mind to unconsidered possibilities' (Lewisohn 2013: 87). Lennon is quoted as saying:

> When I heard it ['Long Tall Sally'], it was so great I couldn't speak. You know how you're torn? I didn't want to leave Elvis. Elvis was bigger than religion in my life. We all looked at each other, but I didn't want to say anything against Elvis, not even in my mind. How could they be happening in my life, *both* of them? And then someone said [that Little Richard was African American]. So Elvis was white and Little Richard was black? 'Thank you, God,' I said. I thought about it for days at school, of the labels on the records. One [Richard] was yellow and one [Presley] was blue, and I thought of the yellow against the blue.

The 16-year-old Lennon went on to 'worship' African American musicians and his obsession with rock and roll continued, as has been well reported (ibid.; see also Riley 2011).

In turn, many music listeners remember their first encounter with Lennon's music, as exemplified by Viv Albertine of UK punk band The Slits. Albertine claims that upon first hearing 'Can't Buy Me Love' by The Beatles at age nine she felt 'as if I'[d] jammed my finger into an electricity socket, every part of me [was] fizzing', while the single's Lennon-sung B-side, 'You Can't Do That', 'pierce[d] my heart, and I don't think it will ever heal' (Albertine 2015: 16–17). A Brisbane-based example of a similarly electrifying experience is provided by singer-songwriter Robert Forster, formerly of iconic indie band The Go-Betweens. In the following quotes provided 18 years apart, Forster discusses his first encounter with the debut single of The Saints, another iconic Brisbane band:

> I heard the record on the radio and the first time I heard it I just *(shakes head)* was just astounded, I was just sort of knocked right out of bed. I thought it was great. And then the announcer said at the end of it, "That's The Saints, '(I'm) Stranded' and it's just come out".
> (My transcription of a filmed interview, Wilson and Faulkner 1988).

> I was immediately bug-eyed. I was Frankenstein on the slab with electricity crackling out of my feet. My body vibrated on the bed as I lay in a catatonic state, listening and absorbing. And then, like a wind gust, it was gone. I waited for the back announcement. [...] My mind tuned out. I couldn't fucking believe it. I thought of Virginia [a friend who had previously recommended The Saints] and cursed myself for not believing her. I got the single [...] the next day [...].
> (Forster 2016: 86)

The stories of Frith, Lennon, Albertine and Forster display common features. Each describes an instantaneous and physical response to a first encounter with particular music. They emphasise their lack of prior knowledge or immediate understanding about what was heard, though each was moved to seek out information and try to make sense of the experience. This helps to present the music's effect as natural, 'like a wind gust' as Robert Forster says, promoting the idea that music acts directly on individuals and framing the specific individual's response as unforced, and therefore authentic. Each storyteller also asserts that the experience challenged their previous ideas about (at least) music and made a lasting impression on their sense of self, demonstrating the typical presentation of first encounters as instantly affecting and lastingly important. This popular elevation of first encounters is also illustrated by Neil Young's song, 'Twisted Road' (2012), in which he recounts the first time he 'Like A Rolling Stone', a Bob Dylan song released in 1966, and insists that 'nothing was as good as the very first time'. This insistence, which is common, makes first encounters an especially clear example of peak music experiences.

The stories presented above are also, to varying degrees, examples of gateway experiences and conversion experiences with music. Gateway experiences are those that open new pathways, in the way that Simon Frith's first encounter with Little Richard made him aware of 'black music' generally and led him to investigate it further. The narrative of the gateway experience, like the first encounter, highlights the contingent nature of musical encounters and their powerful effects, but places greater emphasis on the listener's agency in taking up the invitation that is presented. For this reason, gateway experiences can only be defined as such in retrospect, as part of a personal history. Going a step further, conversion experiences are defined by a change in the listener themselves, most often described as 'becoming' a fan of a musical artist or style. This may be simultaneous with a first encounter or gateway experience (as in Frith's case), though again there is a different narrative emphasis. For example, Robert Forster had heard his friend Virginia speak at length about The Saints and he had even seen the band perform live, but it was only when he heard '(I'm) Stranded' on the radio, alone in bed, that he was astounded by their greatness and cursed himself for not believing his friend. A conversion experience is a moment when 'the penny drops', with this intellectual recognition often bound up with powerful emotion and a strong sense of personal importance. The experience and its consequences become a part of one's personal narrative, causally linked to subsequent attitudes and identity. Conversion experiences highlight the unpredictable and conditional nature of music's effects, particularly when they involve music that has already been encountered before. They also demonstrate most clearly the biographical significance attributed to encounters with music.

Stories about first encounters, gateway experiences and conversion experiences, like the prominent examples presented above, are not only personally significant but contribute to broader popular music discourse in important ways. First, they form part of collective appraisals of popular music, as represented in the lists described at the start of this chapter. There have been numerous anecdotes told and published about the first time someone heard Little Richard, '(I'm) Stranded' or 'Like A Rolling Stone' (for example, respectively: BBC radio host John Peel in Walters 1987; Stafford 2004: 43; Marcus 2005: 32, 146). These songs and artists are canonical within their own genres and popular music generally, and stories about personal experiences with them both respond and contribute to this canon. For example, in *Rolling Stone* magazine's list of the '100 Greatest Singers of All Time', the entry for Little Richard at 12th position begins with that very quote from John Lennon, who also makes the list in fifth place (Rolling Stone 2010). Such lists are acts of cultural consecration, bestowing legitimacy on music and musicians by filtering popular, professional and critical recognition through cultural institutions like *Rolling Stone* (Schmutz 2005). I suggest that personal stories about encounters with popular music assist in this consecration by providing evidence of popular recognition and, in the case of artists like Lennon and authors like Frith, professional and critical recognition, which importantly overlap with the personal. Compared to ostensibly objective measures like commercial success and technical appraisal, peak music experiences justify the cultural status of particular music explicitly by reference to its subjective impact. This is consistent with Stratton's (1983) observation that popular music cannot be defined or judged by articulable criteria, but only by experience. It follows that the 'voice of experience' may be prioritised over the voice of the expert, as Pollner and Stein (1996: 207) observe in Alcoholics Anonymous culture (creating an important role for what they call 'narrative maps', as discussed below). More accurately, in popular music, expertise and professional criticism are openly grounded in experience. Stratton (1983) quotes cultural gatekeepers, including record label and media representatives, who claim to base their judgements around overtly non-analytical and somewhat populist notions of subjective impact, and this can also be seen in the prevalence of first-person perspectives in popular music criticism. In other words, the Romantic discourse of popular music prohibits a reliance on objective criteria, in partial contrast to the worlds of classical and folk music, so that evaluation can only be justified by subjective measures. The reproduction of intimate anecdotes from key figures like John Lennon to support canonical rankings shows that the cultural value of popular music, even in the judgement of experts, is based substantially on the experiences it is seen to create. A reflexive approach to these rules of cultural consecration is apparent in the music journalism trope of a knowledgeable first encounter, in which the narrator admits they have never previously listened to a particular recording (usually an album) despite being aware of its canonical status, in order to set the scene for their actual response. This is the central rule of the blog *Ruth and Martin's Album Club*, which invites celebrity guests to respond to a 'classic' album they have not heard before. In these situations, both the canon and the listener are subjected to an experiential 'taste test'.

The second, important way that stories about first encounters, gateway experiences and conversion experiences contribute to popular music discourse is that they say something about listeners. By describing a listener's response, they offer an evaluation of specific music but also illustrate the listener's taste and relationship to music more broadly. This is why John Lennon's story is reproduced not only in texts about Little Richard, but also in biographies of Lennon himself (for example, Wiener 1984: 147; Riley 2011: 55; Lewisohn 2013: 87). Third, the circulation of these narratives promotes first encounters, gateway and conversion experiences and the stories told about them as important, while providing possible shapes for those stories to follow. For example, a reader who encounters Lennon's anecdote might be encouraged to reflect on their own experiences with Little Richard's music and on their own significant first encounters with music. This is a way that popular music literature and media can awaken people retrospectively to experiences that fit certain narrative forms. Moreover, exposure to these narratives encourages expectations that might inform future encounters with music, particularly when iconic songs or artists are involved.

There are parallels here with Becker's (1953) argument that the effects of recreational drugs are socially constructed, as the apparent immediacy of physical and perceptual experience and enjoyment is significantly shaped and reshaped by exposure to the stories and explanations of experienced users. The stories told about first encounters, gateway experiences and conversion experiences similarly reproduce particular ideas and expectations about music, including how it can affect people and why it should be valued. Where drug culture is somewhat clandestine (though less so now than it was during Becker's fieldwork), resulting in sharper processes of individual enculturation, popular music discourse is a more omnipresent feature of popular culture. As a result, many people are prepared from a young age to recognise and enjoy musical experience in accordance with this discourse. Nevertheless, long-term fans and music scene participants exhibit a stronger and more finely tuned interest in, and commitment to, the values and expectations that are reproduced in group narratives, as reflected in their stories of experience.

Theorising first encounters, gateway experiences and conversion experiences

The narrative tropes discussed here, especially first encounters, have been observed in academic work about popular music, but only among limited groups and they have not been typologised as broader categories. Relevant work in this regard includes Kahn-Harris's (2004: 111) finding that people often describe their initial exposure to the extreme metal genre as separate from anything before, inspiring a new search for more. Similarly, Feldman

(2009) describes people's first encounters with Mod music culture, in which a recurring emphasis on sartorial elements forms a predictable part of Mod biographies and highlights a defining part of the culture. The 'Bruce stories' observed by Cavicchi (1998: 43) and the 'Kisstories' identified by Bailey (2005: 121) (see Chapter 2) include what can be recognised as first encounters, gateway experiences and conversion experiences, presented as key points in fan biographies.

I suggest that the narrative forms identified in these disparate studies share common foundations. First encounters, gateway experiences and conversion experiences are types of peak music experience that are found across popular music styles and cultures. Identifying these sub-categories enables recognition of the shared ways that people make sense of music and life, including differences within and between popular music cultures. For example, comparing the first encounters described by extreme metal fans with those of Mods reveals divergences in how those two subjectivities are constructed. Equally, grouping the first encounters, gateway experiences and conversion experiences of hip hop fans (for example) can help to map their collective understanding of the possible shapes of hip hop fan identity across time.

In studying how individuals narrate their relationships with music, the concepts presented here build on Hennion's (2007) observation that each person's music listening has and forms 'a history'. The interactive model of music listening in his 'pragmatics of taste' (Hennion 2010; see Chapter 2) enables us to understand how particular encounters with the same music can stand out, while also recognising that these encounters can form part of an ongoing personal history upon which the listener may reflect. The collective narrative forms discussed in this chapter provide structure to the individual histories constructed around peak music experiences, while these histories in turn inform continuing identities, by affirming particular values and guiding action. First encounters, gateway experiences and conversion experiences can therefore be understood as 'narrative maps' (Pollner and Stein 1996) for participants in specific popular music cultures and for engagements with popular music more generally. Narrative maps are created when members of a culture talk about and from their own experience, thus representing the dimensions and denizens of a social world and, importantly, 'pre-presenting' them for neophytes. They have consequences for recruitment, by portraying the features of that world in more or less attractive terms, as well as for social reproduction, by transmitting values and norms to newcomers. More generally, these pre-presentations of reality are a part of the very social worlds they represent, so that the 'maps' not only represent but constitute the 'terrain' (ibid.: 204). In this way, the common tropes of first encounters, gateway experiences and conversion experiences both describe and define the cultural spaces of popular music and particular scenes. In both of these senses, they 'map' the twisted roads through which music listeners may pursue their own life's journey.

Locating cultural difference in ideals of experience, which are expressed in the stories shared by cultural participants, contrasts with a focus on indexical homologies between groups and their favoured objects (for example, Willis 1978). We can expect shared priorities of musical experience to be reflected to some extent in objective patterns of consumption, so that narrative analysis provides a way of looking behind the lists that function as shorthand classifications of popular music and its listeners. However, this approach also helps to account for more complex individual taste trajectories, as people are exposed to multiple narrative maps and may develop idiosyncratic combinations as they navigate the intermingling social worlds of popular music. Given this multivocal context, and the tendency for songs and artists to be encountered as part of discursive packages (including artwork, titles, videos and promotional media), different situations and objects might call for different maps or elements. Today's rock or metal fan typically encounters hip hop music with at least some notion of its cultural context informing their expectations, in addition to their more dominant dispositions and capacities. In turn, these may be reshaped by the experience to a greater or lesser extent, informing future encounters and potentially reframing past encounters. Such complexities are explored in the following sections, in the course of defining and analysing first encounters, gateway experiences and conversion experiences based on in-depth interviews conducted during my fieldwork in four Brisbane music scenes.

First encounters: an experience of something new

The defining element of a first encounter is the listener's experience of something new, in the sense of being outside their previous experience. Most simply, this might mean that they were previously unfamiliar with the song, artist or style. An example is provided by hip hop producer and rapper Matt (31), who described his first encounter with the genre of gangsta rap:

> I remember before that I was listening to sort of rock and metal music a lot. And there was a few like Guns 'n' Roses songs I was really into and I thought, this is from a kid's perspective, I thought that was like the bad-ass music 'cause they had a couple of swear words in their songs. And then I walked [down the hallway] like I said, I heard my brother listening to this song where Tupac was dissing Biggie, and he's just like swearing his head off saying, "I'm gonna kill you and fuckin' shoot you" and all this stuff and as a kid I thought, "Whoa! That's, that's way more hardcore, I'm listening to..." and I remember that memory and being struck by that.

Through this quote, Matt explains why this first encounter with both the artist 2Pac (Tupac Shakur) and the genre of gangsta rap was exciting and appealing. Matt was already attracted to 'bad-ass' music, suggesting rebellious and illicit elements, which he found in the rock and metal songs of Guns 'n' Roses. As he describes his first encounter with the song emanating from his brother's room, he was impressed by the even more profane and violent lyrics. His recollection emphasises an immediate thrill ('Whoa!') and a conscious decision to listen to more music of the same kind, which is reminiscent of the first encounters with extreme metal described by Kahn-Harris (2004). However, the story includes details that were probably added retrospectively, such as the identification of the rapper as Tupac Shakur and his target as 'Biggie', meaning fellow rapper Notorious B.I.G., with whom Shakur had a famous rivalry as expressed in threatening 'diss' tracks like 'Hit 'Em Up', which was probably the song heard on this occasion. There are also elements left out of Matt's story, such as the steps he took to find out these details, and any influence his brother may have had on his taste. The emphasis is placed on the chance first encounter between listener and music, marked by an immediate and intense response with biographical significance. At the same time, Matt expresses distance from the former self that is described in the story, noting that his priorities and his reaction were 'from a kid's perspective'. In this way, the first encounter helps Matt to narratively situate his current identity in relation to his younger self, placing both within a history of listening.

A first encounter can be remembered for exposing the listener to music that is new in a more profound sense, challenging previous understandings of music. Ken (58) described his first encounter with hip hop music in 1982, via Grandmaster Flash's 'Adventures on the Wheels of Steel' single, as 'like hearing [hardcore punk innovators] Black Flag or Little Richard', suggesting that it was radically and excitingly new. The song's use of samples challenged his previous understanding of what music could be: 'they were cutting Blondie and Queen and everything in, and I had never thought of music in that way and that was just bloody good'. Thus Ken's story suggests that as well as perceiving new music, he developed through this experience a new way of perceiving music. Further, in rating this as 'bloody good' and placing it in historical sequence with previous first encounters with Black Flag and Little Richard, Ken presents himself as an exploratory music listener who enjoys being challenged by new forms. This example, like the previous one, demonstrates how peak music experiences emphasise particular values.

Chance and expectations

First encounters highlight the operation of both chance and expectations in people's engagements with music. Popular music's mass-mediated form, typically accompanied by a plethora of complementary and explicatory media, reduces the likelihood of encountering a song without prior expectations. However, by virtue of the same mass-mediated form, there is a wide range of popular music in circulation and a wide range of circumstances in which it might be encountered. Even the most well-known, widely discussed works of popular music must be encountered by each listener for the first time. The element of chance is demonstrated in the following story by Lisa (34), describing her unexpected but fateful first encounter with a song:

> In grade 8, so it was like 1994 [...] I found a cassette tape on the bus. [...] And I put it in my Walkman and the first song that played was 'Beercan' by Beck. This would have been just after [the album] *Mellow Gold* came out. And there was that whole like, "I'm sad and unhappy" [manipulated speech sample] bit and I remember just thinking, "Oh my god this is the best." [...] I remember being, like my mind got blown by that song. And then I got obsessed with Beck. So like all through, probably 14, 15, I was like majorly obsessed with him and I would, you know, I got every, I still sort of have every b-side, every seven-inch [record] that he ever released from that time up until he got a bit boring. But I remember that being like a really massive moment that sort of changed my taste.

The circumstances of Lisa's first encounter with 'Beercan' allowed her to listen with a relative lack of prejudice. However, the unusual situation of finding a cassette tape on a bus while carrying a portable player might have produced a more personal kind of receptiveness. Lisa's story exemplifies the phenomenon of a first encounter as a sudden epiphany, as her 'mind got blown', inspiring an obsession with Beck. As in the celebrity stories of radio listening presented earlier in this chapter, Lisa's story emphasises that her effusive response was prior to knowledge about the song's context. The serendipitous circumstances contribute to this emphasis, framing the encounter as if the music found Lisa as much as she found it. The story places Lisa's engagement with 'Beercan' outside the typically mediated spaces of popular music listening and suggests that both her affective response ('Oh my god ... my mind got blown') and her evaluation of the song as 'the best' were more natural. First encounters that involve chance exposure to music promote the ideal of authentic, unmediated relationships to music and suggest that these are possible despite its mass-mediated circulation.

Popular music listeners can engage with a substantial amount of secondary information surrounding music, including promotional media, critical analysis and peer discussion. This creates expectations that inform the experience of music, as acknowledged in the following quote from Sal (27), which echoes the journalistic trope of a knowledgeable first encounter:

> When I first was introduced to [hip hop sub-genre] New Orleans Bounce music, it was basically just on YouTube. And I'd heard all about [iconic Bounce artist] Big Freedia. And the thing that got me was, you know the title of the song, 'Azz Everywhere'. *(Laughing)* I was like 'That sounds great!' [Sal discusses her interest in challenging norms and body positivity.] And yeah anyway so I liked that and I went and checked it out and it was like everything I ever dreamed *(laughs)*. It was like

colourful; the beat was amazing; he was just chanting constantly, like repeating phrases. [...] And then just researching it more I fell in love with it more...

The language used here suggests not only expectations but hopes ('everything I ever dreamed'), based on prior knowledge and reflexive taste. Music fans frequently acknowledge such anticipation yet, as in Sal's case, they still report excitement in their actual experience of music, remaining cognisant of the uncertainty of tasting.

Uncertainty is highlighted even more in those first encounters that differ from expectations. John (25) recalled such an encounter when he was 12 or 13 years old and his mother offered to buy him a CD during a shopping trip:

What do I get? And I remembered that my friend loved Limp Bizkit, so I wanted to get Limp Bizkit. And mum said, 'No, absolutely not, way too mature, you're not getting it'. So the shop clerk said, 'Try Linkin Park'. At the time I had no idea, I was really grumpy, I was like, 'Fuckin' I wanted Limp Bizkit, I didn't want Linkin Park!' So Linkin Park's *Hybrid Theory*, I listened to that on the ride home and twenty minutes later I was in love, I was hooked. So that was a big moment for me. Wow! I hadn't thought of that in a long time. That was a big moment.

The everyday context, for this teenager, of listening to music in the family car is remembered as 'a big moment' more than a decade later because of the peak music experience and its place in John's story of his burgeoning interest in music. A defining part of this experience was the transcendence of his expectations.

Peak music experiences involving expectations, whether they are met as in Sal's story or exceeded as in John's, highlight aspects of how music fans think about music and their relationship to it. Listeners are aware of their own taste, which they see as important but nevertheless open to change, so that one source of music's appeal is the uncertain and sometimes surprising response it elicits. Through this element of surprise, such experiences also underscore the mysterious agency that fans attribute to music, which even when it meets expectations can be memorably affecting. Leaving room for unpredictability and excess in musical experience is another way in which the first encounter narrative allows musical experience to be understood as natural or authentic, despite the heavily mediated preconceptions that listeners may hold.

Immediacy and growth

First encounters that are immediately compelling frame the listener's response as uncalculated, implying authentic good taste. However, first encounters can also anchor narratives of personal development, which instead emphasise individual agency and the transformative power of music.

For example, Allie (27) recalled her negative initial response to a music video by the grunge rock band Silverchair:

> I can remember the first time I ever came into contact with Silverchair. It was, I was at my friend's house, I think I was in grade 3, so it was '96 and [the album] *Freakshow* had just come out. We were watching [television music video programme] *rage* and we were waiting for the new Mariah Carey video to come on. And then they played two Silverchair songs back to back, they played 'Freak' and then 'Cemetery'. And I remember – 'cause my school was pretty like hardcore Christian, it was really full on – I remember looking at it and going, 'Those poor boys' mothers', and just thinking that they were really evil. […] I was freaked out.

Despite the disapproval of her peers, Silverchair became one of Allie's favourite bands during her teenage years, which would explain why she remembers this first encounter with the band. Rather than establishing natural affinity and immediate fandom, Allie's first encounter with Silverchair enables her to tell a story of growth and hard-won identity. This narrative displays authenticity in a different way from a sudden epiphany, by emphasising both individual agency and the power of music in transcending social pressures. A first encounter is therefore useful in constructing a narrative of either natural affinity or personal growth, which are alternative paths to authenticity as a popular music fan.

Gateway experiences: an experience of something more

A gateway experience involves an awareness of new possibilities. This is sometimes the result of a first encounter, as demonstrated by Matt's story about gangsta rap, though it may occur later. The word 'gateway' was used by interview participants, along with related terms like 'floodgates' and 'opening up'. The gateway metaphor is used in popular music journalism, for example in relation to 'gateway bands'. According to the top definition in crowd-sourced online dictionary *Urban Dictionary*, 'Your gateway band is the band you first listened to which completely opened up your world of music' (Lest 2008). Experimental rock band Sonic Youth, who were cited by a number of interview participants, are often described in the music press and in fan discussions as a gateway band because they are known to include references to lesser-known music and art in their lyrics, artwork and interviews, thereby introducing those objects to pop and rock music audiences. It is appropriate to use the same terminology for gateway experiences, which are also claimed by those who have them to open paths to new fields of experience.

An invitation

The defining element of a gateway experience is that it leads to something more, showing the appeal of an area beyond the listener's current sphere of listening. A common instance is when the experience of a particular song seems to equip the listener with a way of approaching a particular artist or style. Jim (44) described such a gateway experience in relation to Bruce Springsteen:

> I was very much a latecomer to Springsteen. He was very big when I was growing up as a teenager, *Born In The USA* came out in 1985 when I was 14. And really when you think about it, being a huge fan of [Australian rock band] Midnight Oil, why wouldn't I like Springsteen? Actually I was sceptical, it was too ubiquitous, it was too everywhere. [...] So it took me a long time to go back and actually hear it for what it was. And a very important moment for me with Springsteen was when an ex-girlfriend played me the song 'Downbound Train' from *Born In The USA*. And the very first listen to that song, this doesn't usually happen for anybody, but I was moved to tears by that song on the very first listen, it just completely broke me to pieces. And from that point I was like, "Okay, I'm ready to let this person into my life". I was in my late thirties by then.

This experience, marked by a sudden epiphany, fits very well with the 'Bruce stories' observed by Cavicchi (1998). It was far from Jim's first encounter with Springsteen, but it marked the point at which he consciously let the artist into his life in an inversion of the usual 'gateway' metaphor. With popular music artists who have a substantial oeuvre, fans are often keen to discuss their point of entry. This occurs in everyday conversation but is especially common and sometimes compulsory in more formal contexts of fandom, such as online forums. By presenting their gateway experience, a fan says something about their history and tastes as a music listener at the same time as making a case for the qualities of the music. For example, Jim's story makes us aware that he is not one to follow popular taste, but also that he distances himself from his history as a music 'snob'. We learn about his broader musical preferences by hearing that he was not drawn in by the upbeat singles from *Born in the U.S.A.*, but was moved to tears by a more subtly arranged, melancholic 'deep cut' (a track that was not a single or hit on its own). Such stories both draw from and contribute to the fan and critical discourse about which songs and albums are more suitable for newcomers or well-versed fans, or for those who tend to prefer one style to another, demonstrating how music both defines and is defined by its fans.

An experience involving one artist can be a gateway to a wider musical genre or approach. Two such experiences were described by Emily (29):

> And then I remember a friend showing me [the punk and post-punk band] Wire and then it was just like, "Oh there's actually a little bit more!" *(laughs)*... ah, I dunno, not-straight-down-the-line music out there. And the same with [the band] Can as well, like I remember when somebody showed me Krautrock and I was just like, "Holy shit, this is amazing!"[2]

Emily described her first encounters with Wire and Can as introductions to much more than those bands, opening gateways through which her listening tastes and creative projects expanded in ways that were 'not-straight-down-the-line'. For a knowledgeable audience, Emily's brief references to Wire, Can and Krautrock provide more specific meaning than general terms like 'alternative' or 'progressive' taste, which might indeed seem gauche. Thus, gateway experiences demonstrate the use of peak music experiences to chart and present narratives of growth. As in the previous examples, Emily described her reaction as enthusiastic and immediate, emphasising direct, emotional response over indirect, rational evaluation and thereby framing the experiences and the longer narrative they construct as natural, unforced and authentic.

Passing through the gateway

The second feature of a gateway experience is that the invitation is taken up, meaning it can only be defined retrospectively. In many cases, the advancement of taste is evidenced by the new field of interest being less mainstream, carrying more of what Thornton (1995) calls subcultural capital. This may be read into Emily's story above and is sometimes acknowledged directly, such as the following quote from Pete (34):

> ...my tastes had gone, like I'd come from the suburbs and come from this background of like a really "Oz rock" [Australian mainstream rock] family, but my ability to think critically about what was going on, what I was listening to, was growing as I was more exposed to it. [...] So I bought those albums [by indie bands Gaslight Radio and Pavement on the same day] because I'd [read] reviews of them that sounded like, in hindsight it's maybe sounding like something I wanted to like. You know it just sounded interesting to me, and kind of maybe it kicked off a few of the things I'd been enjoying in the things I'd been listening to [...] it was kind of a gateway into indie rock I guess, or indie music, but, and then yeah the floodgates opened pretty quickly there...

Self-analyses like Pete's illustrate the reflexivity of some music fans when describing their trajectories of taste. They acknowledge the operation of subcultural capital and media framing, while nevertheless making it clear that their musical experiences were personally significant. A remarkably similar sequence of events from a decade earlier was recounted by Julian (44):

> I read two glowing reviews of these records [by indie bands The Smiths and The Go-Betweens], I had no idea who these bands were. But I went off to the tiny little record store and I ordered these records, at the age of 13. And the woman standing there was like, "You want what?" [...] And that was the moment where I went, "Ah, there's this whole other

thing happening". And I left behind all of my Eighties tastes really, really quickly. And I started becoming an explorer.

As Julian's story makes explicit, gateway experiences are remembered not only for introducing new music to a listener with particular tastes, but for empowering the listener themselves to change through engaging with the music. In Julian's case, this was to leave behind his 'Eighties tastes' and become 'an explorer'. This process of becoming is the central focus of conversion experiences, which are discussed below.

Conversion experiences: an experience of change

A conversion experience is a peak music experience that is credited with a change in the listener's taste or identity. In research interviews, these were often described in response to a question to the effect of, 'Has there ever been a time when your taste in music changed?' While the answer might involve the influence of peers and media, the role of those influences is often to lead a person to the crucial experience with music in which their change of taste is crystallised. Listeners are conscious of the role of their environment and attitude in constructing a musical experience. This makes conversion experiences a powerful demonstration of the situated way that people interpret and evaluate music and, likewise, remember situations by reference to music. These experiences highlight the dynamic nature of people's relationships with music and the active nature of listening and taste, which are processes that must be learned.

Memorably different

An acceptance that the same music can be perceived differently depending on the situation is fundamental to the concept of conversion experiences. The consistency that is implicit in the very concept of taste means that a listener's perceptions will usually differ only subtly, or at least in expected ways. Those experiences that produce a substantially different impression – to adopt Ahmed's (2014) term encompassing both felt impact and reflexive judgement – are therefore surprising enough to be remembered. The following quote from Julie (45) illustrates this:

> I remember it really clearly, I was over at [a boyfriend's] house and he was playing [thrash metal band] Slayer and I was just like, "This is just noise", and then all of a sudden it kind of started making sense. Like I could pick out the structure of the song and it was like, "Oh wow that's actually a tune!" You know, it's not just loud noise that sounds like ridiculous. And then it started to make sense.

Julie explained that she went on to host a heavy metal show on community radio station 4ZZZfm, covering the thrash metal style of Slayer as well as other subgenres. Her story shows how music fans conceive of taste as a co-productive meeting of listener and music, in which a change on the listener's part ('I could pick out the structure') is simultaneous with a change in the object ('noise... started making sense'). This is consistent with Hennion's (2010) proposition that taste is not a static disposition but an active approach, and an object does not 'contain' its effects but responds with effects that are variable and participatory. This variability is how a conversion experience can be surprising and vividly memorable. While Julie's change of taste might be explained convincingly by her intimate relationship with a Slayer fan and associated exposure to heavy metal music, she nevertheless pinpoints her conversion to a precise experience.[3] In this way, a conversion experience can, like Woodward's (2001) 'taste epiphanies', act as a mnemonic and narrative device that condenses and concretises personal evolutions, for both the individual and their interlocutors.

The context of listening

All peak music experiences, but especially conversion experiences, highlight the dynamic, contingent nature of music's meaning and effects, depending in part on the precise setting in which it is encountered. Nowak and Bennett (2014) call this setting the 'sound environment', referring to the assemblage of variables – space, time, body and technology – involved in the consumption of music. The capacity for a physical setting to shed new light on music is highlighted in the following quote from Martin (33):

> I remember in [my housemate's] bedroom one time, he had ['shoegaze' indie band My Bloody Valentine's album] *Loveless* playing super loud, and... I'd never really listened to it before, kind of thought it sounded a little bit tinny and noisy when I'd previously heard it. So I never gave it the time. But he just, he had it cranked in his room, and it was a nice day, and his bay windows were open, and um, it was just – yeah I just thought that sounded amazing, and um, it sort of changed my sensibility a bit straight away. Just by opening my ears to harsher sounds that can also be really immersive and beautiful.

Martin said that he had been aware of the critical canonisation of *Loveless*, but that on its own had not ensured a pleasurable experience. On the contrary, he said that this unexpectedly positive experience gave him more 'trust' in music writers. It is easy to imagine how sunlight through bay windows and loud ('cranked') volume might highlight the immersive qualities of music. At the same time, this example highlights the key element of a conversion experience, that the change of taste (described here as 'sensibility') endures beyond the immediate setting. Martin's confession that he had 'previously heard' the album yet 'never really listened to it' demonstrates again the popular conception of taste as an activity that is developed through practice, consistently with Hennion (2010).

Together with the physical setting, musical experience is informed by the listener's attitude, which might be based on personal or critical recommendations. For example, Liz (26) never thought she would like music as fast, heavy and 'punishing' as grindcore. However, with the recommendation of a friend ('If someone I respect likes a kind of music, I'll listen to it'), in the live setting that she considers crucial to being 'impressed' by heavy music, she experienced her first encounter with Melbourne grindcore band Agents of Abhorrence as 'amazing ... beautiful music that sent me down the road to hell ... it opened me up to being curious about other kinds of grindcore'. Liz's reference to hell is a mirror opposite of the usual language of conversion, but the metaphors of salvation and damnation equally highlight the narrator's devotion to particular music. Consistently with these religious metaphors, the emphasis is placed on an epiphanic experience, which is remembered and discussed as pivotal in the self-narrative being presented. The changes of taste described in conversion experiences might remain abstract and inexplicable without reference to the experiential factors that completed the music in a particular way, but through the prism of peak music experiences such developments can be more concretely explained by listeners and understood by others.

Conclusion

First encounters, gateway experiences and conversion experiences are narrative devices with which people place peak music experiences as milestones in their relationships to music. These experiences are defined by their positions in personal histories of listening, explicitly linking music to biography such that each gives meaning to the other. This demonstrates a popular understanding that the taste and enjoyment of music are shaped through past experiences and reshaped through new experiences. While these particular experiences with music stand out as different and memorable, they are not presented as isolated or random, but as structured and structuring elements in a continuous personal timeline. This history of music listening is an important aspect of identity for people who define themselves as music fans. Through these narratives, people justify their orientations towards particular music and also to past selves. They highlight the specific appeal of particular songs, artists and styles, not abstractly but by reference to the personal contexts in which they were encountered and experienced. As well as identifying and evaluating the objects of taste, these stories explain how and why particular evaluations were made at particular times, constructing narratives of personal growth and developing identity.

While first encounters, gateway experiences and conversion experiences are deeply personal accounts of musical experience and demonstrate highly subjective interpretations and uses of music, they contribute to the discursive construction of collective identities. First, as shared frameworks for the discussion of taste, they make apparent the common and divergent priorities of music listeners. Matt's description of his first encounter with gangsta rap emphasised the appeal of the 'hardcore', 'bad-ass' lyrics that are a defining element of the genre, while Martin's conversion experience with My Bloody Valentine was centred on his new appreciation of the 'immersive' quality of their music, a feature commonly identified in critical appraisals of the band and the shoegaze genre they exemplify. By describing their peak music experiences using shared narrative frameworks, people situate themselves in relation to collective evaluations of music and the values underlying them, while maintaining decidedly individual stories and insisting on their own evaluative agency. Thus, second, the narrative forms themselves promote certain values and limit the ways of being a music listener or fan, acting as narrative maps within particular groups and in popular music more generally. The circulation of these stories promotes an expectation that for someone to be considered an authentic music lover, they should be able to present a convincing self-narrative involving peak music experiences. The tropes of first encounters, gateway experiences and conversion experiences privilege pre-conscious, surprising, emotional and physical responses to music, promoting the idea that people have natural affinities for certain music and that music acts immediately upon listeners. Accordingly, despite popular music's mass, commercial context, the operation of many mediating technologies and the prominence of interpretive discourses in both specialist and mainstream media, the narrative devices explored in this chapter enable and even require people to present their relationships with popular music as both authentic (according to the kind of cultural definitions illustrated here) and quite personal.

Notes

1 Simon Frith was born in 1946 and 'Long Tall Sally' was released in 1957.
2 'Krautrock' is a term used by English-speaking journalists to describe a genre of experimental rock developed in the 1970s in Germany, where it is sometimes called 'Kosmische', including bands such as Can, Faust and Neu! (see for example Cope 1995).
3 Peak music experiences in the context of interpersonal relationships are discussed in detail in Chapter 6.

4 Life-changing moments

Experiences of inspiration and influence

There is a well-worn and widespread claim that music 'changes lives'. This idea and the confident way it is deployed are depicted in the 2004 film *Garden State*, when the female lead Sam places headphones on protagonist Andrew's head and asserts, 'You gotta hear this one song. It'll change your life, I swear', referring to 'New Slang' by US indie band The Shins. Such a belief is subject matter for a number of popular songs, such as when Don McLean's 'American Pie' (1971) asks rhetorically, 'Can music save your mortal soul?', and is perhaps answered by the disco staple, 'Last Night A DJ Saved My Life', first released by Indeep in 1981. As this iconic title illustrates, the claims people make about music's profound effects on their lives often involve singular experiences in which specific music in a particular situation has a lasting impact. The notion that music acts on people is taken seriously in censorship laws, marketing strategies, religious codes, public funding allocations and social movements (see Street 2012). However, the claims made by individuals about their experiences of music's life-changing power have been downplayed in social and cultural studies, due to theoretical assumptions and disciplinary priorities.

Where the last chapter considered how people interpret and evaluate music by linking it to their own lives, this chapter takes the opposite approach, by considering how people understand and explain their lives by reference to music. Peak music experiences are at the centre of these narratives. They provide inspiration to engage in activities and to form commitments, so that they are called upon by people to explain how they 'became' musicians, fans and so on. Peak music experiences also influence beliefs, values and ways of doing things, in both musical practice and other aspects of life. These popular claims demand serious attention, including critical analysis, as memories and stories that both reveal and obscure the innumerable factors in anyone's life. By the end of *Garden State*, Andrew is deeply affected by his relationship with Sam and the reflection it stirs, in the important context of a return to his hometown for his mother's funeral, but this complex set of events is memorably epiphanised in their first meeting and its musical moment: listening to 'New Slang' changed his life. Such epiphanies convey subjective beliefs and meanings, as well as cultural standards of truth and biography.

DOI: 10.4324/9781003093244-4

Identifying experiences with music as sources of inspiration and influence is part of the discursive construction of popular music and its listeners, emphasising the agency of both over more practical, social and cultural factors. At the same time, the specifics of these experiences make apparent the crucial role of affect in the ways people respond to music and therefore its social agency. The following section considers how the question of music's social effects has been theorised to date and introduces the specific theoretical framework for this chapter.

The study of music's effects

Music's perceived capacity to affect people has shaped its treatment in both policy and theory. Street (2012) observes that the urge to censor music for fear of its effects is as old as music itself, recurring across every century and continent. In one of the earliest recorded examples, Plato (1966) theorises that harmonies and rhythms influence character, necessitating their regulation by the state and their careful use in education, while the introduction of a new musical form endangers the whole fabric of society. Historically, most attempts to understand music's effects have distinguished between meaning and affect, and it is the latter that has fuelled the perception of music as problematic, as it seems to bypass reason and cannot be explained through language (Gilbert and Pearson 1999). This negativity can be seen in the pathological and gendered concepts of Lisztomania in the 19th century and Beatlemania in the 20th century (Gooley 2004), along with more recent equivalents like Bieber Fever and 1D (One Direction) Mania.

A parallel prejudice existed for some time within sociology, where music's so-called 'abstract' features, independent of images and words, were seen to be distinct from social realities and impervious to social analysis (DeNora 2003: 152). This resonated in methodologies that overlooked subjective experiences of music, treating culture as a structurally determined constraint and presupposing the meanings and uses of music for particular social groups (Bennett 2008). This impedes the consideration of music as a resource for subjectively navigating those constraints and, as this chapter explores, how music might be said to exert its own social force. Meanwhile, disciplines such as social psychology took up the question of music's effects, for example by considering quantitative correlations between heavy metal or rap listening and teenage behavioural problems (not predictive: Epstein et al 1990), and between country music and white metropolitan suicide rates (indicative of causation: Stack and Gundlach 1992). Such literature established a paradigmatic discourse of music's pathological effects that sidelined sociological inquiry until more recently, with the cultural and affective turns discussed below.

According to DeNora (2003), Theodor Adorno was the first modern social theorist to take seriously the Platonic concern with music's causative properties. Adorno proposes that the internal dynamics of a composition provoke particular modes of engagement from listeners, which can influence their engagement with the world more broadly. For example, Arnold Schoenberg's complex pieces encouraged critical insight into the social character of their period, while the standardised form and repetitive content of contemporaneous popular music invited uncritical submission not only to dance fads, but to authority. Thus, Adorno continues the traditional denigration of physical and emotional responses to music (ibid.: 87), and his method of analysing musical texts in conjunction with critical social theory is criticised by DeNora as ungrounded and abstract (ibid.: 153). However, as she points out, Adorno's work importantly rejects the dualism of music and society, by focusing on music's relation to consciousness as causative and constitutive of social life.

The so-called cultural and affective turns have brought renewed attention to what music 'does' in this social sense. The cultural turn involved the recognition that culture, including popular culture, is not only expressive but constitutive of social identity (Chaney 1994). Accordingly, Street (2012: 173) asserts, 'Music has the capacity to make us do and feel things that we would not otherwise, and it does so with immediacy and directness'. However, post-cultural turn studies have been less concerned with what music does to people, than with what people do with music, as in DeNora's (2000, 2003) use of 'affordances' to describe what music makes possible. Meanwhile, the affective turn involved the recognition that culture and society do not operate entirely at a semiotic level, but through bodies that feel and interact. It is through intensifications of feeling that people recognise and attribute meaning to objects, people and themselves, over a lifetime of encounters that both form and trace impressions (Ahmed 2004). Applying this insight to music draws attention to the non-verbal, physical and emotional effects that were historically feared or dismissed, but which account for so much of music's unique power and appeal. As Gilbert (2010) observes, music is the cultural form that deals most directly in affects, so that its power resides not in its capacity to express existing situations and identities, but in its capacity to make us feel differently and to share those feelings with others. Where an Adornian perspective might lament this abdication of reason and agency, post-affective turn studies reject straightforward dichotomies and hierarchies between mental and physical experience, and between bodies that act and are acted upon. Music affords experiences of the body, time and sociality that enable us to place ourselves in imagined cultural worlds and thereby to construct identities. Accordingly, musical experience can play a social and political role by creating collective identities and motivating commitments and action (Eyerman and Jamison 1998; Bennett 2001). Music allows us not only to perceive and express meanings, but also to experience those meanings as important and worth acting on. The study of music's social agency must therefore have regard to the level of experience at which it manifests, and peak music experiences draw specific focus to this level.

The study of biographically significant musical experiences poses certain research challenges, as the researcher's access is mediated by the very discursive processes that construct those experience as significant. However, the point is not to investigate objective events forensically, but to make their subjective (re)construction a subject of study. We can take seriously the effects that individuals attribute to music, while investigating the social origins of those effects and the performative dimension of their stories. Since experiences are constituted in and by discourse, to understand even music's 'immediate' resonance for individuals requires empirical study of not only its textual properties but its cultural placement. The study of peak music experiences is specifically attentive to the narratives involved in constructing and reconstructing music, listeners and the experiences in which they interact and are produced. To approach them as 'epiphanies' (Denzin 1989; Green 2016) is to consider how people produce stories of experience that accord with collective standards of truth and form. Rather than trying to separate what music does from what people say it does, the two must be recognised as interdependent. Musicians and music fans act on the basis of their perceptions about music's power, including their understanding of peak music experiences, so that this is a way in which music does shape lives. The following sections of this chapter will consider peak music experiences as sources of inspiration to engage in certain activities, including 'becoming' a musician or a fan, and as influences on musical practice and beyond.

Peak music experiences as inspiration

The question of why some people become music fans and musicians has received less scholarly attention than how those identities are performed (Duffett 2013), partly due to the deterministic models of cultural taste and practice noted earlier (Bennett 2008). Recognising more complex links between social and cultural structures opens up questions of origin and inspiration, put by Simon Frith (1992: 184) as follows:

> What pushes people into wanting to be performers or wanting to create? This can't be answered in terms of their wanting to make money, it involves too a desired social experience. How does that differ from the social experience of being a fan? I can't think of a study in any area which addresses this.

However, these questions are addressed directly in popular discourse and often with reference to peak music experiences. Popular narratives of 'becoming-a-fan' attribute quasi-religious conversions to particular musical encounters, as discussed in the previous chapter. In accordance with this tendency, interview participants ascribed agency to specific peak music experiences that 'turned me on to music' (Rob, 40), 'set off my musical tangent' (Dan, 26), provided a 'big kick-along' (Nick, 27) or more broadly 'changed my life' (Sally, 30). In this way, peak music experiences are credited as a source of inspiration to engage in certain musical practices.

Becoming a fan or a musician

Alicia (34), a rock 'n' roll guitarist, commented on the ubiquity of peak music experiences in narratives of becoming a musician:

> Everyone sort of has this, "Oh I heard Fleetwood Mac on the radio", you know, "Neil's guitar lick in this bit of this song and it changed everything for me".

The interview data bear out Alicia's observation. Indie musician Julian (44) was confident in identifying a peak music experience as the genesis of his desire to play the drums:

> One night they broadcast a [The] Police concert. This was in about 1983 or something [...] And I just watched Stewart Copeland drumming and something happened, I just went, "I'm going to do that". And then I just suddenly went, "There's a drum kit here". Dad had kinda taught me a little bit but I just saw him [Copeland] drumming and something just went, click. "I'm gonna do that". And I've been drumming ever since, so thank you Stewart Copeland! [...] I can confidently isolate that exact moment of, you know, before the show I wasn't thinking like that, an hour later I was going, "Tomorrow, I'm gonna do this". It was genuinely that *(clicks fingers)* – the light went off.

Julian's story emphasises the sudden, clear and memorable impact of the peak music experience as an inspiration, which is a common feature of such stories. Upon reflection he teased out some factors, including the appeal of the music performed by The Police, the unique musical and physical personality of Stewart Copeland as a drummer, and the resonance of these factors with the enthusiasm and energy of his 11-year-old self. Julian's story exemplifies a common narrative in which people who had access to instruments and musical training as children, nevertheless, describe their inspiration to become a musician as a separate matter. Peak music experiences tend to be foregrounded over more mundane but practical matters, reflecting the emphasis in popular music discourse on the capacity of both individuals and music to transcend normal social and cultural constraints. By privileging the affective power of peak music experiences, people affirm the transcendent nature of popular music as well as claiming an authentic, personal connection to it. At the same time, this emphasis is consistent with the scholarly recognition that social commitments and actions are driven by feeling (Eyerman & Jamison 1998; Bennett 2001; Ahmed 2004). Accordingly, 'becoming' a musician is not purely a rational calculation of opportunities and benefits, nor the unconscious carrying out of a structurally determined trajectory, but involves reflexive awareness of an embodied feeling that certain things are more valuable and desirable than others. These feelings are produced through experience, with the result that certain experiences are remembered as illuminating and motivating. As Ahmed (2004: 33) says, 'it is a question of *what sticks*, of what connections are lived as the most intense or intimate, as being closer to the skin' (emphasis in original). This is not to discount the structuring role of discourse, but to recognise how it can operate through feeling. For example, the discourse of musical vocation described above contributes to the construction of certain musical experiences as powerful and compelling in certain ways, as well as to the expectation that musicians will provide such an origin story.

In stories of becoming, peak music experiences often mark the emergence or recognition of new feelings, as shown in the following quotes:

> Max (32): I do have a memory of the first song that I ever liked and that is The Models' 'Out of Mind Out of Sight'. [...] My mum bought the 12-inch maxi-single of that song and she played it and I just thought it was wild. [...] That was the first song I was like, "I love music".
>
> Rob (40): The song that actually made me, that I guess turned me on to music, it was like a lightbulb moment. My music teacher played 'Lucy In The Sky With Diamonds' when I was in year eight. And there was something about it, I'd been a bit indifferent to music up until that point, which was a bit weird because my brother was a [radio DJ] but I didn't really care so much about it until I heard 'Lucy In The Sky With Diamonds'. Suddenly I was like, "Fuck that's an interesting song". It just sort of did something.

These examples illustrate the obvious but significant point that a love for music is felt and reflexively recognised through actual engagements with specific music. It is in this sense that Rob is correct in saying the song 'did something' or 'turned [him] on to music'. If listening involves actively setting up the required passivity and taste involves techniques learned through use (Hennion 2007), we can understand how particular encounters with music might be especially instructive in the development of such personal repertoires. They might entail a change in desires, priorities or ways of doing things, so a peak music experience might not merely be representative of personal changes but credited as a cause in itself. For example, Elly (32) remembered hearing a song on the radio not only as her introduction to a favourite musician, but as a 'life-changing' moment:

> I guess one of the key musical influences on my own music is Ani Di Franco and I discovered her music, I think when I was in high school, a teenager some time, and I just remember hearing her on [radio station]

Triple J. [...] I had to find out who it was, and from that moment on I was a fan and it was just, it was immediate. Like it was just an immediate experience. [...] I was in the shower *(laughs)*. On the radio. [...] It was just one of those life-changing moments really. I sort of think, "What if I hadn't have heard that song, what would've happened?" [...] It just put a completely different slant on how I connected with music and it was a much more personal connection from that point on.

In this encounter, Elly experienced a new way of connecting with music, which became central to her identity. As a result, she categorises this peak music experience as a crucial fork in her biographical journey, or what is often referred to as a 'sliding doors' moment, so that she wonders what would have happened if she had not heard that song at that time.

These examples illustrate how peak music experiences can literally embody nascent attitudes towards music and encapsulate them in memory. These attitudes, in turn, reflect on their bearer as markers of developing identity. An experience of being moved by music is evidence of the qualities of that music (and music generally) but also the qualities of the self that was so moved. This is consistent with Ahmed's (2004) assertion that both subjects and objects are recognised and evaluated through intensifications of feeling that are produced in the encounters between them. Through our affective encounters with music, we reflexively learn how we feel about it and thus recognise what it is, and who we are. Such feelings are not reducible to each particular situation but point to a history of feelings within a shared communicative world (Crossley 1998). The concept of peak music experiences is a part of that communicative world for the music scene participants who were interviewed and it refers to those encounters that stand out, by virtue of the singular intensity or character of the feelings they produce within that history. These are the feelings which 'stick' and create lasting impressions on music and the experiencing self.

Seeing, doing and feeling

Inspiration is often found through seeing and doing. This is not to say that every person who enjoys a concert will want to become a musician or even a fan. Commonly reported feelings that go further in explaining such an urge are affinity and possibility. For example, Kim (44) explained that her family 'wasn't musical' and her own interest in music was not 'expected', when a televised performance inspired her to take up the guitar:

I was nine or ten maybe and I was watching TV, like a Saturday morning music show, and I remember seeing Joan Armatrading. You know, this beautiful black woman playing a [Fender] Stratocaster [guitar]. And she was really normal, she wasn't like a rock star, she was a normal looking woman, and I was really taken by her. My dad bought me her album and

I wasn't a massive fan of her music but I just remember going, "She's like really different to everybody else and I want to be like her".

Kim soon began taking guitar lessons and decades later she continues to perform and record, believing herself and her current role models to be 'normal' like Joan Armatrading, meaning unpretentious as opposed to 'rock stars'. She attributes these aspects of her identity partly to her experience of affinity and possibility while watching Armatrading. As Kim acknowledged with some apparent embarrassment, she was a white Australian child when she experienced this identification with an African American woman. This speaks to popular music's well-known capacity to accommodate fellow-feeling across social categories like race, age and nationality, and sometimes to diminish the importance of such difference. In contrast, several interview participants who identified as Aboriginal and Māori said that racial identity was an important aspect of their youthful identification with both local and international Black musicians, including Jamaican reggae artist Bob Marley and US hip hop artists. Racial identity is a more central aspect of these genres of music, but it must also be considered that consumers of music can have unequal experiences of affinity as a result of racist and otherwise exclusionary discourse. Musical experience is not necessarily determined or limited by social divisions, but it can certainly be a way in which those divisions are experienced and reflexively navigated.

Illustrating the compulsion and possibility that can accompany identification in a musical experience, Nick (26) described his reaction to a festival-headlining performance by North American indie-rock band the Pixies, around five years earlier, as follows:

> … and when I saw 'em I was like, *(whispered)* 'Whoa', like, this is, this is it! After that I was like, 'I love this and I wanna, like, get involved in that and do this', yeah. […] I might have been talking about it but I don't think I was actually playing at that time. It was definitely one of the big kick-alongs to get myself organised and get into it.

Nick explained that the singer of the Pixies acted as a role model: 'the way he did things his own way and he was like yelping and screaming and doin' whatever and it's like, "Oh, you can do it", like you can, you know'. This is reminiscent of numerous stories in popular music media and especially those at the heart of punk ideology, in which watching a band shows the spectator that they too can 'form a band' without the means, skill or style that the mainstream (supposedly) demands. Famously, punk icon Joe Strummer of The Clash said in 1976: 'Yesterday I thought I was a crud. Then I saw the Sex Pistols and I became a king and decided to move into the future' (Coon 2012). This reiterates the idea that music's affective power inspires and enables people to transcend typical social and cultural constraints. One way this power seems to manifest is when music creates a feeling of connection between a listener and a performer, even though it may be mediated through television or concert staging, so that the listener believes they could or do share the performer's way of being. In such circumstances, popular music draws unique power from its dual identity as a mass mediated form and an accessible folk culture.

As well as experiences of witnessing musical performance, experiences of engaging in it can be inspiring through the feelings they produce. For example, Trish (37) described a childhood experience in which she became aware that she was a singer:

> I was about six years old or something, and I remember getting on the back of the truck for the Christmas carols and everyone singing these carols all over town and all the lights coming on, and suddenly people started singing in harmony. So I can really vividly remember working out the harmonies and singing along and realising, "Oh, there's this thing that people do". And that was a really, um, that was an awakening I guess in that I could do it easily and I felt confident in this thing, that I wasn't really aware of prior to that moment.

In Trish's story, it is clear how the act of singing was presented to her as meaningful and appealing, then how her own attempt at singing resulted in a positive experience and thus an identification. A similar process was described in bolder terms by Cam (40), a multi-instrumentalist and front person for several bands who said that he 'became a dancer' through a single, memorable experience of dancing:

> When I was 14 I had a kind of, overnight I became a dancer. I don't know how to explain it other than: it was the last school dance of the year and I was really excited. [...] And I get into this dancehall and this girl goes, "I want to dance with you". That blew me over the edge, so I don't really remember what happened, but all I remember is, the night went really fast, and I was in the air a lot, doing splits, spinning around and all that. I sort of realised the next day that was what I was gonna do the rest of my life. Had a sort of a flash of the future: alright, this is my path, I know who I am, this is what I'm gonna do. [...] Dancing and music.

Paradoxically, an experience defined by a loss of self-consciousness and intentionality enabled Cam to realise, on reflection, who he was and who he would be for the rest of his life. This is a rationalisation founded on embodied doing and undergoing.

The inspiration that people attribute to peak music experiences is rooted in the feelings that define them. In the examples presented here, they describe feelings of affinity, love, belonging, confidence, excitement and certainty, which are produced in specific interactions with music that are in turn marked as significant. As recognised in pragmatist philosophy and the sociology of affect, it is through emotions we apprehend the shape and character of events and things, including ourselves. This repeats associations that are already in place but can also disrupt them in memorable ways. Such disruption is a feature of common narratives about peak music experiences. When a specific musical experience creates lasting impressions, it is remembered as a life-defining moment.

The influence of peak music experiences

The concept of influence is well recognised in popular music culture. Musicians are frequently expected to list their 'influences', meaning the artists whose work informed their own practice, while music is often credited with influence on non-musical areas of fans' lives, from style to political attitudes. Ways of doing things and the priorities they enact can be transmitted and absorbed in peak music experiences, highlighting the unique powers of music to affect subjectivities.

Influence on musical practice

Peak music experiences can have an influence at quite a practical level, as they demonstrate both effects that can be achieved and ways of achieving them. Musicians described in interviews how affecting performances or recordings demonstrated the power of a certain creative approach. Musical influence also operates in less practically minded but arguably deeper ways, as artists adopt thematic concerns and even motivations from peak music experiences that intimate what is worth doing and therefore why, as well as how, to do it. Matt (31), a rapper and hip hop music producer, described a listening experience that caused him to reconsider his own artistic priorities:

> I went around to a fella's house who was already doing [youth music workshops] and he was like, "Have a listen to these songs I recorded" [...] with people in detention, youth detention. And I was listening to it and I remember one particular song was a girl, she was singing about love, and it was like a particularly touching, lovely song. And I remember thinking to myself at the time, a lot of the hip hop that was going on around me was from like, middle-class, suburban people rappin' about hardcore stuff, like we're about trying to sound rough, and sound tough, and violence. But then I heard this song from someone in youth detention, who actually had lived a very hard life, you know, really hard, is singing, making this song about love. And I kinda thought, "That's, that's, I wanna help more of this music to happen". You know? That feels realer to me than a lot of this other stuff happening.

Matt said that this experience provoked a change in the content of his own music and also inspired him to begin working in community music programmes. Accordingly, he credited this peak music experience with influence on both his musical practice and other areas of his life. Matt's reasoning shows the close connection in popular music between an artist's musical practice and their identity, so that artistic choices imply deeper values that are expected to be consistent in other areas of life, in accordance with notions of authenticity – in hip hop, being 'real'. In this case, we can see that the judgement of authenticity is not detached, but involves feelings produced in the subjective experience of listening. The recording of a girl who Matt knew to be in youth detention singing about love 'felt realer' to him than his peers rapping about violence. The recorded music and its context, including the singer's background and the situation in which the music was heard, cannot be separated as causes for this feeling, which in turn guided self-reflection and action. This example illustrates the relation between discourse, affect and meaning; the feeling produced in musical experience is informed by discourse, and that feeling informs the meaning of the experience and judgements about the music.

Influence outside musical practice

People claim to have been influenced by music in ways that go well beyond their approach to performing or listening. The link between music fandom and visual style, especially clothing, has been a focus of attention in subcultural studies (for example, Hebdige 1979; Feldman 2009). Some interview participants described how their musical tastes guided their sartorial choices, not only through direct imitation of musical idols but also through the interpretation and adaptation of underlying ethics. For example, Julie (45) said that when she was a young teenager, David Bowie's Ziggy Stardust persona demonstrated 'an anything goes attitude that I really liked, so I picked it up and adapted it to my own wardrobe somewhat'. Music fandom has also been shown to infuse a person's life in less obvious ways, for example in Bennett's (2013) finding that some ageing punks maintain their identification with values such as 'do it yourself', even as they 'tone down' spectacular forms of identification like the mohawk hairstyle. Similar narratives were presented by interview participants, as the following quote from Grant (49) demonstrates:

> [Attending numerous punk rock gigs in the 1980s] has shaped who I am, I can't deny it. Like I wouldn't be probably self-employed, gettin' around in red jeans and that's the only trousers I own, you know, not giving a shit about having a shower some days. [...] I still do shit like shoplift or whatever it might be, just stuff like that that the normal 49-year-old adult in [my suburb] wouldn't do, you know?

As shown here, lifelong influences are often attributed to immersion in a music culture rather than instant epiphanies. However, by emphasising the centrality of music to some people's identity, these narratives underscore the significance of what someone is saying when they attribute their musical taste and practices to specific experiences.

In some instances, people do identify particular music experiences as influential in their broader lives. Liz (26) pinpointed her viewing of a music film as influential in her adoption of punk values in her late teens:

> When I was 18 or 19 I watched the Fugazi [band] documentary, *Instrument*. And that was like super influential. When I was getting more involved with like, my musical participation of like how I want things to be and I was trying always to be a bit more like, all-ages where possible, and if I was gonna go to a hardcore show and I saw that one of my friends was like acting rough in the pit then I would like talk to them about it. Just be like honest or whatever.

Instrument (1999), which was also cited as influential by another interview participant, consists largely of live performance footage, intercut with band interviews and footage of touring and recording, without narration. It includes footage of all-ages shows at non-traditional venues and of band members castigating individuals for rough behaviour at concerts. Liz adopted the politically charged practices and values she perceived in the film and therefore credits her first experience of watching the film as 'super influential'. She claims that this guided her response to behaviour she encountered in local settings. Indeed, Liz emphasised the importance of sources of information like this film, along with zines and intra-scene conversations, to a young person without access to 'a sociology degree', opining that 'it shouldn't be hidden away in libraries'. For her, as a politically minded member of a punk scene, musical experience is closely associated with moral and political education. Her viewing of the concert film *Instrument* was a memorably influential peak music experience within that ongoing education.

Musical content and especially lyrics are often cited by listeners as influential on their thought. Interview participants described the formative impact of lyrics and extra-musical statements by expressly politically engaged artists like Ani Di Franco, Bob Marley and Midnight Oil. For example, Dan (26) said that after becoming a fan of folk-rock artist John Butler, when he saw a performance that also inspired him to 'pick up the guitar' himself, the artist's influence extended into political commitment through both practices and lyrics:

> I started going to like, protests and stuff where those bands would be playing, because I'd see them playing. John was always talking about certain things, like ref[ugees] – you know, I ended up writing a song about refugees, and all that stuff.

Since music and its presentation can have such influence, it follows that a musical experience might be credited as decisive. This is demonstrated in the following story told by Lily (25), who was moved to rethink her priorities and quit her job after hearing a particular hip hop song:

> I remember working a job that I really hated. It was just like a cafe job that I worked a couple of days a week while I was studying still. And [rapper GDP] had a song called 'ReEvaluate', which was like, I guess the main message of the song was - it seems pretty cliché of a message, but like it's touched me super, super deep - like what's the point in going to work if you're not really happy at the end of the day or if you're just watching the clock waiting for the time to be over? 'Cause all those little bits of time that you spend working for somebody else unhappy and unfulfilled, they end up connecting together and forming like the big chunk of time that is your life. And that really hit me and really, really affected me. And I always had a weird relationship with working and I knew I didn't really like it, but then this song just put it into words that were so obvious and made, I don't know, my approach before then was just to like slog it out until something better came along. But I listened to this song and was like, "Oh yeah!" Like, nothing better is gonna come along, I need to actually change my circumstances. So I ended up quitting that job and going fruit picking for a couple of months and working on farms. So that definitely was a big like turning point in my life.

The lyrics of the song were clearly central to Lily's response, as they put an idea 'into words that were so obvious'. However, in seeking to explain how hearing a song could come to be such a 'turning point' in her life, Lily emphasised the importance of the feeling that music induces:

> I'm a very, like, emotional thing. And so I can't like intellectually understand something and be moved to act, it has to like channel me from that emotional element of myself. So music is really helpful in that way, in that it kinda gets you inspired about an issue and then I'll go and like research the fine details of it. Whereas the music is, I don't know, it kinda like ignites the flame of like, "Oh yeah! This is messed up, we need to do something about it!"

Lily said that she thought about this capacity of music to convey meaning at an emotional level in relation to her own songwriting, when working on her separate folk and hip hop projects. She gave the example that instead of singing, 'We must save the trees', it would be more effective to induce people to feel something about trees. Her analysis here closely echoes the ideas of Eyerman and Jamison (1998) and Jane Bennett (2001), that the feelings produced by music are a crucial motivator in social commitment and action. These feelings inform the meanings derived from lyrics and other signs, marking those meanings as important. Accordingly, music's influence must be located in the embodied experience of reception, into which peak music experiences offer critical insight. When it is remembered later, a peak music experience represents the strength of feeling associated with an idea. For example, Lily remembers the inseparable emotional and rational aspects of her decision to quit her job by reference to the time she listened to 'ReEvaluate' by GDP. Thus, peak music experiences can be epiphanies that both drive and mark major turning points in people's lives, in their musical practice and in other aspects of identity.

Conclusion

This chapter has considered how music can be said to inspire people to 'become' musicians and music fans, to engage in particular activities and to hold particular attitudes, as well as how music can influence people in terms of their musical practice and in other aspects of their lives. Such inspiration and influence are not entirely inherent in songs as written or recorded, though music and lyrics afford certain kinds of response. These work together with the associative affordances derived from the music's presentation and surrounding discourse, as well as the situations in which the music is encountered. In an experience of music, these combined factors are met by a listener with dispositions formed through a history of encounters. Such embodied, situated experience is the ultimate source of the meanings taken from music, the judgements made about it and the feelings that infuse both. Those feelings are crucial in motivating subsequent perceptions, dispositions and actions, so that the affective aspect of musical experience accounts for music's unique reputation as a driver of identity.

Peak music experiences offer a window into music's social agency by placing focus on the situated, embodied experiences from which its meaning and effects derive. People often credit particular experiences with the inspirations and influences they draw from music. These stories both respond and contribute to the discourse that constructs music, listeners and the experiences in which they meet, so that what music 'does' is inseparable from what people say it does. It is therefore important to consider the narratives of peak music experiences that present music as such a powerful driver of identity and position it in relation to, and often above, other social and cultural constraints. Further, these narratives construct an authentic music lover, at least within the local music scenes studied here, as one who has been moved in such profound ways by music. This ideal of music listening is in direct contrast to the aesthetic philosophy of Theodor Adorno and others that holds intellectual contemplation to be superior to physical response, but is closer instead to Romantic ideals in which the value of art is bound up with the feelings it produces. By attributing biographical force to emotionally charged experiences with music, which might involve downplaying more practical or mundane factors, people present themselves as authentic musicians and fans while also investing music with substantial power. The aim of this analysis is not to disentangle these discursive constructions from music's 'real' effects, but rather to show the real effects that follow from them. People think, feel and act according to their conscious and embodied understanding that in certain experiences, music did things – for example, it expressed, explained, revealed, connected, endorsed, decried and affected – with inspiring and influential consequences. In this very real sense, experiences with music change lives.

5 Why music?

Peak music experiences as motivation

The song 'Everything Is Free' by Americana performer Gillian Welch, co-written with David Rawlings and released in 2001, has been adopted by commentators as a poignant summary of the position of musicians in contemporary cultural industries (MS 2012; Wood 2012). The song describes the expectation that music will be given away, observing that an unnamed someone has scored big by figuring out, 'we're gonna do it anyway / even if it doesn't pay'. These words were recited to me by Jim (44), a music writer, whom I interviewed together with Elly (32), a singer-songwriter who cited Welch as an influence. Jim quoted the words in discussing his view that some musicians, like Elly, seem to have no choice but to create music, which made them 'authentic' but also vulnerable to exploitation in 'the culture of free in the age of the download'. Elly, who at the time derived her income from outside music while maintaining a profile as a recording and performing artist, described her own motivations as both a performer and a listener in terms of self-expression, interpersonal connection and a therapeutic outlet. Two years later, I recognised 'Everything Is Free' during a live performance by another Brisbane act, Feeding Fauna, and discovered a recorded version on their album *N Is for Then* (2017). These scene participants found personal relevance in Welch's song, in which the rueful acceptance of economic reality leads to the more positive conclusion that the singer has also figured it out; she is indeed going to 'do it anyway', by staying home and singing a love song to herself. The idea of music as a gift to oneself and an end in itself is at the core of how people explain their investment in music and scenes, as musicians and workers as well as audience members and listeners. Peak music experiences are central to these narratives of motivation.

Peak music experiences provide motivation as embodied experiences, as memories and as sought-after ideals, representing to people what is important and their reasons for doing what they do. This chapter considers how peak music experiences fulfil this role for music scene participants including performers, organisers, technicians and listeners. These experiences provide incentives and justifications for everyday activities and long-term investments by offering both transcendence and affirmation of the self. They are described as both therapeutic and addictive, illustrating the nuanced

DOI: 10.4324/9781003093244-5

ways that people understand their agency in relation to music. In the long term, peak music experiences anchor narratives of fulfilment, vindication and success, as well as a somewhat opposite narrative of authentic enjoyment that places the direct pleasures of musical experience ahead of other, extrinsic motivations like social distinction and financial reward. In these ways, peak music experiences offer particular insights on the question of why some people grant music a central status in their lives, devote considerable resources to musical pursuits and base their social lives around them.

Ascribing motivations for musical practice

Motive is a fraught topic in sociology, where people's self-reports of motivation are received with care and suspicion in accordance with differing theoretical positions. Generally, motives have not been approached as identifiable causes, analogous to forces in physics, but as justifications and explanations for past and future action (Campbell 1996). Thus, 'motive talk' is not taken as evidence of objective causation, but as an interpretive performance that follows normative grammars to connect disparate events into an intelligibly differentiated collection of experience: a person, of a certain type (Blum and McHugh 1971). Over the long term of social careers, however, the interpretive and causative aspects of motive may converge as people's self-accounts reinforce or reconstitute their subjective motivations for ongoing and future action, especially during moments of ambivalence (Winchester and Green 2019). Accordingly, the stories told by music scene participants about the causative impact of particular experiences (see also Chapter 4) are partly performances of identity and belonging, reiterating their commitments to collective values through the grammar of motive talk; at the same time, these stories are part of an ongoing process of self-calibration such that the experiences actually motivate long-term commitments, actions and identities.

Another critical perspective on motivation is the notion of fields of cultural production, such as music, as spaces of struggle within a broader context of class relations (Bourdieu 1983). Even and perhaps especially where direct economic motivations are lacking, participants in such fields are seen to pursue cultural and symbolic power, while such struggle is obfuscated (including for the actors themselves) by a shared 'interest in disinterestedness' (ibid.: 321). Accordingly, the participants' belief and investment in the face value of the practice, which Bourdieu calls 'illusio' (ibid.: 354), is both a product and an enabling condition of deeper forces and struggles. This casts suspicion on self-reported motivations. Some criticism of this model regards it as a Hobbesian reduction of human sociality to competitive self-interest (Sayer 2010; Banks 2012; Crossley & Bottero 2015), though more recent adaptations allow more room for reflexivity (Sayer 2010; Threadgold 2018) and for meaningful difference between the illusio of a specific field and broader society, as Threadgold (2018) observes in Australian DIY music scenes.

Another criticism is that this model on its own is insufficient to explain people's motivation to participate in musical activity, without attention to intrinsic rewards or internal goods including embodied pleasures (Banks 2012; Crossley & Bottero 2015). These intrinsic motivations are themselves seen to be structured by convention and learnt through social immersion in 'worlds' and 'practices' (ibid.). This chapter will consider peak music experiences as manifestations of both symbolic capital and internal goods, which reflect and reproduce the social fields or worlds from which they arise.

Turning from theoretical debates to ethnographic findings, some studies of music scenes have specifically considered the motivations of participants, especially focusing on musicians. Regarding non-professionals, Cohen's (1991) ethnographic research among Liverpool rock bands in the 1980s finds that music provided band members with an escape from the everyday, an outlet for creativity and a space for friendships. The participants *enjoyed* playing, performing and socialising in bands, although many were also significantly motivated by and preoccupied with by the possibility of 'making it' (ibid.: 3). The somewhat parallel study of Swedish 'garage' bands and fans by Fornäs et al. (1995: 251–255) identifies three main motives: collective autonomy, alternative ideals (in comparison to family and school, for example) and the 'narcissistic enjoyment' of creative self-expression. This enjoyment is facilitated partly by the 'volume, beat and sound' of music which afford particular kinds of experience, including the dissolution of ego boundaries; therapeutic feelings of life, involvement and wholeness in one's own body; and the experience of the individual self as greatly enlarged by merging with the band and being mirrored by audience response. In his ethnographic study and insider account of Brisbane's hobbyist indie musicians, Rogers (2008) observes that beyond the dreams of 'success' that tend to be present in early music-making activities, acts of creation and listening bring pleasurable engagements with music as a creative canon and as a social binding agent. Each of these geographically and historically diverse scene studies identifies both instrumental and hedonistic motivations for participating in music-making, with a subjective emphasis on the latter in a range of perceived benefits.

As for listeners, Grossberg (1994: 52) postulates that rock music offers 'a way of making it through the day' by providing empowerment, guidance and a means to navigate and respond to their lived context. Beyond everyday survival, other authors acknowledge the occasionally transcendent qualities of musical experience. As discussed in Chapter 2, several studies have shown the importance placed on extraordinary and memorable experiences of music and the self in cultures oriented around extreme metal (Kahn-Harris 2004), punk (Tsitsos 2012) and dance music clubbing (Malbon 1999; Pini 2001). These provide diffuse recognition that people engage in musical activities partly in pursuit of specific kinds of experiences, which resonate throughout their lives by affirming aspects of identity and empowering social action in response to their specific contexts. This chapter builds on these analyses in considering specifically how peak music experiences are a conscious motivation for various forms of participation in a music scene. Focusing on these experiences enables a detailed phenomenology of how a person can escape, be empowered or experience belonging through musical activity.

The consideration of peak music experiences also helps to answer the question, how unique is music in this regard? There are many other ways for people to seek and experience self-affirmation. For example, Fornäs et al. (1995: 254) refer specifically to diary-writing as an alternative source of creative self-expression in adolescence, besides playing in a garage band, while Green (2010: 192) observes increasing recognition of sport as a way for young people to develop lifestyles and enhance identities. However, music offers unique affordances for experiences that define and affirm self-identity. First, music is an especially physical medium and evokes the kind of affective response that marks ideas as significant and motivates action. Second, music's meanings are especially social, due both to the collective processes of its production, distribution and consumption (which in the case of popular music are mass-mediated processes) and, once again, to its non-verbal affordances for interpretations that are as varied as they are deeply felt. People's engagements with music always work to define them, for themselves and others. Third, music is experienced with particular regard to context, such as places, times and situations, which it imbues with meaning and to which it becomes linked in memory. These factors together make music uniquely amenable to being implicated in deeply felt, socially oriented, specifically remembered experiences of the self. These peak music experiences persist in memory as reminders of identity and justifications for action, while the pursuit of such experiences motivates and shapes ongoing participation. The following empirical analysis demonstrates these processes and shows how music scene participants consciously reflect on them.

'Why I keep doing it'

The interviews for this project, which were semi-structured along biographical lines, concluded by asking why each person continued to engage in the musical activities they described: listening, attending events, performing, organising, etc. Their ensuing reflections provided a sense of closure to the interviews, although in many cases the question had already been more or less answered. Several major themes emerged, often within the same interview. One common answer was that making and listening to music is part of 'who I am', which was typically described as an embodied knowledge such that engaging in the activity feels right while not doing so feels wrong or even painful. More than one interviewee claimed they would die if they stopped. A related theme was the celebration of the specific qualities of musical experience, as uniquely engrossing, therapeutic and energising. Another major theme was the desire to 'be a part' of something, with music facilitating connections between people, including between performers and audiences, between fellow listeners and between creative collaborators. Peak music experiences were cited as exemplary for each of these themes. Such experiences also punctuated narratives of personal and professional success and fulfilment, commemorating particular achievements and encapsulating feelings of validation, or 'making it'. However, among long-term music scene participants there is a common narrative in which the motivating effects of financial and social success are de-emphasised in favour of direct musical experience, which is presented as an authentic motivation for ongoing commitments in the face of practical difficulty and everyday mundanity. As will be discussed, this narrative might be somewhat specific to the long-term 'hobbyist' (Rogers 2008) and professional-amateur or 'pro-am' (Leadbeater and Miller 2004) musicians and workers who were interviewed, although it is consistent with broader notions of authenticity in popular music. Each of these themes will now be explored in detail.

Self-awareness and connection

When explaining the appeal of music, people emphasise their embodied experience. Typical elements of this experience include an absorbing focus on music with a corresponding loss of other concerns; a loss of self-consciousness together with an increased feeling of connection to others; and, somewhat paradoxically, an increased sense of inner wholeness, power and identity. These are elements of the flow experiences described by Csikszentmihalyi (1975), the strong experiences with music described by Gabrielsson (2011) and the trance-like deep listening studied by Becker (2004) (see Chapter 2), demonstrating how musical experience is widely seen as its own, profound reward. The elements of exclusive focus and self-dissolution are explicitly cited as motivations in the following quote from singer and multi-instrumentalist Trish (37):

> I think, for me, it's the one thing that I disappear into completely. Yeah, when I'm doing it. And if I do, even though there's anxiety maybe leading up to a show or lots of work involved in getting it together, there's that bubble that I enter when I play that only happens when I'm doing it in front of an audience and it's like nothing else for me. So that's why I keep doing it.

Trish's quote also demonstrates a common claim that the sacrifices involved in musical activity, such as the work of organising a gig and the (sometimes severe) anxiety suffered by musicians prior to a performance, are justified by the singular experiences that music creates. Rapper and singer, Nat (34), described a connection to others and to herself as the definitive elements of her euphoric on-stage experiences, in the following terms:

> There are moments I can remember having euphoric experiences on stage. Probably every show I have one, very strong, like a meditation at the height of meditation; that feeling of, where I feel like I'm connected

to the universe and connected to the people who are listening to me, and connected to my music and my heart and my soul and it just feels like no other feeling I've ever had.

Once again, these experiences are described as unique to music (although Becker (2004) draws physiological parallels to religious ecstacy), as well as ephemeral, so that the everyday activities and investments involved in being a musician are justified by feelings that might be experienced once in each show. This accords with Malbon's (1999) observation that club dancers' experiences have effects that extend beyond the moment and into everyday life, which I would extend to peak music experiences more broadly, across genres and scenes.

Paradoxically, the loss of the awareness of time, self and surroundings can ultimately affirm identity, by showing what is valuable and worthwhile. People come to know and trust these properties of music and self through their experiences and, sometimes, a particular experience is seen as exemplary. Alicia (34) told the following story about a peak music experience in which she both lost and found herself:

> I got asked to play an improvisation guitar relay in Melbourne, so sixteen ladies on guitars; one of my absolute heroes Penny Ikinger was one of the musicians. I was terrified of that every second until it happened. But closed my eyes, two and a half hours later, went "Oh shit! I'm still in this room, this dark room with all these people". And I got off and said to someone, "Whoa, that was a weird twenty minutes". They said, "No, that was two and a half hours". And I had no idea. But afterwards I had this overwhelming, like I had this wonderful feeling again with the guitar. I knew about how I was the guitar player in that two and a half hours and it was just about that. I think sometimes with bands and stuff it's about performing a show and you get all these other pressures. But that one sort of unlocked this, just playing guitar is where it's at.

This example helps to clarify how a loss of self-awareness can affirm self-identity. Alicia says she was aware of nothing other than the music to which she was contributing, to the extent that she seemed to lose more than two hours. Afterwards, she interpreted this as embodied knowledge of her identity as 'the guitar player' and the experience had an afterglow in her overwhelming, wonderful feeling with the guitar. Reflecting on this memory reminds Alicia of her identity and the feelings that playing music can produce. The affective transcendence of individuality in musical experience can thus contribute to the rational construction of a coherent self-identity over time.

Therapy and addiction

The immersive, self-affirming, world-connecting experiences produced in engagements with music can be therapeutic. The restorative properties of musical experience are cited by some as a reason for their ongoing investment in musical activity, with specific peak music experiences offering potent, concrete examples. Kim (44), who plays bass guitar and sings in an indie rock band, gave the following example to explain how playing music anchors her:

> I find going to practice to be like a really cathartic experience. If I feel anxious or stressed in life and I go and have a practice, I feel like I've had a shower, you know I feel like it's all washed away. Loud noise, I guess that's what it is. [...] I've gone to work and been so stressed out that, I had to go to practice afterwards and I pulled over on the side of the road where a park was and I sat on the grass because I couldn't breathe, I had lots of anxiety. I calmed down a bit and went to practice and then after practice I was normal. Because it was just, I don't know, restorative rock and roll. But that's how it anchors me, it's just what I know.

Here, Kim attributes the therapeutic effects of band practice to the 'loud noise' of rock and roll which washes away other stressors. This is consistent with the previous discussion of how music, as a multi-sensory, time-based medium, can physically and mentally consume a person's attention, offering a flow experience with similar benefits to meditation. Rock 'n' roll guitarist Tracy (39) came to her interview with a similar story in mind:

> As I've been thinking about it the last few days, trying to sort of sum it up in my head and reflect on it, it does end up sounding a bit spiritual in a way. It's sort of that feeling of belonging, that feeling that you've got something in your life that drives you to move on. And last night at band practice we decided to work on some new stuff, 'cause we've been stuck playing gigs for a year and we hadn't gotten around to writing new stuff. And within about half an hour we had this awesome song mostly written, and it's awesome! And I felt really flat at the beginning of band practice and by the end of it I was so fucking excited and happy and inspired. And that is what drives you in life. So those moments in particular, like in the practice room, are some of the most profound I've had I think, rather than playing live even. Creating that in the room, with your best mates, sharing that and communicating without words. So I wanted to mention that to you. I thought last night, "I should tell Ben about this", 'cause that, you know, it physically and mentally drove me from being quite flat and uninspired and unmotivated, in all aspects of my life, to this morning being really fuckin' excited and having energy. And seeing the world in a more positive way. It's really that infectious.

In this experience of collaborative songwriting, Tracy felt belonging, creativity, friendship and drive, which persisted at least until our meeting the following afternoon. Her story illustrates how a peak music experience, even in a clearly defined context like band practice, can have an afterglow that infuses other aspects of everyday life. This afterglow can be felt physically and mentally, as excitement, energy and a positive way of seeing the world in general. By describing her mental preparation for our interview, Tracy explicitly acknowledges what is implicit in all of the interview data: that peak music experiences endure as ways to remember and explain such feelings about music, one's self, other people and so on, including for the benefit of a researcher but also for one's own benefit. They are, as Woodward (2001) notes in relation to 'taste epiphanies', resources for the construction of self-narratives. On this basis, it is unsurprising that when people are asked why they persist with musical activity, they respond with reference to peak music experiences.

The language of 'therapeutic', 'restorative' musical experience coexists with pathological metaphors of infection, disease and addiction. Such language is not used disparagingly, beyond largely tongue-in-cheek comments about the amounts of money and time invested in musical activities, or the indulgence in alcohol and drugs that often accompany those activities. Indeed, music fans relish its dominance over them, as shown in the following quote from Alicia (34) that cites some of the less healthy aspects of rock 'n' roll culture to illustrate the energising effects of a peak music experience:

> You can feel like you're dying of the flu or something, all you wanna do is go home, you never wanna see another cigarette or a beer in your life. And the band [that you are watching] has something so good about it that you just go and get six beers, start chain smoking, you know. It's so exhilarating, that moment.

Pathological language serves to emphasise music's relative agency over the people who claim not merely to benefit from the experiences it provides but to need them, as shown in the following interview excerpt from rock 'n' roll musician Ally (27):

> It doesn't make any sense but you feel compelled to do it and you know, I get really antsy, I get really anxious if I don't play for a while. I think it's, like it's a really, it's a physical thing. I s'pose maybe I should exercise, but why exercise when I can drink beer and play guitar?

Some people come to appreciate their reliance on music when it is unavailable, as in the following quote from punk and indie musician Liz (26):

> I think I only just like came to terms with like, "I guess I'm a musician". Like last year I broke my leg [...] and it was so frustrating to me that I couldn't do that. [...] I think that was like "Oh, I guess like I'm some sort of musician".

These musicians describe a deep fear of losing their involvement in their music scene, similar to what Rogers (2008) observed in the Brisbane indie rock scene. Music for them is an essential technology of the self (DeNora 2000). They take motivation and self-identity from peak music experiences, and by the same token they fear that without music their experience of the self would be so deficient that they would not be alive at all. While music has an inescapable power over them, they can use this power actively to navigate life and to experience it more fully. Tracy (39) illustrates this simultaneous enslavement and empowerment when she says:

> ...music motivates me to do things. So if I'm angry, I can put on an album and I can get that anger out. If I'm happy I can put on an album and celebrate my happiness. So it's like blood, it's in my veins, it's like this integral thing in my life that I don't think anything else could re-place. It's like a god. It's like I'd imagine people who are really religious would feel the same way.

Tracy experiences her self and world through music, describing this in lan-guage that slides between choice ('I can put on an album') and necessity ('it's like blood'). In this way, music functions 'as a prosthetic device, to pro-vide organising properties for a range of other embodied experiences and in ways that involve varying degrees of deliberation and conscious aware-ness' (DeNora 2000: 102–103). The religious analogy captures the mixture of devotion and empowerment, as music fans experience their subservient dependence on music as joyous and self-affirming. As in religion, this deep personal connection is revealed and understood through moments of revela-tion or epiphanies, which concretise and encapsulate aspects of identity for self-reflection and communication to others (Denzin 1989). Peak music ex-periences, such as the rejuvenating rehearsals described by Kim and Tracy, and the transcendent live performance remembered by Alicia, epiphanise one's relationship to music. They crystallise the subjective value of music in embodied experiences, which are felt and remembered as moments of revelation.

Satisfaction and fulfilment

The previous chapter considered how peak music experiences provide in-spiration and influence for nascent musical activity. Peak music experiences can later be sources of satisfaction and fulfilment that reassure people and confirm their choices. A physical feeling of achievement from performing music is expressed in the following quote from rapper Daz (32):

> I think 'cause it makes you feel good. Doing something productive. At the end of the whole gig, the whole set time, you'll get off feeling like wow, you're feeling good about yourself. It's something like finishing a

nice home-cooked meal, like damn I feel settled now, I feel good so I'm laid back, just relaxing when the breeze comes through that window. Just like that, that's the feeling I get. Come off stage feeling like damn, I did my job.

While satisfaction is presented here in the everyday sense of doing one's job, musical experience can also involve more profound fulfilment such that participants feel their life is complete. For example, rapper and singer Nat (34) remembered thinking that she 'could die happy' after her euphoric experiences participating in a local, weekly hip-hop event:

> I do remember one moment thinking in my head, this is pretty epic, I don't know if I could even tell [the organiser] this because his head might blow off. But I just remember thinking that I could die happy, because I'd really just had some euphoric musical experiences, especially the freestyling stuff. [...] I was singing, and playing guitar, and rapping, and it was just like, this is the coolest thing, how could I want more? It was exactly what I didn't know that I wanted.

This illustrates how the moment-to-moment feelings produced in the experience of music can contribute to a longer-term sense of identity and fulfilment. It is notable in Nat's story that she 'didn't know' what she wanted; it was through her euphoric experience of participating in particular musical activities that she experienced them as 'the coolest' and herself as capable and fulfilled. Reflecting later on this peak music experience reminds Nat, and helps her to explain, what music means to her.

Listeners and audience members also have fulfilling and reassuring peak music experiences. For example, Ally (27) said that attending live performances by her favourite local rock 'n' roll band, HITS, evokes an experience that affirms her own trajectory as a musician and more broadly as a person:

> I find going and seeing HITS play is almost like a, I don't wanna say religious experience but it's like going to church. 'Cause I love every single one of them so much and each individually. And they'll play and, you know, even if it's a bit loose it's always fucking great. But it's really, I find it really life affirming. 'Cause you know, it's like that's what you wanna do. And you're just as messed up and fucked up as I am, and you're doin' fuckin' great. You know, that's why you do everything. I think I really, I like that. It always, whenever I see those guys play, I kind of go, "Yep, I have made the right decisions with my life".

The affective response produced by watching and listening to music informs judgements about the performers and performance, but also about perceived values. The embodied judgement that 'even if it's a bit loose it's always fucking great' might apply to the band that is playing and, by analogy, one's own musical activities, but also to other activities and to a lifestyle more generally. Accordingly, an exciting experience of live music can be felt to justify not only the direct investment of time and money to attend, but also a person's broader commitment to music listening and/or creation as well as associated lifestyle choices, confirming they have made 'the right decisions' with their life. A similar experience was described by Liz (26), a music fan, musician and promoter who experienced a feeling that 'this is why we do this' when watching the onstage interaction of Turnpike, a band who are respected as veterans of Brisbane's indie music scene:

> They just blew me away and I was just standing there like, every time I watch that band I am reminded of like, the perfect times you've been in a band. And that band has been together for like fifteen years or something and they still play a lot of the same songs that they've always played, but it still sounds so fucking impressive. And they still like, sometimes fuck up. And, boy howdy, and it's just like, they've got each other, they're all like watching each other. It's, it was perfect bandship, for me, when I watch that band. And I was just like watching it like this and then [my friend] came up around me and put her arm like around my waist [...] she was hopefully seeing what I was seeing and feeling, like "This is why we do this". It's like you want to make something interesting, with a group of people that you admire, and maybe are friends with, or you become friends with. And you want to support each other, you want to like, get to know each other in this way. And that's why you would do, like, be in music. Or heavy music in particular. Because like nobody else would do it with you except for these people. And like, yep. That's like, the best way I can describe how I feel about that.

This peak music experience involved Liz's perception of 'perfect bandship' in the visible and audible interaction of the performers, which reminded her rationally and emotionally of what can be gained through participation in a music scene. This and the other emotional experiences of 'bandship' in this chapter demonstrate an important, affective dimension to these micro-social relationships and microcultural spaces within larger music scenes, building on existing analyses of bands by authors such as Cohen (1991), Fornäs et al. (1995) and Finnegan (2007). In Liz's case, once again, judgements about a musical performance are linked to judgements about ways of being and socialising more generally, while these are both bound up with feelings to which music gives shape. In this way, peak music experiences can affirm sets of ideas and feelings about 'why we do this', providing motivation for ongoing commitment and action. While this chain of understanding can be described at length, the actual feelings are not fully articulated and may be inarticulable, although they are subjectively remembered through the embodied, musically structured experiences. Liz's story shows how these feelings can seem to be communicated between people most effectively when they share a musical experience ('she was hopefully seeing what I was seeing and feeling'), which will be explored further in Chapter 6.

Success and vindication

Participation in popular music involves normative milestones. Some of the milestones of music listeners are first encounters, gateway experiences and conversion experiences, as discussed in Chapter 3. Some of the milestones commonly cited by musicians in Brisbane music scenes include joining a band or group, first performance, first released recording, performance at a favourite or iconic venue, meetings and collaborations with respected artists, and so on, as will be illustrated in below. These milestones structure understandings of what a successful life in music should look like, and they provide specific motivation to reach particular goals. Indie musician Emily (29) acknowledged this when she was asked why she continues to play and listen to music:

> I do think about it a lot. I think, you know, my parents make me think about it a lot, especially my dad. But it's those things that, those dreams that you don't wanna give up on. Like, I've always wanted to tour overseas, so until that happens I don't wanna stop.

Reaching a milestone is experienced by those involved as 'an event' involving a 'great feeling', in the words of former musician Ken (58). Ken said that even though the punk band to which he belonged in his youth harboured no expectation of becoming professional, they experienced the production of their first record as such an event. These personally meaningful experiences become justifications of a continuing commitment to music.

Performances at culturally significant venues or to large or visibly engaged crowds, especially for the first time in a musician's career, are often remembered as peak music experiences involving feelings of validation. A number of instances arose in interviews, including the following experience described by Julian (44) when remembering the burgeoning success of a band in which he played drums:

> [I remember] seeing this huge mob of people and it was the queue to get into the Zoo [a venue in Brisbane] and it was several blocks long. And I was like, "What are all these people doing here?" People were starting to wave at me. And I'm like, "Holy shit, this isn't happening." But it was! And we sold out, people couldn't get in, the Zoo was just full up to puss's bow as they say and it was just so unexpected. We just were astounded. And it was such a great night. So I would nominate that as being a major night, and a real, I guess I was sort of five years into being a musician and being in bands and stuff like that, and it was this real vindication of going, I had done something right.

Singer-songwriter Elly (32) drew a similar sense of validation from her first performance at the Zoo, which was a memorable experience for 'the opportunity to play at one of the longest running music venues in Brisbane and also on a decent-sized stage', 'having a fair few people rock up for the show' and having 'some really, you know, important people come along, special people to me'.

What a gig means to a musician depends on where they are in their trajectory as well as the specific cultural values with which they identify. Keyboardist and singer Jane (26) felt her performance to less than 20 people in Real Bad, a DIY venue in a decrepit suburban building, to be 'a stand out moment':

> Just because it's like, it's Real Bad. [...] Obviously it's this incredible space that people from all round Australia talk about like, "Oh you're gonna play Real Bad", it's got this reputation. [...] And just 'cause it's in Moorooka, like the journey there, it's all this mix, this special experience.

Gigs can also have such personal meaning for people in other roles, such as event organisers. Jim (44) organised a festival including the reunion of one of his favourite bands, and credits this personal connection as a major source of his enjoyment of the gig:

> [C]ertainly for me it was one of the best five gigs I've ever seen. But not necessarily because it was the best musically or anything like that, it was because it had so much else attached to it, for me. [...] I just went around that day wearing a grin the size of a fucking planet and I just really couldn't believe it was happening. In some ways I've never quite come down off that personal high. [...] These days I can go "Well at least I did that!" You know. So it meant an awful lot. It was a really big thing.

As these examples show, performing and organising gigs has personal and social value for participants, manifesting in feelings of affirmation, that motivate them in addition to (or instead of) financial reward. These are remembered as peak music experiences, by which those involved chart their own history and from which they can draw ongoing motivation.

Experiences involving a sense of recognition by role models and belonging with desired peers are cherished. Sal (27) said that after being criticised for incorporating twerking[1] into her DJ performances, her dance performance with a cult figure of what she regards as the true twerking culture of New Orleans Bounce music:

> ...felt like a big fuck you to everyone, and very satisfying. It's basically like the highest goal of anyone who loves twerking [...] to get asked to dance for the whole show of Big Freedia with his dancers, is like, yep.

That's the ultimate goal and I'm proud of myself for getting there. Probably sounds really dumb like, "Oh! I got to shake my arse *(laughs)* onstage with this obscure New Orleans hip hop artist". That was like a big deal for me.

Sal's story of success as revenge lends itself to analysis in terms of symbolic struggle in a cultural field (Bourdieu 1983). As well as the symbolic capital of joining a celebrity of the field on stage, Sal emphasises the accompanying feelings (satisfaction and pride) that can be attributed to illusio, as well as a level of reflexivity about this illusio and its relation to the broader social field and its doxa, consistently with Threadgold's (2018) development of the concept. Similar experiences are reported by musicians who have been booked as the 'support' act for major or personally admired artists. For keyboard player Lisa (34), touring in the support act for iconic synth-punk band Devo carried a range of additional, personal meanings related to her identity, which she thought about as she performed onstage:

I remember we supported Devo and that was a real dream for me because, you know, they were one of the reasons why I loved synthesisers. And that was pretty special. And also seeing them play a few times and talking to them about stuff, felt really special to me. And also like playing on that bill, I thought a lot about my connection to synths and I thought a lot about my history and my, like what I love about that band and why I'm doing it and it was a real sort of self-realisation tour. And I thought about it a lot onstage too. So that was kind of really special.

This quote underlines the personal value of certain gigs for musicians, even at a relatively professional, well-compensated level. Such value can be experienced at the time, so that motivation is embodied directly in the act of performing, and also remembered later. Alongside the accumulation of symbolic capital within a field, these experiences offer a palpable sense of self-identity and become the focus of reflection, exploration and narration in the long term.

People who are not musicians but undertake other work in music scenes celebrate the cultural value of particular jobs and events that they are involved with. For example, Mick (49) described how 'moments' from his work as a concert lighting technician provided him with a sense of satisfaction and even privilege:

Yeah I mean the last one was the Rolling Stones. They're those moments where you go, "Wow, this is exactly where I wanna be, doing this, getting paid". You know, I would have bought a ticket anyway but here I am in this privileged position, getting paid and maybe I'll get a T-shirt later for nothing.

This highlights an important point about the cultural value attached to work in the popular music industry. If a concert is seen as desirable, working at the concert is considered a privileged position in comparison to being an audience member, in an inversion of wider social norms around technical and service work in leisure industries and elsewhere. This contrasts specifically with the hierarchies in place at classical music events as described by Small (1998), where ushers, attendants and technicians are seen to perform a service role for audiences, who in turn are separated from the rarefied arena of artistic performance. Popular music, especially in local music scenes, involves a different and less hierarchical experience of social interaction and cultural status than other art forms and non-artistic industries. This is most obvious when the same individuals inhabit various roles in the scene, as musicians, audience members, technicians and, for example, bar staff at venues. Popular music culture promotes the desire to 'be a part' of popular music or a particular music scene so that, for example, record store assistants and concert technicians have more glamour attached to them than other shop clerks and event technicians. The perceived value of these desired positions is embodied and remembered in peak music experiences.

As careers in popular music are notoriously insecure, memories of high points take on importance as motivations for subsequent effort and investment over long periods of time. Mick (49), who as well as working as a lighting technician has been a musician for several decades, referred explicitly to this when recalling the experience of supporting a high-profile band:

> We ended up going away with INXS just before their Wembley thing [stadium concert in 1991], so we toured with them for two weeks solid as a Brisbane three-piece, unsigned, which was mind-blowing. [...] We were playing every night to five thousand people [...] and actually hanging with those guys. [...] That was a real eye-opener; that was a good turning point. Again, you can look at those big moments and go, "Oh well that spurred me on for another ten years".

Later in the interview, Mick returned to this idea:

> You get those little things that, like, spur you on for the next period. You go, "This is good. I love this shit. I'm gonna keep doin' it." Those little, you know, highs along the way and you just know that that's what you do. "This is why we do it." You love it.

The ease with which musicians are able to recall their experiences of success and fulfilment bears out Mick's point that such high points are held onto as a source of motivation, in some cases for many years. Guitarist Tracy (39) noted the frequency with which she reflects on one such experience, when her band toured in Europe:

Standing in a venue in Paris watching these amazing rock 'n' roll bands and meeting all these people, yeah, it was just a dream come true. I still can't get it out of my [mind], I think about it almost every day. This was in 2012 [three years ago]. I still think of that being such a significant thing in my life.

These experiences of success, fulfilment and vindication stand outside the everyday life and mundane work of music scene participants but have an afterglow that infuses day-to-day thought and feeling. In this way, peak music experiences are a subjective resource for sustaining investment in musical activities and identities for years to come.

Better than success

As well as the narrative of career success punctuated by memorable experiences of affirmation, music scene participants share another, sometimes conflicting narrative of authentic enjoyment that is overtly dismissive of extrinsic motivations. In this narrative, peak music experiences are explicitly cited as the goal of musical activity and the reason for ongoing commitment despite its costs. John (32) drew on this narrative when describing his recent focus on dance music production, after working mostly as a DJ for some years:

When you're producing and you're making your own stuff, you're going back to the core of why you loved music and that was because of the way it made you feel. [...] As a kid you'd hear the music and you'd feel the music and you're like, "This is the best song ever!" and it would make you feel like you were king of the world. And then it would make you feel like a god when you used to play the music that made a whole room feel like they were kings of the world. And then you hear that song being played four times a week and other people doing the same thing, you kinda lose the love for music, or the music sort of doesn't affect you in the same way. So when you start making music, it becomes like this internal process where you're just making music and this is the other side of it, like there was the recognition but the other side of it was the way it makes you feel, regardless of the recognition.

In this narrative, the affective experience of music is cited as the initial motivation to become involved as a performer and, later in life, remains a more important driver of participation than social recognition. If the feeling wanes, recognition is not a sufficient motivation on its own and it becomes necessary to find new ways of engaging with music to achieve the desired experience. The inspiration experienced as a 'kid' (a theme discussed in Chapter 4) is a touchstone to which music scene participants consciously return when their commitment is challenged. In a further example, Pete (33) said that transcendent moments of musical experience helped him to overcome exhaustion and disillusionment as a DIY venue operator:

> ...we went on a journey of going 'This is *awesome!*' and then, kind of, towards the end going 'Fuuck, I'm tired, I don't wanna go!' [...] and in the end, like it just seems like it always comes back full circle to those same experiences of enjoyment that you started with in, like you know as a teen, those things that, when you really enjoy playing music or putting something on like that's, that's all there is, like there's not a lot of the other aspects that you thought were gonna be there, I dunno. [...] And the only way to kind of sustain it is to, um, come back to that feeling that you had as a kid of you know, really seeking out just what you really enjoy.

This quote underlines again the primacy afforded to experiences of musical enjoyment and the dismissal of 'the other aspects you thought were gonna be there' in musical practice, such as social distinction and career success. According to these music scene participants, their ongoing activity is in large part a search for peak music experiences, motivated by the memory of past experiences and the belief that more will come. When these experiences are found, they affirm people's ideas of what they hold important and who they are.

This motivation for participation in a music scene aligns with what Fornäs et al. (1995: 254) call 'narcissistic enjoyment' but, importantly, such a hedonistic focus is considered virtuous and sociable by scene members. Enjoyment pays respect to the power of music and the similarly pure intentions of other scene participants, while extrinsic motivations like fame and financial reward are narcissistic because they disrespect the art form as a means to less noble ends, placing individual gain above the common goal of positive musical experience. For hip hop producer and rapper Nathan (35), the best musical experiences are defined by a feeling of connection to other people, while the financial aspects of the music industry are challenges that he and his collaborators are forced to overcome in order to achieve that feeling. This understanding of his own musical practice is encapsulated in a peak music experience in which his hip hop crew performed at a festival, following frustrating dealings with the organisers:

> ... we weren't getting paid, we were like losing money to this corporate scum, but the gig was like incredible. It was everyone's best gig that they'd ever had in their life and there was probably fifteen of us involved within the whole scope of the two-hour show, and yeah it was everyone's best gig they'd ever had in their life. So that's kind of the trade-off or pay-off of dealing with these corporate fuckhead accountant, bottom-feeding scum is that you have to reach people some way and unfortunately they, a lot of times own the stage that you wanna get on. So yeah that feeling of like connecting with people, providing like

a unified feeling of happiness, for thousands of people focusing on one note or punchline or, like, dancer or whatever, when they're all doing that together, it makes it worth it even though you have to go through very humiliating, financial strife with these fucking dogs. To connect with people.

This quote illustrates how the experience of music, including the experience of self and others that music makes possible, is celebrated as an end in itself rather than a means to or product of other rewards. On this view financial dealings are a necessary, though sometimes unsavoury and frustrating, practicality in pursuit of the true end of musical experience. In this narrative, the sacrifices and investments required to create a musical event are motivated by the desire for a particular kind of experience and, accordingly, peak music experiences are felt and remembered as moments of fulfilment and justification.

By privileging the affective experience of music over other rewards, the participants present a natural, uncalculated and therefore authentic relationship to it. This can be analysed critically in terms of symbolic struggle (Bourdieu 1983), as a way to establish rightful membership of the field and social distinction from those who participate for less noble ends. From this perspective, such self-interested manoeuvring is both obscured and underwritten by the illusio of the field, or shared belief in the game, which stipulates enjoyment as a worthwhile goal and even an ethical obligation. This anti-materialist ethic might downplay actual power differences between those who must think about money and those at leisure to disregard it, while also maintaining those inequalities by incentivising musicians and other music scene workers to provide their labour for inadequate compensation or acknowledgement. However, two important points must be added to this Bourdieusian analysis. First, music scene participants exhibit reflexivity about what is described here as illusio, acknowledging to a degree their various types of motivation and the tensions between them. This becomes a resource for questioning and challenging the doxa of the wider social field, like the Australian DIY music practitioners studied by Threadgold (2018) who reject fundamental neoliberal assumptions and 'embrace' poverty. Apart from de-prioritising financial success, a subversive ideal demonstrated in the celebration of peak music experiences is the pursuit of connection and collectivity. Music, as it is described by these scene participants, exemplifies the investment in collective experience over (or more correctly *as*) self-interest. Many of the quotes in this chapter celebrate experiences of the self in relation to others, and experiences of collective pleasure and identity are highly prized. The reflexively perceived contrast between this pursuit and wider social values is clear in Nathan's account of his hip hop crew knowingly losing money and pride to 'corporate scum' in order to transcend, through musical experience, the very terms of that competition: to connect with people.

Second, there is no reason to doubt that the peak music experiences described in this chapter, along with others throughout this book and in other literature (not least the large-scale study of Gabrielsson 2011), actually provided the subjective pleasures, therapeutic benefits and sometimes profound meanings described by the people who had them, and that no illusion is necessary for these things to be valued highly. The field of music therapy is testament to the contributions that musical experience can make to human well-being in its physical and social dimensions, which may be considered priceless. As argued by Crossley and Bottero (2015), the concept of illusio requires at least elaboration to account for the intrinsic rewards of musical activity (and such elaboration is also offered by Threadgold [2018]). Critical attention to the symbolic struggle involved in music scenes is necessary, but may not be sufficient, to understand what drives them. In this chapter, we have seen how peak music experiences can be manifestations of both symbolic capital and internal goods, working to motivate and direct participation in music scenes.

Conclusion

The findings presented in this chapter are drawn from a research sample in which all of the musicians were working at the hobbyist (Rogers 2008) or professional-amateur (Leadbeater and Miller 2004) level, although some were full-time musicians in the past. Caution must be exercised in extrapolating beyond this group on matters concerning music careers. It may be the case, for example, that long-term professional musicians have a different relationship to the narrative that values 'authentic', intrinsic enjoyment over extrinsic reward, especially when it comes to compensation for their services. However, this narrative is tied to an idea of authenticity that is known to be widespread and fundamental in popular music culture, involving a genuine love for music that transcends typical social, cultural and material constraints. A further caveat is that the research sample is drawn from active participants in a local music scene, so that care must be taken in applying the findings about motivation to people with a more casual or solitary relationship to music. However, even such sporadic engagements with music may also be driven by a search for a particular kind of experience, as the following quote from Peter (52) about concert attendance suggests:

> I've talked to mates of mine, guys in their fifties now, late forties early fifties, who don't see much live music; a lot of them have got kids, they don't get out as often as they used to. And if I had a dollar for every time a guy said to me, you know, "I don't go and see much live music but I've really gotta see more bands because it makes me feel so great". I just think, especially for those people like me who started watching live gigs years ago, it's therapeutic.

This is consistent with DeNora's (2000) finding that music listeners who do not necessarily identify with a local scene recognise music's affordances for regulating and exploring feelings. However, in addition to the everyday uses of music observed by DeNora, such as getting ready to go out or winding down, music can afford extraordinary experiences of transcending everyday concerns and going beyond one's everyday self. This may be precisely what drives less everyday, more consciously special engagements with music, such as soundtracking major ceremonies and parties, going clubbing and attending concerts. The uncommon efforts that are required to organise these musical activities might be consciously justified, for the wide range of people who undertake them, by the uncommon experiences they produce and the broader significance of those experiences in everyday life.

The main contribution attempted by this chapter, however, is to show the centrality of peak music experiences to the motivations of local music scene participants. For these people, the extraordinary and the everyday aspects of musical activity and scene belonging are consciously related. Long-term identification with the music scene and day-to-day activities associated with it are justified by the promise of peak music experiences in which the everyday self is both transcended and re-affirmed. These experiences are said to be therapeutic and also addictive, showing how music lovers conceive of their well-being and agency as bound up with the affordances of music. Personal fulfilment, vindication and success are embodied and remembered through peak music experiences, making them a key resource in the construction of self-narratives. Peak music experiences are also foregrounded in narratives of authentic musical identities, according to which the powers and pleasures of music itself are placed ahead of other goals associated with music scene activities. In these various ways, peak music experiences have a crucial role in motivating the substantial, long-term commitments to music by which some people define themselves.

Note

1 Twerking is a dance style that involves the vigorous thrusting and shaking of the dancer's buttocks, often in a squatting stance. Sal refers to the understanding that the dance originated in the New Orleans hip hop style known as Bounce, which is associated with African American and LGBTQ communities.

6 Listening together

Peak music experiences and interpersonal relationships

The preceding three chapters have focused on how peak music experiences are related to individual identity, as a resource for the reflexive understanding and presentation of the individual self. They can be turning points in people's relationships with music, epiphanies in autobiographical narratives of inspiration and influence, and motivations for ongoing practices. The next three chapters are concerned with peak music experiences as an aspect of belonging, in micro-social relationships, collective events and music scenes. This chapter will consider how such experiences can reflect and inform relationships between people, such as family, friends and romantic partners.

As will be discussed, the close association between popular music and romantic relationships in particular is so widely accepted as to be the subject of clichés. In theorising the interpersonal functions of music, existing sociological literature has largely focused on what music signifies through its lyrics and semiotic associations. By contrast, this chapter will consider how music also creates an affective space in which people can experience and express feelings with and about each other. These musically structured and shared experiences can stand out as peak music experiences that become emblematic of certain people and relationships. These are epiphanies that help to construct interpersonal narratives, in the same way that they contribute to the narrativisation of people's relationships with music and themselves, as shown in previous chapters. This chapter will also demonstrate a reflexive element to these ways that music contributes to relationships. While I have emphasised that peak music experiences may occur unexpectedly and cannot be commanded, people sometimes plan or consciously take advantage of shared experiences of music to communicate, explore and celebrate certain ideas and feelings. For example, this can be an aspect of planning a group concert attendance, or enjoying a favourite song on the radio together. In these ways, peak music experiences perform a specific role in relationships while exemplifying music's broader interpersonal functions.

DOI: 10.4324/9781003093244-6

Popular music and relationships

Popular music has a close association with interpersonal relationships and especially romantic ones, through both its content and the ways it is used. A great proportion of popular music has been ostensibly 'about' love, so that the three main categories identified in Peatman's (1942) content analysis of popular song lyrics – 'happy in love', 'frustrated in love' and 'novelty song with sex interest' – remain familiar to a modern listener. In fact, this consistent subject matter has helped to define popular music in contrast to other forms such as folk music (Frith 1989), and has drawn criticism on the basis that it promotes passive consumption, superficial emotions and even ideological submission, in comparison to both folk and art music (Adorno 1990 [1941]; MacDonald 1953). Such criticisms are broadly echoed by those popular musicians and fans who shun clichéd love songs as a way of positioning themselves against the mainstream, a method of distinction that was significant in the first wave of punk rock (Laing 1985: 68–69; see also Reynolds and Press 1995: 87–88). In addition to the content of popular music, its common uses have been oriented, historically, around romantic and sexual relationships, most obviously through the popularity of dancing as a form of social interaction. This, too, is so widely understood that it is regarded as a cliché and avoided by some. For example, 'hip' clubbers claim to reject the supposedly mainstream practice of going to a dance club to 'pick up' (Thornton 1995).

Beyond these general associations between popular music, love songs and dancing, Horton (1957) offers a detailed consideration of popular music's constructive role in relationships among post-war youth. In his analysis, the formulaic content of popular songs is what makes them socially useful. Based on the lyrics of over 200 songs published in popular magazines, which he finds overwhelmingly to be 'conversational songs about love', Horton categorises their lyrical themes into acts and scenes in the drama of dating: from 'Courtship' through 'The Honeymoon' and 'The Downward Course of Love' to the final act, 'All Alone'. He proposes that as well as illuminating a panorama of emotional possibilities, these songs provide a conventional language to young people who tend to lack skill in the verbal expression of profound feelings. This language need not be used in direct discourse, 'for, if two people listen together to the words sung by someone else, they may understand them as a vicarious conversation'; thus 'the audience of lovers finds in [the singer] their mutual messenger' (ibid.: 577). The singer may also demonstrate 'the appropriate gestures, tone of voice, emotional expression – in short, the stage directions' for transforming the abstract, conventional possibilities of the verse into personal expression. Through popular songs, a young person learns various roles and identifies some as their own as they associate them with lived experience. In these ways, Horton argues that popular songs promote a sense of identity, to which we might add a sense of belonging from micro-social relationships up to generational groups. Horton's study was replicated 11 years later by Carey (1969) and, subsequently, in a comparison of popular music songs released in the years 1977 and 1986 by Bridges and Denisoff (1986). Using the same approach, these studies found new and changing elements in the drama of courtship as represented through popular song lyrics. Frith (1989: 93) cites Horton in arguing that '[p]op love songs don't "reflect" emotions, then, but give people the romantic terms in which to articulate and so experience their emotions'. He expands Horton's strict focus on lyrical content by adding that the non-verbal aspects of music such as beat and melody give vitality to lyrics, while performing conventions construct the listener's sense of both the singer and themselves. Nevertheless, on the basis that people's access to songs is primarily through their words, Frith concludes that lyrics give songs their social use.

DeNora (2000), who is also concerned with how music both shapes and captures people's experience of relationships, decentres lyrics in this process. As discussed in previous chapters, she argues that music can not only express but structure emotional states. Its affordances in this regard are partly inherent (such as lyrics as well as musical elements), as well as by common association (such as the conventions noted by Frith above) and personal association (such as memory). This means that although lyrics and their delivery may be significant depending on other factors, they do not exhaust music's affordances. DeNora observes that one of the primary uses of music for the respondents in her study was to remember key people in their lives, including family members as well as lovers and former partners, whose memories were often associated with emotionally heightened phases or moments. One of these respondents proposed that 'everyone has their relationship songs' and DeNora considers how listening to such songs enables people to reconstruct and relive crucial times and events that are linked to those relationships (ibid.: 64). In the examples she presents, music is interlinked with phases or times in people's lives, such as a season spent travelling or a romantic affair. This chapter will build on this observation by showing how a single musical experience might be significant to someone's idea of a person or relationship, by giving shape and quality to particular feelings and therefore enabling them to be recognised, expressed and remembered. In turn, this may be a peak music experience and an epiphany in which certain, subjective truths and feelings are encapsulated.

The recognition that music gives form to feelings on an aesthetic and therefore intersubjective plane explains how listening together can create a sense of affinity or intimacy. In proposing musical experience as a model of social interaction, Schutz (1951) observes a process of 'mutual tuning-in'. Listening to music is therefore a way of consciously 'being together' and people can feel that they 'share' musical experiences. The existence of a common affective space also permits and encourages certain kinds of interaction, most obviously in the case of dancing in time together, but also less overtly by influencing perceptions of mood and time. Besides music itself, the often ritualised activities oriented around it enact relationships and express values (Small 1998), based on collective understandings but with potential micro-social significance, for example when a concert ticket is offered as a gift or invitation. The historical and widespread association between popular music and love might contribute to the music's affordances, by creating expectations about what may take place between people in the setting of a concert, dance or other shared musical experience. Taking these various affordances into account, it is possible to return to and expand Horton's (1957) concept of popular music as a tool for navigating relationships and thereby constructing identity. As he notes, musical content can be used for vicarious conversation and also makes available to listeners a conventional language and typical narratives for their own expressions. On top of this signifying capacity, music structures experience and can thus enable and encourage people to relate to one another on multiple levels, which are often non-verbal and sometimes ineffable. Music can provide shape to feelings about and between people, create an appropriate setting for the expression of particular feelings, and supply a lyrical, gestural, tonal and symbolic language through which feelings can be expressed. Again, and importantly, music is also a way of simply being and feeling *together*.

The emotionally charged, interpersonally significant experiences to which music contributes may have a unique importance and thus be peak music experiences – *that* time we danced, *that* time we listened together, *that* gig we saw. Such peak music experiences can act as epiphanies in the sense described by Denzin (1989), as they illuminate underlying aspects of relationships or mark significant changes in relation to them. A peak music experience can come to encapsulate particular aspects of people and events, playing a key role in the narrativisation of relationships. The following sections of this chapter consider some of the ways that peak music experiences have significance for people with regard to their relationships with family, friends and romantic partners. These are also considered as especially visible demonstrations of the broader, subtler role that music plays and the ways it is used in relationships between people.

Constructing and remembering family

The majority of interview participants made reference to their family when narrating the development of their own interest in music, for example by noting either that music was 'always around' or that their family was 'not musical'. This suggests a common belief that a 'musical' family is sufficient explanation for one's own identification with music while the absence of such an explanation must be noted. This is a popular notion of what Rimmer (2012) calls 'musical habitus', involving socialisation towards music in the family and home. Rimmer draws a distinction between objects of taste, such as artists and genres, and the practices that people bring to them, arguing that musical habitus is more concerned with the latter. Consistently with this distinction, only a minority of participants in this project claimed a direct 'cultural inheritance' (Smith 2012) of the knowledge and objects of fandom, such as following their parents' taste in specific artists or songs. Instead, there was generally a separation between interest in music, as measured in intensity and defined by practices, from the more specific question of taste in music as characterised by the objects of interest. More participants claimed to have inherited the former without the latter from their families. Interview participants identified a variety of ways that music was experienced in domestic settings, bearing out Grácio's (2016) observation that despite a historical lack of sociological attention, family and domestic spaces are relevant when analysing 'everyday musicking'.

Music fans often remembered their families by reference to musical experiences. This is demonstrated in Kim's (44) description of how she associates a particular album with a family ritual:

> My family wasn't musical but there were certain records that I grew up listening to [and] every Christmas we would always listen to [Neil Diamond's 1972 live album] *Hot August Night*. The first song is like a string quartet playing this, it's called the 'Prologue' I think and then it goes into 'Crunchy Granola Suite', and it's just this amazing piece of music. And when it starts to change into like the rock song, it gets so exciting, and I just always remember that as being, I connect it to Christmas. Because I'd always be putting the Christmas tree up listening to that record [and] that's a big memory of childhood for me. [These days] I would only ever listen to that record at Christmas... maybe when no one's around I might put it on.

This is an example of an enduring connection between particular music and memories of family. Through a series of listening experiences in the setting of family Christmas preparations, Kim formed an association between that setting and a piece of music that has no ostensible connection to Christmas through its lyrics or other content. To that extent, Kim's story shows how music can accrue affective powers through its mere co-presence with other things, such as people and events, with such links enduring as a result of the wider significance of the moment. However, Kim also refers specifically to the 'amazing' musical passage when a string quartet is joined by other instruments to begin the rock song, with the effect the music 'gets so exciting', and it is this passage in particular that she connects to 'putting the Christmas tree up'. This bears out DeNora's (2004) further observation that music might not only memorably accompany a heightened moment but also help to create the moment as one that is heightened. In this case, the music's general affordances are shaped partly by the formal connotations and anticipatory tone of the opening string arrangement ('Prologue'), the dynamic entry of rock drums and a strummed acoustic guitar, the ensuing acceleration of tempo and the cheers of the audience when the 'Crunchy Granola' riff is first played. When Kim was a child, the album may also have had common or at least family associations with Christmas, as *Hot August Night* was released in December 1972 before charting as the number one album in Australia for 29 weeks (according to the ARIA Albums Chart). Accordingly, this piece of music might have not only accompanied or reflected but also given shape to Kim's excitement while decorating the Christmas tree, combining with that setting to produce a memorable experience. Reflecting on the experience now, including by re-listening to *Hot August Night*, allows Kim to remember her family and the settings, events and practices they shared, partly by reproducing the same feelings. This shows how a peak music experience can have a lasting effect on the subjectively perceived affordances of a song, by adding to its personal associations in quite specific and emotional ways.

In another example, Lisa (34) described how a particular song consistently drew her thoughts to her parents in a way that illustrated their love of music:

> Well I remember my parents were always really big music fans [...] I always remember my parents are obsessed with 'It's All Over Now, Baby Blue', but the Them version, the Van Morrison [-sung] version not the Bob Dylan version. And they played that song all the time and they used to like dance around the lounge room to it together, 'cause they do like rock and roll and ballroom dancing. And my dad's Van Morrison and Them record has a skip in it, and forever to this day, every time I hear that song I expect the skip and I think about my parents dancing. And that's a serious emotional connection to that song.

Lisa's past experiences of hearing 'It's All Over Now Baby Blue' with her family render it uniquely meaningful and emotional for her to this day. Listening to the song now evokes the setting of her parents' lounge room, their activities within that setting and the people themselves. The experiences associated with the song punctuate a particular narrative about Lisa's parents, providing a colourful image symbolic of their status as 'big music fans'. Thus, a set of musical experiences has become emblematic of something that Lisa remembers about her parents. Music was a key factor in the construction of these moments as memorable in the first place, as the activity of dancing was overtly oriented around music and, specifically, 'It's All Over Now, Baby Blue' as recorded by Them (1966). This use of the song by Lisa's parents probably owed more to the musical arrangement than the lyrics written by Bob Dylan, which are commonly interpreted as a firm farewell ('You must leave now...'; see for example Williams 2004: 138). While Dylan's version released in 1965 foregrounds the singer's voice somewhat starkly over an acoustic guitar, Them's recording adds drums, bass guitar, tambourine and a prominent keyboard melody that together create more obvious affordances for slow dancing and feelings of romantic or familial love, perhaps despite the lyrics. Lisa's further comment about expecting 'the skip' (a jump to a later or earlier part of the recording, caused by damage to the corresponding part of the physical record) also highlights the role of this specific music, as she heard it, in constituting her own experience and her subsequent recollection of it. Expecting the same skip, even when the song is heard through a different format, illustrates how a piece of music might not only reference but also reconstitute subjective experience, as the listener's response traces paths formed in past encounters with that music. The tendency of a piece of recorded music to produce and reproduce particular experiences can be informed by factors intervening between the recorded content and the listener, including playback technology, as part of the 'sound environment' (Nowak and Bennett 2014).

The stories told by Kim and Lisa demonstrate ways that families and romantic couples use music to be together. Songs are chosen to soundtrack activities, to recognise occasions (perhaps most notably in the tradition of the 'first dance' at a wedding), to reflect and create shared moods and to create the possibility for certain kinds of interaction. The latter use is obvious in the case of dancing but can be seen more subtly in each of the other uses. The divergent descriptions by Kim and Lisa of their families, as 'not musical' and 'really big music fans' respectively, suggest that such domestic uses of music are somewhat universal although they may vary in frequency and importance. These kinds of musicking bear out Horton's (1957) notion of popular music as a relational tool that offers dramatic shape and common language to micro-social interactions. However, to account for a song's affective, expressive and mnemonic possibilities and therefore its role in relationships, the focus must be both broader and narrower than Horton's focus on lyrical content and delivery. Both listeners and the settings in which they listen imbue music with power and meaning. Consequently, the focus must be broad in the sense that it is not limited to the inherent (composed, performed or recorded) content of a song, but also narrow in the sense that musical experience is shaped by specificities of the sound environment and subjective histories of listening and association. Unique conjunctions of these elements create peak music experiences that, in turn, become significant to the future affordances of a song, so that they are recalled and recreated in the act of listening. Accordingly, peak music experiences offer close insight into the construction of personal and interpersonal musical meanings and effects.

Epiphanies about relationships

Peak music experiences involving significant relationships, such as those with family and friends, demonstrate how peak music experiences operate as epiphanies (Denzin 1989) through which people realise and remember specific biographical facts and meanings. An experience of music might memorably capture one's perception of a person or crystallise a particular characterisation of a relationship. For example, Holly's (26) recollection of her family's shared interest in music and their practice of 'singalongs' was punctuated by a specific event:

> There were lots of kind of impromptu sing-alongs. Yeah I remember, I think mum and dad were cooking dinner and my brother and I were sitting at the kitchen bench, and [it] must have been the radio 'cause I remember, all of a sudden Pearl Jam came on, 'Black', and we all just kinda went "Ohh, yes!" And then we just sort of sung every word of the whole song together, really loud, it was just, yeah. It was an awesome moment. Really cool.

Holly's story begins with everyday activities in an unremarkable setting, before the unexpected arrival of a favourite song provokes a meaningful, shared experience that she remembers years later. The family's reaction to the song demonstrates how music can create possibilities for interaction and expression, in this case the act of loud group singing and through it the mutual expression of exuberance, shared fandom and closeness. Once again, these affordances are probably shaped less by the lyrics of 'Black' (which would fit within the 'All Alone' act of Horton's (1957) drama of courtship) than by other factors. These probably include the shared recognition of the song as a favourite as well as the melodramatic style of Pearl Jam's singer Eddie Vedder, which invites a hearty singalong. Bennett (1997) observes the collective selection of particular songs for singing along to in a public bar, by way of requests made to performers, showing that this practice involves the production and celebration of local, group identity. Similarly, the family singalong described by Holly both draws on and contributes to the shared history they associate with 'Black'. When Holly recalls this peak music experience, it carries information about her family, symbolising their shared taste, their manner of interacting and her feelings about them, which might be difficult to describe directly or in the abstract without this concrete example. It can be seen as a minor or illuminative epiphany, which is symbolic of underlying aspects of a relationship (Denzin 1989). Accordingly, Holly was able to use this peak music experience in the interview setting to help present characteristic details about her family.

Another function of peak music experiences as epiphanies is to enable people to explore and recognise the nature of their feelings, both as they occur and in memory. In a potent example of this, Maddy (35) described a peak music experience that gave shape to uncertain feelings:

> This is the most powerful experience I've ever had. My mum was dying in 2005 and I was at Woodford [Folk Festival] and saw Dirty Three. And um, just like, it explained, and I can't even, I don't know if you, I can't ever explain what that is or what that feels like. Yeah, it totally made sense, I don't know, yeah. I just was like, "Wow". Like, I can actually... I can't even explain it. [...] Yeah the total loss, just was like, yeah

that's what it is. I always wondered how I was gonna feel, after she died. She had a week out. Yeah that's when I knew. And it was super sad. [...] I understood the past and the future and right now.

Maddy's powerful experience, through which she understood her past, present and future as connected to her mother's terminal illness, could be seen as a major epiphany, defined by Denzin (1989) as an experience which touches every fabric of a person's life and changes it irrevocably. Music was essential to this epiphany by giving it form, so that Maddy could recognise and then engage reflexively with her own emotions. The Dirty Three is an instrumental three-piece band, with a melodic focus provided by expressively played violin, accompanied by drums and electric guitar in semi-structured songs. Their music ranges dynamically between delicate, lyrical passages and intense, loud tumult. It is understandable that the inherent and associative affordances of this music could offer shape to Maddy's strong feelings about her mother and to anticipate how she would feel after her death. Thus, feelings which she says she could never explain in words 'totally made sense' when expressed and reflected back to her in musical form. This highlights the point made at the start of this chapter – that lyrics do not always limit or even dominate what popular music can express or facilitate (cf. Horton 1957; Frith 1989). This experience involved instrumental music, like Kim's memory of the 'Prologue' on *Hot August Night* and some other pieces of popular music discussed throughout this thesis. A better model for understanding what occurred here is DeNora's (2000) claim that music contributes to the shape and quality of feelings on an intersubjective plane. To understand 'the past and the future and right now' requires that a profusion of lived and remembered experience be rendered aesthetic, that is, selected and ordered perceptibly (in John Dewey's terms: see Chapter 2), and in this case music provided the necessary structure. In memory, this peak music experience continues to be a resource for Maddy to remember and even to relive an emotional journey that she remains unable to verbalise. In turn, this remembered experience has significance to Maddy's relationship with her mother. As her 'most powerful' experience, it also represents more generally the power of music and its importance in her life, which is the context in which she told the story.

The presentation of the foregoing peak music experiences by research participants exemplifies, in addition to the subjective impact of such experiences, their use as a narrative resource. They condense and convey otherwise abstract, subtle or complex meanings associated with relationships. In this way, the ideas become mobile and can be passed between people. Demonstrating this mobility, Holly (26) described a peak music experience that was not her own, but nevertheless had significance for her: 'It was kind of music that brought my parents together, like they first met at a gig, a Violent Femmes gig, which Nirvana was supporting'. Holly's parents must have told her this story, which she can now share for her own purposes. To an audience with some knowledge of the artists mentioned, her short anecdote might convey significant meanings, for example that Holly's parents were popular music fans; that they had somewhat 'alternative' taste and are probably relatively young parents, having attended alternative rock concerts in the early 1990s; and that they spoke to their children about music and its role in their lives. This illustrates how, by condensing a bundle of meanings into a mobile form, peak music experiences are a powerful narrative resource for talking about people and relationships.

Sharing music experiences

Interviewees suggested that they are well aware of music's powers as a relational aid, including its capacity to create meaningful and memorable experiences. As I will now consider, it is apparent that people sometimes plan and orchestrate shared experiences of music, or seize upon them when they arise, as a way of enacting, exploring and celebrating aspects of their relationships. This is consistent with Horton's (1957) description of popular songs as a mutual messenger and of listening together as a vicarious conversation, enabling the expression of profound feelings. However, as already noted, music's affordances for shaping and reflecting emotion go beyond the content and delivery of lyrics that concerned Horton. John (32), a DJ and dance music event manager, described becoming aware as a child and teenager of how music could create a mood or atmosphere, beginning with an interest in the soundtracks to Disney and Star Wars films:

> And I think that sort of filled my love of music and brought it into another dimension in terms of how to use it to gauge or even force emotion. Like you can play it a little bit softer and the right type of chords and then you've got the perfect sad scene in a movie. I would always be the person who would play the music at a house party or something, I'd bring the CDs as a kid. And then I was able to dictate the feeling or the mood of the party for the whole night. [...] Gettin' the lady with some sexy music whenever you came home from a date. And that was cheesy as all hell!

As John pointed out, the use of music to invoke certain kinds of affective atmosphere is so well recognised it can be considered 'cheesy'. However, this shows an awareness that music can enable feelings to be shared between people, with the potential to create intersubjective experiences that are memorable in their own right.

A uniquely memorable, shared musical experience is demonstrated by Holly's (26) description of her attendance at a concert with her father and brother:

> [I saw] the Fleet Foxes with my dad and my brother. We bought the ticket for his birthday and yeah, he was just kind of floored that we wanted to do, like go to a gig with him, 'cause he has this thing in his

head that his gig days are gone and he's too old now [...] And yeah, we all really, really loved Fleet Foxes and it was a great night, and there was a lot of moments just, yeah, the three of us just looking at each other with these massive grins just going *(whispered)* "Shit!" It was nice, it felt great. It was special. [...] And I also went just with dad to see Wilco [...] and that's a similar experience. It felt like a real kind of bonding. Yeah, it was great. We were just on such a high afterwards.

The shared experience of the Fleet Foxes concert was meaningful for Holly's family in several ways. First, through the act of giving their father a ticket and thus proposing to share a particular musical experience, Holly and her brother expressed ideas about him and their relationship in relation to social norms of concert-going. Their father's surprise indicates the significance of this act of non-verbal communication. During the concert, the three family members expressed their responses through facial expressions, in 'moments' that Holly remembers, so she recalls the event as a shared experience. Her recollection that this 'felt great' and was 'special' suggests that through expressively enjoying the music being performed, she and her father and brother were also expressively enjoying each other's company, perhaps highlighting their shared love of music and the shared values underlying it. Consequently, by planning and sharing experiences of the Fleet Foxes and Wilco concerts, Holly and her brother and father 'bonded' in ways that might not be expressed verbally. For Holly at least, these are peak music experiences that continue to have an effect, as her memories of the concerts enable her to reflect on her family and her feelings for them.

Holly also recalled being taken by her mother to her first concert, featuring singer Vanessa Amarosi. She described this as another occasion when a shared experience of music was significant in the context of a particular relationship:

I remember that just feeling really special as well, 'cause it was like me and mum going to see this powerful woman. And she was, she actually blew me away, I still stand by that, she's a powerhouse. She was, crazy voice, insane.

The identity of the singer and qualities of the musical performance are central to what this experience means, along with the form in which the music was experienced. While Holly and her mother might have listened to Vanessa Amorosi's music together in other situations, attending a concert (and especially a first concert) is a deliberate and even ceremonious way of experiencing music together. As in the previous example, the very act of 'going to see' a concert together can express ideas about each other based on the meanings associated with the event, which in this case are centred on the singer's identity as a powerful woman. This meaning was underlined by the musical and especially vocal performance, which created affordances for powerful womanhood to be perceived, experienced and celebrated. Notably, Holly emphasises the singer's voice rather than what she sang, or as Barthes (1989) puts it the 'grain of the voice', which is part of the geno-song (the materiality or body in the performance) rather than the pheno-song (the communicative aspects of the performance). Beyond the lyrical focus exemplified by Horton (1957) and the communicative meaning of a song more generally, this grain and other corporeal aspects of music performance can be important in contributing to a certain kind of experience. In this case, the singer's voice contributed to the concert being a peak music experience for Holly which now encapsulates, among other things, particular values that her mother shared with her as a child, including by sharing music (an instance of 'musical mothering': Grácio 2016).

Deliberate attempts to set up and share a special experience with music are perhaps most clearly demonstrated in the use of recreational drugs. Gomart and Hennion (1999) find similarities between 'drug addicts' and 'music amateurs', as both go to some lengths to actively abandon themselves to the arrival of particular pleasures. This active passivity is apparent in the following quote from Pete (34), but with both the efforts and the outcomes being consciously shared between friends:

> [I remember] driving around in my mate's Datsun Stanza [car] listening to *OK Computer* [Radiohead, 1997, "within a week or two of its release"] on acid. Um, taking turns to drive so you know, the other two of us could be in the back, sort of heads on the speakers and... I think that sort of connected pretty deeply too.

Pete said that the aim of this elaborate, cooperative endeavour and others like it was to 'listen to how far we can hear into this music'. This intention echoes the hippies observed by Willis (1978), who also combined psychedelic drugs and progressive rock music to explore 'inner space'. Notably, however, Pete speaks in the first-person plural: 'we'. This is reminiscent of MacDonald's (2005: 247) observation that The Beatles, who often spoke in the first person plural (for example, George Harrison's statement that 'we don't know about that yet' when asked by a fellow musician in 1965 about his belief in God), 'advanced through their twenties as a sort of sensory phalanx, picking up facts and impressions and pooling them between each other'. While The Beatles may have been uniquely bound by the extraordinary circumstances of their youth together, their collective self-image is to some degree exemplary of that shared by ordinary groups of young friends experimenting with music, drugs and other aspects of culture together. The intention of Pete and his friends was to use drugs, specific music and a car to synchronise and share a subjective experience. They succeeded to the extent that Pete remembers this as a peak music experience some two decades later, partly as a moment that represents that group of friends and what they shared in that time of life.

Engagements with music can present unforeseen affordances for particular ideas and feelings, as well as those that might be planned or hoped for. In response, listeners may spontaneously seize opportunities for interpersonal expression. This can be seen in Holly's earlier story of her family singing along to 'every word' of a song on the radio, which would surely have been recognised as a 'moment' while it went on over several minutes. In another example, Liz (26) described how a night of live music provided a setting for her to explore her own feelings and then to share them with a friend. First, Liz went to see a band in which she used to perform, which was a 'super surreal' experience involving conflicting feelings of belonging and disconnection. She then crossed the road to another venue where she watched Turnpike, a local noise-rock band. As described in Chapter 5, this performance demonstrated 'perfect bandship' to her, reminding her of 'the perfect times you've been in a band'. Turnpike are regarded as veterans in the Brisbane scene and they are also known for performing sporadically and improvising some sections of their songs, with varying but occasionally transcendent results. I was present at this show and spoke to a number of people who agreed that it was an impressive and even inspiring performance. For Liz, however, there was an additional, personal resonance in light of the earlier part of her evening watching her own old band. Liz described how she shared these reflections with a friend, in terms it is important to reproduce in part for the present discussion:

> And I was just watching it like this and then [my friend] came up around me and put her arm like around my waist and, I, was, yeah, we both would have been like, fairly drunk, but I whispered all these thoughts I was having into her ear and she was like, "Aw! Aw." 'Cause she's also a musician who's been through the shit with bands, and also been in bands with partners where it's not worked out so well… but also had like the good times. And also she was hopefully seeing what I was seeing and feeling like, "This is why we do this".

When Liz sought to communicate her thoughts to her friend, she relied on the assumption that they shared perceptions of the show and associated feelings, in the same way that they shared certain histories. This demonstrates an understanding that music creates a common subjective space, in which the communication of intimate thoughts and feelings might be both more appropriate and easier than in other circumstances. Liz's judgement of this musical performance is bound up with the uncommon levels of self-reflection and self-expression it enabled. The result is a peak music experience that represents, among other things, her idea about 'why we do this' and her understanding that this motivation is shared by her friend, as well as the longer personal and interpersonal narratives in which this experience has a place.

As the foregoing examples demonstrate, people use music to communicate and relate to each other in ways that depend, to a large extent, on music's experiential affordances. The lyrical and other content of music can provide a language for the expression of feeling, but it can also shape feelings as they are experienced. Thus, listening to music together can engender emotional closeness and lay grounds of possibility for particular kinds of action and interaction, including uncommon expressions of emotion. Activities besides listening but oriented around music, especially ritualised activities such as those involved in concerts, can subtly or ceremoniously express ideas about relationships. For example, giving tickets, 'taking' a guest or 'going together' to a concert can be meaningful gestures in themselves; the extraordinary setting of the concert can permit extraordinary expressions of feeling; and the music itself may provide extraordinary shape and qualities to those feelings and aid their expression. More ordinary settings and uses of music, such as listening to music during a family activity and singing along to a shared favourite song, can give rise to equally extraordinary experiences of being together. People can both plan and grasp these opportunities to share certain kinds of experience with others as a way of exploring, expressing and celebrating their relationships, which can sometimes create peak music experiences of lasting significance.

Conclusion

This chapter has considered the role of peak music experiences in relationships between people. It has been shown that in families, music is used to soundtrack activities and recognise occasions, based to an extent on its capacity to structure emotional experience. This can heighten the experience of certain events and, in turn, forge lasting links that inform the meaning of certain music well into the future. Thus, a major element of music as a social resource is its capacity to refer to and also to reconstruct experiences that have significance in relation to interpersonal relationships. It has also been shown that music can produce a common affective space for people to interact in potentially exceptional ways, which can create memorable moments within relationships. The intersubjective setting that music produces depends on its inherent and associative properties as well as the socially significant, collective activities oriented around it, such as rituals of concert-going. Finally, it has been shown that people take advantage of music's capacity to enable uncommon experiences and expressions of feeling, by using shared experiences of music to acknowledge, explore and celebrate aspects of their relationships with friends, family and romantic partners. Opportunities for such shared experiences can be planned or seized. Musical experiences that are imbued with personal significance and emotional resonance in this way can be peak music experiences, through which people and relationships are remembered and narrated in retrospect. By considering these peak music experiences as exemplary of broader practices, this chapter has argued for an expanded understanding of how music is involved in relationships between people.

7   Live music experiences

Presence and affective space

Peter was a 52-year-old Brisbane man who I encountered regularly in the audience of live shows by local and touring indie musicians. When I interviewed Peter and asked why he devoted time to seeking out new music and attending gigs, he began by saying that he and his wife had compared their ideas of a 'great musical experience'. She was not interested in 'just standing there nodding at the music', but wanted to dance and to see a 'show', exemplified by a Prince concert they attended together. Peter, by contrast, was interested in 'the song', including how it was performed and how it sounded; being 'physically present in the environment'; and a venue with some 'atmosphere' along with reasonable acoustics, although some 'crappy pubs' had 'done it' for him over the years. He then answered my question more directly with reference to a peak music experience:

> I reckon it just transports you, away from your normal regular life and it takes you somewhere new. And you're a part, more than something which has been created and is put on the screen in front of you, you're there as it's happening, and you may just actually influence what's happening. You know, your enthusiasm and the collective enthusiasm of those around you may just have an impact on what happens on the stage. And clearly they have an impact on you. And I love that idea! You know, I saw at Bluesfest this year, one of my guilty pleasures of music, the Counting Crows. [...] And at the end of the concert [the singer] just stood there, and he sorta said you know, "I've just had the best night tonight". And they played really well and it wasn't the best thing I saw at Bluesfest but I just got that sense of us lifting him and lifting the whole band. And you know this is a band that's been around for twenty years, a bit of a journeyman band, you know, had their really big hits a long time ago, been slogging it out, and ah, you know that sense that everything can come together, the songs sound great, the band feeds off the [audience]. I love that sense that, you know, we're helping to create that moment as well. And I don't know where you get that anywhere else.

DOI: 10.4324/9781003093244-7

This illustrates some key points about live music. Peter identifies multiple elements that complement the music itself, including practical and symbolic factors such as acoustics, atmosphere and a visual 'show'. His comparison with his wife demonstrates that people may place different weight on these elements, or evaluate them by different standards. For both of them, presence and participation in collective activity were essential, although these were manifested in different ways and exemplified by specific memories. Most notably, Peter emphasised that live music could create a unique kind of collective and individual experience. This, ultimately, was his reason for investing time, money and energy in listening to music and attending gigs.

Live music is the setting for the greatest number of peak music experiences reported by the music scene participants who were interviewed. Music fans typically remember and talk about their first and favourite live music experiences as part of their listening histories (see Chapter 3), while 'getting to see' a favourite artist is an especially celebrated experience. This reflects the special status of live music in popular music culture. These peak music experiences, as specifically celebrated instances of live music, reveal what people value most in the live context and how this differs between groups. This chapter considers common elements of peak live music experiences, including the role played by venues, sound and physicality, performance and presence, favourite artists and collective affect. Musical genres and cultures bring different expectations to bear on each element, but there is an underlying emphasis on the experience of presence. Accordingly, peak music experiences provide a new perspective on what defines 'live music', which is a topic of both popular and academic debate. The various elements create an affective space in which people explore individual and collective identity, including through otherwise uncommon expressions of self and belonging. Live music enables extraordinary feelings and behaviour, resulting in especially affecting, memorable and meaningful experiences. These peak music experiences help to account for the special status of live music and for people's investment in music generally.

What is live music and why is it special?

The special status of live music is recognised in popular music studies. Frith (2007b) asserts that despite immense cultural and technological changes since the time of classical music, the concert continues to be the experience that defines the values of most music lovers across genres. He observes the growing importance of live music as one of the more buoyant sectors of the 21st century music industry in the United Kingdom. This is consistent with literature regarding the Australian context, which places live music within the so-called 'experience economy' (Pearce 2013). Campbell (2013) observes that Australian independent music, for example, has since the 1970s shifted from a commodity-based economy with a focus on the sale of recordings, into the experience economy with a greater focus on live performance. Beyond economic value, the live experience also motivates people to invest their time, bodies and emotions, especially at the level of local scene participation in which this book is empirically grounded. Major ethnographic studies of local and global music scenes highlight the central and special status of live music (Finnegan 1989; Cohen 1991, 2012; Cavicchi 1998; Kahn-Harris 2007). While Thornton (1995) suggests that dance music culture marked the decline of (a particular notion of) live music in favour of pre-recorded music, she nevertheless describes the centrality of collective musical events such as discotheques. More recently, Frith (2007b) observes the rise of the 'superstar DJ' centred on 'in person' appearances. These points invite the question of how live music is defined.

In performance studies, liveness is regarded as a quality of the relationship between performer and audience (Fritsch and Strötgen 2012). Some scholars in this field assert that physical presence is essential, excluding performances that require media to be perceived (ibid). However, Auslander (2002a) argues that the relationship between live and mediatised performance is neither ontologically given nor technologically determined, but historical and contingent. He argues that in fact the concept of liveness was an effect of mediatisation; recording technology made it possible to label music as 'live', then broadcast technology made it necessary by blurring the experiential distinction, which had to be reinstated discursively (2002b). It is now widely accepted that live music may incorporate mediatisation in the form of amplification and video screens, and a prominent category of recordings is described as 'live' (Auslander 2002a). Changing media have led to further redefinitions, including webcasts of musical performances (Duffett 2003) which achieved new prominence during the global COVID-19 pandemic of 2020, and concert presentations of pre-recorded music with animated performers such as the cartoon band Gorillaz (Fritsch and Strötgen 2012). Dance and other electronic music have drawn complex appraisals of liveness, as the gestures of a performer in these styles may not seem commensurate to the sonic output for some observers (d'Escriván 2006). Some electronic performances are promoted as 'live' or 'live P.A.' (personal appearance or performing artist), referring to performers using electronic music gear to manipulate pre-programmed or pre-recorded material, as opposed to DJs who play more or less complete tracks, even though both involve physical presence and moment-to-moment creative decisions (see Fritsch and Strötgen 2012: 55). d'Escriván (2006) suggests that differing expectations regarding liveness are based on a technological generation gap, although this may be less important than music-cultural differences, such as between rock and dance audiences or between traditionalist and experimentally minded spectators. This chapter builds on the recognition of liveness as socially constructed, but instead of distinguishing between discursive and experiential understandings (per Auslander 2002b), it is shown that evaluations of liveness continue to be based in the experience of the audience and the performer. This is where discursive constructions of liveness take effect and are confirmed or challenged, consistently with theatre scholar Wolf-Dieter Ernst's extension of Auslander's theory (according to Fritsch and Strötgen 2012, who discuss Ernst's German-language work in English). Peak music experiences in the live domain demonstrate that experience is central to how live music is defined and why it is valued.

After defining what is meant by live music, the next question is how to account for its importance. Live music has been seen as a barometer of authenticity, which is a central value term across musical genres (Moore 2002). In the live setting, musicians and listeners can judge and be judged on whether what they do is 'real' (Frith 2007: 8; see also Gracyk 1996: 74–75; Auslander 2002a). However, this authenticating function does not fully account for the significance of live music. Frith (2007b) notes that successful live acts like the Rolling Stones reached peak record sales years ago and now release records to promote a tour rather than vice versa. He argues that as, over the last hundred years or so, the Western experience of music has been individualised and further entwined with people's sense of self, there has arisen an equally passionate drive to share our musical tastes. Live musical performance therefore matters as a deeply pleasurable event at which our understanding of ourselves through music is socially recognised. This is consistent with Small's (1998) theory that through the 'musicking' activities involved in any musical event, a group explores, affirms and celebrates their relationships and values. As Cavicchi (1998: 37) finds for Bruce Springsteen fans, a concert represents a powerful meeting of the various forces, people and ideas involved in their fandom, shaping and anchoring their sense of who they are and where they belong. This chapter builds on these explanations for the importance of live music, as the peak music experiences examined here demonstrate how the live setting can be especially revelatory, enabling strongly felt and lasting interpretations and evaluations of music, performers and audiences. These experiences also exemplify live music events as occasions for the pleasurable recognition and celebration of individual and collective identities. These in turn are reasons why so many peak music experiences arise in the live setting.

After identifying why live music is so valued, we can ask more specifically what makes some live music experiences stand out. Research has identified a number of important elements in creating the sought-after social space, including the practical and symbolic affordances of venues; the musical, gestural and visual aspects of performance; the presence and behaviour of audiences; and the anticipatory and commemorative activities surrounding events. The relevant literature in this regard is discussed through the following sections. Participants bring specific expectations to each of these elements and audience studies have begun to identify common qualitative axes, such as intimacy versus spectacle, the unique atmosphere and character of a venue versus the predictable and comfortable running of a show, surprise and the unexpected versus confirmation of already held tastes, and inward versus outward audience participation (Behr et al. 2016). However, across these divides, participation in live music and collective musical events involves a common desire for an extraordinary kind of experience, which has been described in various terms: immersive and transcendent (ibid); being taken out of oneself (Frith 2012); oceanic and ecstatic (Malbon 1999); collective, participatory, unpredictable and unique (Cohen 2012). Behr et al. (2016: 411) note that '[w]hile the concert/gig does not need to attain this "transcendence" to have value, it is the potential for that which keeps people going back', whether as part of their regular activities or on special occasions. These extraordinary experiences are expressed outwardly, so that people 'behave in ways that they would not outside the performance ... things which would be inappropriate in the context of everyday life' (Cavicchi 1998: 89). Once again, ways of engaging vary greatly, 'from rapt silence to noisy sing-alongs, intense mental concentration to the physical exertion of dance' (Behr et al. 2016: 411). The uniting feature is the exceptional experience and expression of identities in a collective setting. Accordingly, peak music experiences of the kind considered in this chapter are central to understanding the social significance of live music. They illustrate the unique affective space created in live music events and the ways that extraordinary live music experiences inform ongoing practices and everyday identity. Further, as idealised but actual instances of live music, they provide insight into the elements that comprise it and the measures by which it is valued. The following sections consider live music experiences in terms of place and space, sound and physicality, performance and presence, crowds and collective affect, and the resulting experience that sets live music apart from the consumption of music in other contexts.

Live music venues

Despite the proliferation of media through which music can be experienced from a distance, venues remain central to most people's idea of live music. While all musical experience is informed to some extent by setting as demonstrated throughout the previous chapters, live music emphasises and ritualises this physical context. Behr et al. (2016: 404, 414) found that audiences for 'classical, folk, jazz, singer-songwriter and indie music performances' at the Queen's Hall in Edinburgh, when planning their attendance, thought about whether a venue would enable 'the sorts of transcendence' they prized. Both the practical and symbolic affordances of venues play a role here and they are evaluated through audience expectations. For example, Forbes (2012) shows that some (mainly rock) acts and audiences revelled in the physically dilapidated state of the Glasgow Apollo as a sign of authenticity, while 'pop' audiences such as those who attended a Neil Sedaka show complained of a squalid experience. Some venues accrue iconic status, as observed in relation to the Glasgow Apollo (ibid) and various unofficial venues in Australia's local music scenes (Bennett and Rogers 2016). This can inform the meaning and memory of events that take place at those venues. One of the most iconic venues in Brisbane history is the Cloudland Ballroom. Cloudland, as it is known, was built in 1940 and became a post-war 'social Mecca', hosting resident dance bands and touring artists from Buddy Holly in 1958 to punk and new wave bands in the early 1980s, before it was controversially demolished overnight in 1982 (Stafford 2004: 117–118, 125; see also Bennett and Rogers 2016: 97; the demolition is referenced in Sydney rock band Midnight Oil's 1987 single, 'Dreamworld'). 'Ken' (58) provided the following recollection of a concert at Cloudland from the perspective of more than 30 years later:

> I saw The Clash play Cloudland and that was a great show. But Cloudland was a great venue. Reading about the sprung floor is not the same as bouncing on the sprung floor, that was a fantastic experience!

This quote highlights both the reputation of the venue and the embodied experience on which it is partly based. Specifically, the sprung floor was well suited to the 'pogo' dance style of punk fans (see Laing 1985), despite being designed decades before this phenomenon. Accordingly, the physical properties and cultural status of a venue can be interrelated and both may imbue a live music experience with significance.

An iconic venue that still operates in Brisbane is The Zoo, a 500-capacity, licensed room which has been associated with local and alternative music since it opened in 1992. For many local musicians, their first performance, first headline performance and first sold-out performance at The Zoo are remembered as career milestones and peak music experiences (see for example Elly's and Julian's stories in Chapter 5). Smaller, unofficial venues in Brisbane are also 'invested with a high degree of importance, authenticity, and aesthetic value' due in large part to the emotional work that goes into them (Bennett and Rogers 2016). Simply knowing about such venues can mark the inside and outside of a particular community (Shank 1994: 120). An example is Real Bad Music, a 'squatted' space with capacity for no more than a few dozen people in a dilapidated building in the outer suburb of Moorooka, which was destroyed by fire in 2016. Jane (26), quoted in Chapter 5, describes her band's performance at Real Bad Music as a peak music experience, with reference to both its reputation and the unusual journey to its suburban location.

Venues can embody the zeitgeist of particular genres and times (Bennett and Rogers 2016; Feldman-Barrett 2017) and therefore resonate thematically with the music being performed there, imbuing experiences with significance. For example, an artist might perform in a 'home ground', as demonstrated in the following story by Jim (44):

> A very important one, one that really stands out as amongst the most moving and uplifting gigs I've ever seen was actually Yothu Yindi. I

saw them in 1999 at the inaugural Garma festival in North Queensland. Look it up, it's a longstanding thing. And Yothu Yindi are from the north east of Arnhem Land, they're Yolngu people. And I was seeing them play on their home turf, on the beach, with the stage kind of crowded eight deep in Aboriginal kids who were, you know, tiny, less than ten years old; they were heroes to them. And it's one of the most moving things I've ever seen. I cried at that show too. I've cried at a few shows but that would probably stand out in the top five, you know. And part of that of course is politics, social conscience, all of that kind of clichéd stuff. That was important.

Jim's story highlights the importance of setting to the experience of live music, as well as the various factors that inform the meaning of a setting. In this case, Yothu Yindi's reputation as musical ambassadors for Yolngu people and culture made their performance in an iconic part of Yolngu country especially meaningful to Jim, an informed visitor to that place. The association of music and place imbued Jim's experience of the concert with political and social resonance. I understood Jim's description of these factors as 'clichéd' to mean that he considered them obvious in the circumstances, while perhaps also expressing some embarrassment at his own sincerity, of which I was in no doubt. Similarly, singer-songwriter Elly (26) cited her performance at a women's prison as a peak music experience, calling it her 'little Johnny Cash moment' in reference to the country singer's career-defining performances at US prisons such as Folsom Prison (1968) and San Quentin (1969). Accordingly, it can be seen that one element that distinguishes live music is a ritualised emphasis on meaningful settings. The following section considers a more physically determined attribute of live music venues, their treatment of sound.

Sound and physicality

An important element in experiential accounts of live music is the character of the musical sound, especially its volume, which tends to be significantly louder than in other listening settings. While venues were valued for their acoustic properties before electronic amplification (see Sabine 1923), popular music concerts are now associated with far louder volumes than unamplified musicians could produce. The technological and aesthetic valourisation of volume can be traced most clearly in rock music, as it progressed from ballrooms in the 1960s to arenas and stadiums in the 1970s and beyond (Frith 2007).[1] High volume increases the materiality of sound and the corporeal nature of musical experience (Gilbert and Pearson 1999: 44), which can result in a qualitatively different experience of musical elements. For example, Jones (1988: 156) posits that it was at high volume that 'reggae's drum and bass rhythms, and the sensual "feel" of the music, were at their most effective'.

Listeners tend to be conscious of volume as an aspect of live music and it is not unusual for music fans to specifically remember the loudest performances they have attended. In this regard, local concerts by US band Dinosaur Jr and Irish band My Bloody Valentine featured prominently among indie rock fans in this study, including more than one reference to physical illness. May (35) remembered the physical experience of volume as central to her 'second big concert' in her early teens, finding it shocking at first but later appealing.

> Janet Jackson was crazy 'cause it was the first time I experienced like bass actually interrupting your heartbeat. It was so loud. I was like, "What is this?" [...] And the bass was not like that for [my first concert] Roxette. It's a shed! It's a fuckin' shed, the [Brisbane] Entertainment Centre. Can you imagine Janet Jackson bass in her prime? It was like, I was shaking.

This description illustrates how high volume enhances particular aspects of musical experience, such as the physically perceptible vibrations of bass and sub-bass frequencies. This highlights musical differences, such as the more prominent bass in Janet Jackson's hip hop and dance-influenced pop as opposed to Roxette's guitar-based pop-rock. Fans sometimes claim that certain music must be experienced live in order to fully appreciate it, as demonstrated in the following quote by Aaron (25) about Australian noise-rock band feedtime (the name of which is uncapitalised):

> I guess for years I'd heard that feedtime never translated on a record, like the strength and the grit of the live sound could never be reproduced through a recording. And that's what I found on that day [that I saw them]. So on one hand that question was answered, like "Why can't it be reproduced?" Because, you know, the guitar just like buzzes through parts of your brain that you'd never experienced before.

The collective wisdom Aaron had heard over the years, that feedtime 'never translated' in recorded form, also suggests that attending a live performance can be a way of accruing symbolic capital. This is described by Forbes (2012) as 'I Was Thereism'. As in the earlier discussion of venues, discussions of sound show again how practical and symbolic factors are difficult to disentangle in live music experiences and consequent evaluations. Other research participants cited volume and quality of sound among their reasons for valuing the club setting in dance music. For example, Martin (32) said that he first got 'really big into' dance music when he started hearing it 'in a proper club, with good DJs being able to manipulate the hardware that they had in a club to make it sound great'. This highlights again the differentiation of musical elements at sufficient volume, which is usually only experienced in the live setting. Accordingly, a practical reason for the preponderance of peak music experiences in the live setting is that the greater bodily impact of music at loud volumes highlights unique qualities, as well as imbuing them with affective power, creating memorable experiences of feeling and meaning.

Performance and presence

People's descriptions of their peak music experiences as audience members tend to highlight the proximity and activity of performers. In accordance with Auslander's (2002b: 21) observation that liveness is first and foremost 'a relationship of simultaneity', experiences of live performance are often marked by uncertainty as to what will occur as the performance unfolds. This entails both the risks of disappointment and the pleasures of satisfaction or surprise. There is an associated focus on the skill and effort of musicians, which are evaluated according to various cultural standards. Some people's experience of live music is elevated by their perceptions of technical proficiency and professionalism, as shown in the following quote from Lily (26) about Joanna Newsom, whose music is situated in the indie market but incorporates both folk and modern classical elements:

> I've only seen Joanna Newsom play once but that was probably one of the best shows I've ever been to. And that was more, I think, just how polished it was and how nice it is to go to a show when someone is just so well-practised and such a... I guess a professional at everything that they do. So she's just an amazing harpist, she's got an incredible voice that is doing the most, just really really complicated vocal melodies that are completely in contrast to the really complicated harp parts and then her lyrics just tell the most vivid, evocative stories. [...] The kind of experience that can be created from just being really good at what you do, really technically proficient, can be really great for a spectator.

Joanna Newsom's skills as a composer and performer are highlighted on her recordings, which have a naturalistic aesthetic that largely emulates an intimate live performance. Lily's emphasis on these skills in concert demonstrates the heightened focus that is placed on performers and performance in the live setting, due to their increased visibility as well as the higher risks associated with making an error before a simultaneous audience.

The different interpretations of liveness in electronic music, as discussed earlier, tend to revolve around ways of evaluating performers' skill and effort (see d'Escriván 2006). Dance music fan and event organiser John (25) focused on these elements when describing an 'amazing' performance by the electronic music producer Trippy Turtle:

> He was ridiculous, he was incredible. He was bouncing around, he was doing it all live on the fly, hitting samples and MIDI controllers and this

and that, blending all his tracks. I knew all his tracks by heart, he was [performing] new songs that I'd never heard. [...] And this guy was just on a whole other level and it really showed me the difference between what a DJ set could do and what a live set can do and the level of control you can have in the room. 'Cause everyone always says that a good DJ controls the room, controls the flow. But this guy took it above that, he was creating songs at the time with all of his different samples, it was amazing.

This peak music experience highlights again the significance of simultaneity, which is experienced through uncertainty ('new songs that I'd never heard') as well as the visibility of active performance. John found it exciting that the songs were being 'created' in the moment and that this involved substantial activity on the part of the performer. Notably, these are the same elements that some rock fans find lacking in electronic music, based on different definitions. By placing increased focus on the acts of performance, live music highlights such cultural differences.

The liveness of a performance can also be made apparent by imperfection, so that mistakes can create a memorable experience for audience members. This is demonstrated in Peter's (52) experience of a concert by the alt-country band Wilco:

They played a gig at the Tivoli and it was obvious that they weren't quite prepared for the gig, that they were very much early on in the process of playing that album and integrating the band. And so what made that gig amazing to me, as someone watching a gig, was the fact that it wasn't polished. So I seem to recall on a couple of occasions they stopped playing a song after a few bars and went back and played it again. And so you got a real sense, it was like being in the garage as the band were playing.

Peter's comparison to 'being in the garage' with the band illustrates how imperfections can contribute to a sense of intimacy with performers, even at a theatre-style venue like Brisbane's Tivoli, by foregrounding simultaneous human activity. Such perceptions are shaped by cultural criteria; for example, in indie music, imperfection contributes to the valued sense of emotional directness and authenticity (Fonarow 2006). Accordingly, when Aaron (25) described his stand-out live experience of seeing grunge-rock band feedtime, he expressed relief that their performance retained the roughness he enjoyed in their recordings. He observed, 'That would have almost been like the cardinal sin, like the drummer getting really tight. They just started and stopped when they liked [...] the songs are kind of these organisms that just have to be awakened'. Such expectations and their significance in audience experience illustrate how aesthetic and social values are performed in live music (Small 1998). The live setting therefore provides unique opportunities for musical experiences that reveal, affirm or challenge values.

Extra-musical aspects of performance also contribute substantially to the experience of live music, including physical gestures, verbal communication and visual style, assisted by lighting and other stage effects. Performers' clothing has been identified as especially important in, and partly definitive of, the genres of glam rock (Auslander 2006) and Mod (Feldman 2009). However, such extra-musical elements contribute to musical meaning in all genres (as Small 1998 argues using the example of classical music). Musicians can take advantage of these in the live setting to achieve greater control over the reception of their music, which helps to explain why live music experiences are often described as revelatory. However, cultural expectations are involved in the perception of what could be called stagecraft. As Auslander (2002a: 70) observes, '[t]ightly choreographed unison dance steps may be necessary for a soul vocal group to establish itself as authentic but would be a sign of inauthenticity in a rock group because they belie the effect of spontaneity rock audiences value'. People's descriptions of their peak music experiences highlight such distinctions, but also demonstrate a reflexive attitude towards them. DJ and dance club organiser Joe (32) recalled a peak music experience in which obviously staged elements of a performance combined with his interpretation of a song to create an emotional response:

> When I was a kid and Basement Jaxx had that 'Good Luck' track, I remember going to Big Day Out [festival] and [the highlight] was when they started playin' the song, and then the [guest] singer would surprise the crowd by coming from backstage and would sing it to the crowd as like a surprise vocalist. And you'd be like mind blown cause you're like *(mock screaming)* "Oh wow!" Especially that song 'cause it's such an empowering song as well. So that was one of the genuine moments where the music really made the hair on my back of my neck stand up, and gave me goosebumps. See it gives me goosebumps thinking about it just now, because of such, of the impact that it made.

As this quote shows, music fans are often well aware of the calculation involved in live performances, but may nevertheless be moved deeply. Stagecraft itself may be appreciated as a display of skill or a gesture of generosity, which was the interpretation offered by music fan and critic Jim (44) when describing part of a Bruce Springsteen concert:

> A lot of this is cheese, you know, this is showmanship, this is vaudeville. But he got this kid, who must have been 10 or 11, maybe 12 at most, got him onstage, he'd obviously seen him with his parents down the front, the kid must have known the words to the songs, and he probably does this every show 'cause there's always one, right? [...] The E Street Band are pounding away and he takes this kid to the side, next to the drum riser I think, and he's sort of dusting his knees down with some talc

[talcum powder] of some kind. You sort of go, "What's going on here?" He takes the kid back to the front of the stage and this is all timed right at the crescendo of the song, they go running down the front of the stage and they do this power slide on their knees together. This is the corniest thing you have ever seen. On the other hand it's one of the most moving things I've ever seen on the stage. He's given that kid an experience he'll never forget. He's given everyone else in the audience – I'll never forget it. And you just go, that is a beautiful thing to do. That's like, this is the anti-snob. If you were there and you were not moved by that I'd be like "You curmudgeon! You arsehole!" You know? That was the ultimate act of inclusiveness I've ever seen.

While Jim's analysis is uncommonly thoughtful, perhaps due to his perspective as a music critic, Springsteen's talcum powder routine plays to his audience's reflexivity about rock performance conventions. His exaggerated stagecraft is a way of performing a deeper relationship with his audience, which Jim described as inclusiveness.

Musicians at the local and amateur level also demonstrate awareness of performance conventions and their significance. For a performer, a well-executed stage move can be part of a peak music experience by creating a feeling of achievement, as illustrated in the following story told by rapper Dee (35):

When we did a show at [small Brisbane venue] the Bearded Lady a little while ago […] we have a bit in one of our songs where it's like, "Have a rest". And usually we just sit on the ground and have a rest. I like to do theatrics as well. And there was two couches, so we just sat on the couch and I was like, "Have a rest!" And it was just kind of perfect, the joke, and I wish there were things like that all the time. Yeah, that feeling when you know you were right, I know I'm right, I did it, everything's working right now, a couple of seconds and yeah. That's satisfaction.

Dee's performances include humour alongside more serious musical and lyrical content, which is common in hip hop music. This and the previous quotes show that neither humour nor theatricality is necessarily inconsistent with genuine feelings on the part of audiences and performers. They also illustrate that all participants share an interest in the successful creation of a convincing and moving live music event, along with a tacit acknowledgement that there is in fact a performance taking place. To an extent, participants in a musical event willingly acquiesce to performance conventions in search of moving and memorable experiences.

In some genres such as punk and indie, theatricality is shunned in pursuit of authenticity and unmediated expression (Hibbett 2005; Fonarow 2006). Nevertheless, these very ideals are performed through particular conventions. For example, the punk values of total commitment and spontaneity can be displayed through bodily abandon, as demonstrated in the following peak music experiences:

> Tracy, 39: I'll never forget seeing Fugazi at the Roxy. That sort of clicked my brain over, that night. It was just the most perfect sound, this was sort of back in the Nineties, and the performance as well. Guy from Fugazi just, you know, scaled up to the balcony and did this huge stage dive and got carried around by the crowd and things like that.
>
> Ken, 58: I saw [Iggy Pop] in Berlin in '81 or '82, which is probably the best time I've ever seen him, he was fully engaged. And you'd never ever realise, he really is 5 foot 1 [the title of an Iggy Pop song]! Because the energy coming off him just makes him feel like he's six and a half feet. So you really do feel like you're part of something when you see an Iggy Pop show.

Physical performance is a form of musicking that enacts relationships, including between performer and audience (Small 1998). In contrast to more overtly rehearsed displays, the above examples depict relationships built on shared values of immediacy and direct expression. As well as physical exertion, performances are also valued for perceived emotional effort, which is perceived as generous as the following quotes illustrate:

> Nat, 34: [R&B singer] D'Angelo at Soulfest [...] just gave to this little Brisbane crowd, like I think they only sold a third of the tickets that they wanted to, but he just absolutely killed it and just gave so much.
>
> Holly, 25: Definitely every time I've seen [indie-folk artist] Conor Oberst play, I've always come out of it really moved. And I feel like he's someone who, again, like is really conscious about being at every performance that he does. I mean it may be like one show in a huge tour, but I feel like a lot comes out of it from him. I almost marvel at the kind of emotional stamina he would have to give that kind of performance at every show.

These quotes refer to the emotional presence of musicians, described by Fonarow as 'beingness' (2006: 192). The peak music experiences considered in this section show the experience of presence as a common, underlying goal of the various conventions of theatrical performance, physical expression and emotional display. Presence is performed and interpreted in different ways; the grand gestures of Bruce Springsteen that are seen as inclusive by his audience might be considered by a punk audience to lack the authenticity of spontaneous action, while an indie crowd might perceive emotional distance in rehearsed moves. The experience of presence is definitive of live music, while the different ways in which such an experience is produced help to define popular music cultures such as rock, indie, dance and so on.

Identity and fandom

Audiences speak of the live experience in terms of 'seeing' musicians, just as musicians advertise their upcoming 'appearances'. The persistence of this language, despite the proliferation of images outside of live performance, suggests that visibility represents the more fundamental concept of presence in defining and valuing live music. Popular music fans will list the artists they have and have not seen, presenting the mere fact of attending a live performance by a given artist as a goal in itself. As Fonarow (2006) notes in relation to indie music, fans 'collect' significant gigs. Accordingly, seeing a famous or favourite artist is often cause for anticipation, excitement and remembrance as a peak music experience, as the following quotes illustrate:

> Tom, 22: D'Angelo's set at Soulfest was pretty hectic, I'll never forget that. I was sort of right behind the VIP area, directly in front. It was just incredible, I never thought I was gonna see him and I'm pretty sure most people here [in Brisbane] never thought they'd see him live so that was definitely memorable for that.
>
> Julian, 44: [The Police] reformed and I saw them when they came out in 2008, so that for me was like: I'm getting to see Stewart Copeland drum. "Yeah, hi Sting, I just wanna hear the drummer", you know?

Seeing a favourite artist is partly an occasion for reflection on one's past and present taste, acting as a milestone for a continuous and developing identity.

A related priority is seeing a favourite song performed live. The study of popular music consumption and fandom has tended not to focus on songs, but on artists and genres more generally (although DeNora (2000) provides an exception as discussed elsewhere). It is a popular music cliché that live audiences want to hear their favourite songs even when the artist has tired of performing them. This suggests that while fandom might be understood as a relationship with a musician, fans also have a direct relationship with their favourite music. Accordingly, the fulfilment of the wish to see a favourite song performed live can be a peak music experience. In one example, Jill (32) went to some expense and effort to see her favourite band, Radiohead, at multiple concerts on their first Australian tour that she was able to attend, recalling 11 years and nine more concerts later:

> Time just goes by and you forget things, but I guess you remember the general feeling of being there and maybe you remember certain things, songs or whatever. I think they played 'Lucky' in Melbourne, and I was really happy because I really loved that song and I really wanted to see that live. So I guess I remember things like that, going "Yes, I got to see the song I liked!"

Similarly, when Lisa (34) was asked if she could think of any highlights among gigs she had attended, she described how her long wait to see a favourite band culminated in an emotional response to a familiar song:

> I was trying to think of something on the way over here that really affected me. In 2008, which is not that recently, Ween toured that year and I'd not seen them play before [...] So I was really excited to see Ween and they started the show with that song 'Buckingham Green', I don't know if you're a Ween fan but I was really excited. And that's one of the only times I can remember where I've been moved to tears. 'Cause they played, there's this guitar solo which is a kind of simplistic solo but it's so familiar to me and I think it meant so much to me that they were playing it, and it was the first song and I was so excited, it was at the Tivoli, that I just started crying when they started doing the guitar solo. So I remember that really affecting me.

These examples show how the experience of hearing a favourite song 'live' is marked by memories and feelings about both the artist and oneself.

Live peak music experiences with favourite artists come to represent past selves and contexts, particularly when they are evaluated differently over time. For example, Peter (52) described his first Bob Dylan concert as a peak, although after seeing more concerts he rated that performance as relatively poor:

> Probably the defining early musical experience was seeing Bob Dylan play at the Myer Music Bowl in about 1979 I think. He was touring off the back of his *Bob Dylan Live at the Budokan* album and this was an album he made, it was like a greatest hits album live, where everything was played slightly to a reggae beat. So it actually was, in retrospect because I've seen Dylan many times since, probably not his greatest concert because everything had that sort of reggae flavour to it and the live album's not very good. But that didn't matter to me. I mean, seeing Dylan as a 16 or 17 year-old, that was, without any doubt, the big musical experience of my life at the time. Yeah huge, just huge.

Re-evaluating a peak music experience in hindsight is a way of understanding personal growth. As shown in Chapter 3, peak music experiences are milestones of fandom as an aspect of long-term identity. Live music events, as settings for celebrating the objects of fandom, are especially productive sites for such biographically significant experiences. These aspects of long-term music fandom are also demonstrated in the practice of seeing a favourite artist on multiple occasions. In an extreme example, Georgie (45) said she has seen her favourite rock band from the United States, Monster Magnet, almost 20 times, having followed them on every Australian tour. Another example is Jill (32), who had seen the bands Radiohead and Belle and Sebastian on multiple occasions and explained that this was partly a way of tracking her life:

> You sort of have memories I guess, listening to a band like that, where you've really loved them for like a long time and you know all their records, so just going to see them live is sort of like a flashback to lots of times where you've listened to them as well; last times you've seen them and where you were and what you were doing then as well.

These examples suggest a special role for live experiences alongside the domestic listening discussed in DeNora's (2000) theorisation of music as a technology of the self. Peak music experiences with favourite artists and songs show that live music provides a unique opportunity for people to engage with those objects of fandom, as well as with their past and present selves, within a context of collective performance and celebration. These experiences are defined to a large extent by their rarity and the anticipation leading up to them, making them quite different to seeing local bands on a weekly or even more frequent basis, as is common in the local music scenes of Brisbane. However, at such non-celebrity performances, other factors may still create peak music experiences, as will be shown.

'Surrounded by people': crowds and collective affect

A defining feature of the live music experience is the presence of an audience. Frith (1988: 7) notes that in the live context we can see music in the making 'and in the receiving – the audience was always crucial for my understanding and enjoyment of a show'. The attention, enthusiasm and exuberance of live music audiences can be as important as the musical performance itself (Pearce 2013: 7–8). Live music involves what Urry (1990) calls (in the context of tourism) the collective gaze, involving the celebration of people being together to appreciate what they are experiencing. Beyond merely witnessing an event together, the enjoyment of live music involves a feeling that we have been 'in the company of like-feeling people, in an ideal society which musicians and listeners have together brought into existence for that duration of time' (Small 1987: 67; see also Hesmondhalgh 2013: 106). Live music can demonstrate the peculiar subjectivity of 'the crowd', which Henriques (2010) describes as a corporeal but collective subject, an entity that is not singular but plural, or both at the same time: the one who-is-many and the many-who-are-one. This phenomenon is partly explained by music's synchronisation of people's experience of time and emotions (see Chapter 6). Hesmondhalgh (2013: 118–119) suggests it is also explained by the primal orientation of humans towards shared experience, as recognised in Durkheim's concept of collective effervescence and Maffesoli's theory of neo-tribes. Bennett (1999a) argues that neo-tribalism with its focus on site-specific belonging is a useful framework for understanding consumption-based youth cultures, using the example of an urban dance music event to which people bring various sensibilities and ways of participating. Within this framework, live music can be seen to offer an essential social space for identity and belonging.

The experience of being in a crowd emerges as a common element in peak live music experiences. Jill (32) cites this as the determining factor of her 'best concert', by the band Chic:

> That was amazing. Everyone was dancing. I just wanna dance, yeah. And they just had so much energy on stage that it comes, everyone has that same energy, it's really good.

While Jill says she wants to dance, it is important that 'everyone' is dancing. To dance alone is not the same as dancing in a crowd. Dancing is an especially clear example of how music synchronises subjective time and orders collective action (DeNora 2000). As Jill's quote shows, this can be experienced as the sharing of energy between performers and audience members. The sense of collective affect is also central to a peak music experience described by Tom (22):

> I remember a number of years ago going out to Good Vibrations festival down the Gold Coast and seeing Nas and Damian Marley perform together. And being in a massive big crowd and yeah, really, really in those situations when you're really feeling the music, like not just hearing it but, you know, feeling ah, like a physical, um, sensation of sorta rush during the peaks of certain songs and things like that. And the thing of being in a crowd when you hear the whole, you know, you feel that and then you also feel that all the people around you feel the same thing and then everyone makes noise together and you feel it rise up. Yeah very memorable experience that was, yeah.

As this quote shows, crowd members can experience collective affect as quite immediate and physical – 'you also feel that all the people around you feel the same thing' – although at a rational level this might only be gleaned from outward evidence such as noise and movement. This is the crowd as a corporeal and collective, singular and plural subject (Henriques 2010). Tom's description of a shared physical rush during musical peaks and people making noise together illustrates again a shared sense of time. These peak music experiences show that the simultaneity of liveness (Auslander 2002b) is not only between performers and audience, but also between audience members. Tom's peak music experience, along with others in this chapter at festivals, arenas and stadium concerts, challenges any assumption that these large-scale events and the additional kinds of mediation they involve (such as video screens and crowd control measures) prevent the experience of affective simultaneity or emotional intimacy among those present. This too is a matter of cultural preference, such as the virtue that pub bands and punk bands of the 1970s attributed to 'bar-room' venues and the particular kind of intimacy these allowed and imposed (see Laing 1985: 8). By comparison, Tom's experience and some of those described by performers below seem to be enhanced by the size of the audience.

While live music can create a sense of collective identity based on presence at an event, it also provides opportunities to celebrate pre-existing forms of belonging. Liz (26) described a peak music experience at a gig in which her interpretation of the music, her identification with the audience and her perception of unanimous passion were related:

> One of the favourite gigs I've seen is this band Limp Wrist. There's something that makes you, like, euphoric when you see a band like that. I don't know, I feel like 'cause I felt everyone in the room felt exactly the same thing because of the music. It was like, super unique, crazy-fast, Latin-inspired hardcore with queer-focused and uplifting lyrics. And it's a packed room of people that, lots of people that I knew who had travelled interstate for this show. Lots of gay people, lots of women. So there's like a hundred people in a moshpit and totally like, not violent but just like pummelling into each other out of like, aggressive passion. And that's like a part of the music as well. I like, almost passed out in that moshpit. [...] That was one of the last times I've like, stayed in the moshpit for like that long. And came out all battered and bruised and my glasses were broken and everything. It was really great, I did not regret.

For Liz, this experience involved the celebration of pre-existing community, based on friendship as well as gender and sexuality, as well as a shared affective experience with 'a hundred people in a moshpit' and indeed, 'everyone in the room'. This illustrates how live music is a site for both the consolidation and formation of social connections.

The peak music experiences described by performing musicians also depend to a large extent on the audience. The experience of performing to an especially large crowd is often a memorable one, occurring for example at festivals:

> Lisa, 34: And then another kind of amazing show was the first Big Day Out that [we] did, I think it was in 2008. [...] The third time I played [the biggest hit as a new member of the touring band] was in front of 30,000 people and when I started playing that intro, the whole audience just erupted and my hand started shaking *(laughs)*. So that was really affecting, 'cause that was an instant reaction from the audience that was crazy.
>
> Nathan, 35: It was the last rap of the thing and there was like three thousand people, could have been ten thousand I don't know, it was a lot of people. [...] Yeah just the full energy of like three to ten thousand people, whatever it was, knowing the lyrics that I was rapping.

Lisa's story shows the experience of simultaneity from the performer's perspective, when an audience responds immediately to musical cues. Nathan's quote includes another use of the term 'energy' to describe his experience of rapping to, and with, thousands of people. Crucially, both of these examples describe a crowd that is not only large but engaged. In the peak music experiences of performers, the most important feature of the crowd is that it is receptive to the music being performed. This collective energy can be produced in much smaller audiences with physical intimacy playing a role, as the following example from hip hop musician Tom (22) shows:

> The place was packed, everyone was within about half a metre from us; we were crammed in the corner, outside onto the street we had the windows open, the whole crowd was blocked up and the music, the feelings of that, probably one of the most memorable shows for me because everyone was going nuts. It just drove the energy; everyone was, you know it felt like we were all sort of one at that time. Which is pretty crazy.

This and the preceding quotes show that the collective subjectivity or 'oneness' of the crowd can be felt by performers as well as audiences.

Across genres, live music is seen to hold the potential for an experience of reciprocal exchange between performers and audiences. Musicians are quick to point out that a memorable live performance is not a 'one-way thing', as shown in the following interview excerpt from rapper, Matt (31):

> There was lots of people there and they loved the music and there was people singing along, rapping lyrics, and lots of familiar faces in the crowd and everybody just really, really felt like we were together. I mean, you know they use the term, "You feel like you have the crowd in the palm of your hand", which is how it felt, but I don't think that term's quite adequate 'cause it kinda sounds as if it's just a one-way thing, like "I've got them", but it's not like that at all, it's like they feed back.

This exchange of energy is enacted in quite different ways across different musical styles and settings. This is shown in two contrasting peak music experiences described by Holly (26), a regular attendee of local gigs. The first example involves a raucous performance by a dance-punk duo with guitar and drums:

> I went to this, like, house party in East Brisbane and DZ Deathrays were playing there and I'd never heard of them and found out that they were big later. But they had kind of set themselves up in the middle of the lounge room and then people were just going psychotic, all around them and, yeah, I dunno I just thought that was really cool, it felt really like… a mutual process, you know they were really like getting off on just being surrounded by people who were getting off on their music, you know? It felt really like symbiotic, it was awesome.

The second example involves another 'house show' of subdued, folk-style solo performances to a seated audience, which is where I met Holly:

> I loved that. I think what struck me the most was how vulnerable I felt that the artists were, and made themselves. And I kind of felt as soon as I walked into that house and into that room, I felt like it was a really, um, like warm and, just really like non-judgmental space. And I just felt everyone like, enter that room and just kind of be really, feel really comfortable with themselves. And I felt that with the artists as well. And I think that's why they felt like they could be a bit, you know experimental and try songs that they didn't have down fully, and it just felt really supportive and respectful. I just think there was so much respect for the artists and so much gratitude that they were choosing to share that. [...] I felt like there was kind of a shared vulnerability.

While these two live music experiences involved markedly different styles of music and physical activity, each was made special for Holly by her sense that the performers and audience worked together to create an affective space in which to feel and act. The metaphor of symbiosis and the notion of 'shared vulnerability' suggest that in a live music event, the collective subjectivity can extend not only to fellow audience members, or fellow performers, but across all participants. These claims, which are not uncommon in relation to live music, stand in contrast with Auslander's (2002a: 57) idea of a gap between performer and 'spectator'. He asserts that while live performance 'places us in the living presence' of performers 'with whom we desire unity', it reasserts 'the unbridgeable distinction between audience and performance [and] foregrounds its own fractious nature and the unlikelihood of community in a way that mediatised representations, which never hold out the promise of unity, do not'. On the contrary, in many of the peak music experiences described by both performers and audience members, these roles remain clear but are transcended by a community of feeling. While this experience is temporary by nature, it may nevertheless inform enduring ideas about relationships, such as the sense of belonging to a scene (see Chapter 8) or, as Jill (26) said with regard to her attendances at multiple concerts by Radiohead and Belle and Sebastian, 'getting old together' with favourite artists and fellow fans.

Among the Brisbane music scene participants who were interviewed, experiences of collective affect were claimed far more often in situations of physical presence than in more distantly mediated representations. The connection between physical and emotional interaction is especially clear in Holly's description of the 'psychotic' DZ Deathrays lounge room audience and Liz's recollection of the Limp Wrist mosh pit, which recall Shank's (1994) observations about the punk scene in Austin, Texas. He states (ibid: 125):

> The importance of this intense bodily stimulation cannot be overemphasized. [...] Within this fluid stream of potential meanings, the

audience and the musicians together participate in a nonverbal dialogue about the significance of the music and the construction of their selves. Gestures of the performer contribute directly to the meaning of the musical experience, generating and being generated by corresponding physical responses in the listeners.

These cues can also be identified in less physically intense styles of interaction, for example in Jill's experience of an energy exchange between funk band Chic and their dancing audience, and in Holly's enjoyment of the supportive and respectful space generated by a seated audience in a folk-style house show. The contribution of collective bodily action to the experience and meaning of music helps to explain the special status of live music events.

Peak live music experiences show that the experience of physical and affective community among audiences and performers is valued across popular music genres, emerging as a defining ideal of live music. These are occasions when desired social relationships are performed and experienced, including relationships between audience members, between performers and between both, as well as between individuals and the world, and between individuals and their selves over time. Such peak music experiences are thus embedded in narratives of belonging and identity, featuring significantly among the experiences of motivation discussed in Chapter 5. The affective space produced by these collective interactions enables particular experiences and expressions of individual identity, which are considered below.

'In the moment': experiencing and expressing feelings with live music

It is apparent that while various factors contribute to peak music experiences in the live setting, these ideal experiences share a particular quality, namely an abundance of feeling. At least some fans consciously evaluate live performances by the feelings they engender. Ken (58), who reported seeing hundreds of live music events over several decades, judged his favourites as those where he was 'lifted' or 'elevated'. Similarly, when regular live music goer Peter (52) was asked if any recent gigs stood out, he explained: 'The way I make this judgment is, how did I feel immediately after that gig, and how did I feel for like a week or two after it'. These criteria recognise the afterglow of a peak music experience. The special status of live music is based to a large extent on its enhancement of music's affordances for the exploration and ordering of emotion. This experiential promise is used in the marketing of concerts and festivals in the experience economy (Pearce 2013).

An especially valued kind of experience with live music is being 'in the moment'. Descriptions of this experience resemble the state that psychologist Mihaly Csikszentmihalyi (1975) describes as 'flow' (see Chapter 2).

The many stories told by musicians about experiences of flow are exemplified in the following quote from rock guitarist and singer Alicia (34):

> I can think of a recent [gig] we played in Adelaide where it just, like we'd had a really bodgy [sic] one the night before and just everything felt like it was happening without you having to be present for it. And the crowd sort of, maybe we were giving that off, but they were just with us from the start [...] Sometimes you just get in there and you're feeling it and they just want it as well and off it goes. But the moments that are memorable, I can't even remember the gigs for it, it's just that lost, that foggy moment thing you get as a player. Where you're hyper-aware and unaware of what you're doing and why you're doing it. You almost sort of log out. Sometimes when [the other singer] and I will hit a certain harmony I just feel like I'm sort of lost in the atmosphere for a second.

This echoes Shank's (1994: 126) finding that Austin rock musicians value most the 'magical' shows where they do not have to think and experience a holistic feeling. While performers and audiences make various efforts to achieve this state using intoxicants, preparation and rituals, the arrival of flow is ultimately regarded as an unpredictable instance of music's power. For audience members, simply watching and listening to live music can induce a narrowing of attention and loss of self-consciousness, as Holly (26) described:

> I remember going on one date [...] and we went and saw this band at Black Bear Lodge. And I remember just kind of sitting on the floor and, um, yeah was just really like zoned in on the music and just absolutely loving them and I can't even remember the band's name but I remember thinking, "These guys are incredible". And then after a while just becoming aware of [my date] like looking at me and smiling at me and watching me just being like: *(mimes open-mouthed expression, laughs)* and then that just kinda turned into a really nice moment and it just, I realised how kind of, yeah, authentic I was in that moment.

Holly recalls being unaware of her own appearance and surroundings while she 'zoned in' on the music of the band she was watching, demonstrating music's capacity to enthrall and the absorbing, active nature of listening. While it is shown in other chapters that people can engage deeply with recorded music, the live setting in particular directs people's full attention towards music by way of complementary sensory input, social conventions and a lack of competing demands. It follows that the relatively single-minded setting of live music is conducive to experiences that approach the state of flow.

Holly's claim that she was 'authentic' while she was unselfconsciously absorbed demonstrates how live music is understood as a setting for the experience and expression of particular versions of one's self. By creating a space apart from everyday life, defined instead by the temporary performance of ideal social relations (Small 1998) and sensual immersion in music, the live setting enables people to explore alternative or ideal selves through uncommon physical and emotional expression. In an especially colourful example, hip hop musician Cam (40) spoke of dancing experiences in which he could see music and move at superhuman speed:

> I've had these experiences that when you're dancing inside the dance bubble, with the sound bubble, and you combine 'em – that takes a bit of time to do, you don't just get there, you've gotta work it, warm up your body and all that – but when they link up, then I feel like I can slow time down, or time distorts. Alright? And when I feel like time is distorting, like this is gonna be out there, but I've actually felt time stop, with dancing and listening. *Really* intense, I can't describe it. [...] I've actually felt myself stop time and move within metres, and it starts up again it's like "Whoa, how'd I do that!" It freaks people out, freaks myself out.

Less fantastically, performers often speak of succeeding at musical or physical manoeuvres while they are 'in the moment' that they might not otherwise attempt, including risky group improvisations and acrobatic moves. Cam also described performing experiences in which he seemed to control the movements of audience members with his singing:

> I feel like I'm building an energy. My voice can go inside a human body and make parts of their body I've actually done freaky things with my vocals. Like go, "Tiki-dee tiki-doo didi-dee didi-da", like that with a beat, and the girls were going [moves body rhythmically to that beat] and I'd go [makes vocal sounds that slow down and speed up] and their bodies would go [collapses then comes back up]. And they're looking like, "How did you do that?" And I go, "I don't know but that was rad!"

The stories told by Cam make especially bold claims about musical affect. However, other people's peak music experiences demonstrate wide support for the idea that live music can, at least, permit or encourage a loss of normal inhibitions. Jim (44) elaborated on this:

> I've done some absolutely nutso shit as an audience member. I remember being so caught up in a gig by an Adelaide band called King Daddy that when the singer, a guy called Nazz, was talking about the merch they had, how it was twenty bucks for a CD or something, I was down the front and I retrieved twenty dollars from my wallet and I stuck it down his pants. And that was the kind of showman that Nazz was too, he was completely out there and sticking twenty bucks down his pants was completely appropriate to that show, I swear. Um, what else. I remember seeing a gig by the Vegas Kings [...] there wasn't enough room

to dance down the front at Ric's but there was a speaker stack, so I got on top of the speaker stack and I was just going nuts on top of this speaker stack, dancing like crazy. I mean obviously I couldn't move too far 'cause I would've fallen off. The security guard was keeping a close eye on me but there I was. What else. Yeah, I kinda got into stage-diving a bit again recently too, when I was probably drinking a little bit too much and I realised that I don't bounce quite the way that I used to and I came up with very sore ribs, so I thought I'd better stop that.

As Jim suggests, a range of conduct is considered appropriate at a live music event that would not be attempted in other situations, due to social conventions or physical caution. In particular, live music invites the uncommon performance of emotion, such as through gazing, cheering, crying and dancing. A central theme emerging from peak music experiences with live music is that it creates a space in which people can experience and express alternative selves, such as a more powerful, confident, emotional or demonstrative self and perhaps a more authentic self, accompanied by a strong sense of belonging to a like-minded collective. This embodied exploration of different relationships to the self and others is a way in which musical experiences can be considered life-changing, and a significant reason why the live setting is idealised by music fans.

Conclusion

Peak music experiences involving live music present a number of factors as important. The variety of these factors demonstrates the multiple, multisensorial elements of musical experience, which can be identified in other settings but are most apparent in live music. As a result, the live setting invites deep and committed engagement with music and, in turn, reveals meanings, similarities and differences in music and people. This goes some way to explaining why the live context is regarded as ideal for musical experience and gives rise to the greatest number of peak music experiences. By creating a collective focus on music and co-presence, live music enables collective values to be communicated and explored through the actions of all involved. For individuals, live music permits the experience and expression of extraordinary feelings and therefore enables the exploration of alternative or ideal identities. Peak music experiences in this setting show that music fans anticipate and celebrate these affordances and valourise live music as a result. It is apparent that the cultural value of live music and its consequent economic value stem partly from its capacity to produce particularly affecting and meaningful experiences. This contributes to the understanding of live music's social value, which has been identified as an important but under-researched question for policy development (Behr et al. 2012; Frith 2012). Considering live performance as an ideal setting for music also provides insights into the power of music more generally. Live peak music experiences can be understood as 'peaks among peaks', demonstrating most clearly the reasons why people engage with music and rate it as important.

Note

1 In the 1970s and 1980s, the *Guinness Book of World Records* contained entries for the 'loudest' live performance, including rock bands Deep Purple at 117 decibels in 1972, The Who at 126 decibels in 1976 and Manowar at 129.5 decibels in 1984. While KISS and Motörhead later claimed volumes well above 130 decibels, Guinness stopped including this category in their records, supposedly in recognition of the dangers of hearing damage. Excessive volume is not unique to rock music, as electronic dance act Leftfield is said to have reached 137 decibels at London's Brixton Academy in 1996, allegedly causing audience members to faint and plaster to fall from the ceiling (Drozdowski 2014).

8 Ideal experiences

Scenes, aesthetics and belonging

Peak music experiences are intensely personal, involving subjective responses to embodied and situated encounters with music. However, music is known and valued for its capacity to generate shared experience, as the previous two chapters have demonstrated in different ways. Alicia (34), a rock 'n' roll guitarist, described some of her memorably 'amazing' moments as a performer in the following terms:

> Just that you kind of know you're lost to it and, if you can have the moment to glance up, you know that the majority of people there are too. And it sort of takes, it's not even about sound or anything at that point, everyone's sort of given themselves up to that exact moment. Those bits are not always easy to catch if you're not in that space yourself.

Besides echoing some points made about live music in the previous chapter, this quote gives voice to the idea of a musical moment as something that can be shared, though not necessarily by everyone, creating an inside and an outside. Some people might give themselves up to a particular moment, while others might not even catch it if they are not in the right subjective 'space'. In this way, peak music experiences manifest belonging, most obviously in the temporally and physically bounded collectivity of a live music audience. However, the observation that musical moments are not always 'easy' to catch, but require a certain disposition highlights the importance of what a person brings to their encounter with music. Peak music experiences are the outcome, and proof, of more enduring and internalised forms of belonging.

Peak music experiences reveal what people value most in musical experience. As this chapter will show, comparing peak music experiences across a number of people reveals clusters of shared ideals associated with particular scenes. These experiences are a way that scene participants identify with and reproduce such collective values, and therefore how their belonging manifests. It is partly through the strong feelings involved in musical experiences that participants are aware of their affinity for the defining elements of a particular scene. This chapter will show how music scenes can be

DOI: 10.4324/9781003093244-8

understood partly as shared concepts of ideal experience, which represent not only common objects but also shared ways of experiencing, which are known and reproduced through peak music experiences. Thus, peak music experiences contribute to an 'ethic of the aesthetic' (Maffesoli 1991) within music scenes, adding to the growing understanding of affective scene belonging and the operation of collective memory in music scenes. This theoretical framework will be discussed in the following section.

Music scenes, collective memory and the ethic of the aesthetic

The scholarly concept of a music scene, as discussed in Chapter 2, can be distinguished from community, place and genre, although each of these interacts with scenes. According to Straw's (1991: 373) influential definition, a scene is a 'cultural space' in which a range of musical practices may co-exist and interact, within various processes of differentiation and according to varying trajectories of change. Consistently, a substantial amount of research has identified local, trans-local and virtual dimensions to music scenes (Peterson and Bennett 2004). All three of these can be found in the preceding chapters of this book; while the fieldwork took place in Brisbane, the research participants situated their tastes and practices within trans-local contexts and many used virtual spaces for practical and symbolic aspects of their participation. Peak music experiences relate most closely to the newer concept of an affective scene, which refers to a shared sense of sceneness between individuals who are not directly visible to each other, but knowingly consume the same music and related media and, above all, make 'a similar sort of sense out of what they are hearing, reading and watching, based on their shared generational memories and cultural experience of that music' (Bennett 2013: 60). This chapter considers how peak music experiences, as shared ideals and frames for making sense of musical experience, connect this affective dimension to localised activity.

One way in which affective scene belonging has begun to be explored is through the study of collective and cultural memory. This approach, as developed in the 1920s by sociologist Maurice Halbwachs (1992), recognises that individual memories are constructed through and for group contexts, while groups maintain continuity and cohesion through the mutually supportive recollections of their members. From Halbwachs's focus on the mediation of memory through everyday communication such as conversation, the concept has expanded to include cultural memory, in which cultural objects and practices carry the meaning of collective experiences through time and have formative and normative roles in group identity (Assmann and Czaplicka 1995). Individual memories and identities are constructed using these group frameworks and individual biographies are located in relation to collective stories. According to Bennett and Rogers (2016), literature about popular music scenes has tended to avoid the predominant past-tense and memory-based nature of the relationship between scenes and participants. However, they argue that as the articulation of music scenes is often based on past events, ideas and histories, cultural memory should be a primary concern for scene studies. Based on research in Australian cities including Brisbane, they show that cultural memory, maintained largely through personal, informal archives and interactions rather than institutional settings, is a major part of scene identity and shapes current practice.

Peak music experiences further illuminate the operation of collective memory as an important aspect of scene identity and belonging. The focus here is not on collectively significant objects or events from the past, although peak music experiences could shed light on how these are meeting points for individual experience and cultural memory. The more central issue is how individual memories of musical experience, even when they are quite personal, are constructed and communicated with cultural forms. That is to say, every memory is to some extent both a means and a product of social identification. The remembrance of particular musical experiences reveals priorities, which align an individual with collective values. In turn, the stories that people tell about their peak music experiences contribute to the communicative reproduction of those collective values.

The following sections of this chapter will show that the peak music experiences of scene participants reveal shared ideals, which help to define scenes by shaping collective practice and providing common frames for interpreting and evaluating musical experience. The dance, hip hop, indie and rock 'n' roll scenes of Brisbane are defined in part by preferred ways of experiencing music, as epitomised by peak music experiences. A useful theoretical framework for this form of belonging is Maffesoli's (1991) ethic of the aesthetic, referring to a common faculty of feeling and experiencing that binds a group. This aesthetic cannot be summed up as a question of good or bad taste, nor of specific content, but the way in which the collective sense is experienced and expressed (Maffesoli 1996: 85). Accordingly, this is a way of conceptualising how music scenes that are not limited by clear musico-stylistic nor physical boundaries are held together by a shared framework for understanding and evaluating musical experience. As an 'ethic', or value system, the aesthetic imposes no obligation on members besides sharing it, and no sanction other than being excluded should the shared interest end (Maffesoli 1991: 16). This concept is a part of Maffesoli's (1996) broader theory of neo-tribal sociality, involving fluid identifications based on shared emotions instead of future-oriented, rational projects. Neo-tribal theory has been taken up in post-subcultural studies of popular music consumption, especially in relation to dance music culture (e.g. Bennett 1999a; Malbon 1999; Riley et al. 2010). However, while scenes have been identified alongside neo-tribes as key post-subcultural concepts (Bennett 2011), the specific theoretical links between the two are little explored (see Green 2018). The following sections of this chapter show through empirical analysis how peak music experiences exemplify the ethic of the aesthetic that underpins belonging in the dance, hip hop, indie and rock 'n' roll music scenes in Brisbane.

Brisbane scenes and styles

Many interview participants struggled or declined to identify with a 'scene'. Their answers suggested that contrary to academic usage, they understood that term to refer to a fixed community defined by a specific musical genre. However, the scholarly conception of scenes is appropriate for the more fluid and loosely bounded collective settings in which their musical practice took place. Some participants said that they felt like part of a community oriented around particular venues or key people, but often there was a lack of exclusive commitment to one music-based social network or, especially, one musical genre. Many expressed an omnivorous approach to genre in both their private and public musical activity, as typified in the following quotes:

> Ken, 58 (former punk musician, former radio DJ): I would say that I enjoy all music except for opera.
>
> Ivy, 29 (guitarist and singer): It was something I really struggled with when I was younger, because I never really fitted into one of the scenes. Like I always loved experimental music, so I would go to those shows, and I loved punk and hardcore music so I would go to those shows, and I would go to, you know, indie shows as well. I guess to me it's just a banner of underground music. But also, I could float in between them which is what I wanted. I don't like the idea of being stuck in the same, ah, same scene or same movement of music or whatever.

As Ivy's description of a 'banner of underground music' demonstrates, the downplaying of stylistic divisions tended in many cases to play up the idea of an overall Brisbane scene, particularly at the 'underground' level in the sense of small-scale, overtly alternative music. This is consistent with Bennett and Rogers's (2016: 113) contention that scenes are not necessarily clustered around specific genres but may be categorised under broad headings such as 'independent' or 'alternative', especially in 'peripheral cities with smaller populations, where the boundaries between the audiences for given music styles are more porous'. In comparing Brisbane to other places for musical activity, there was a widely expressed view that the local music scene is especially 'multicultural', as musician and recording engineer Barry (32) put it. This was consistently attributed to Brisbane's relatively small size and peripheral location, resulting in a limited audience and range of venues, compared to the larger cities of Melbourne and Sydney. For example, Lucy (35, singer and keyboardist) explained that she felt a connection to dance music and did not 'like guitar bands at all', but frequently shared bills with them as 'it's kind of Brisbane sometimes, you can't choose, you know'. Other participants professed to enjoy this diversity, both as producers and consumers of music. Genre and style are sometimes described as evolving elements within a broader scene, as illustrated in the following excerpt from an interview with two members of different electronic music groups:

> Jane, 26 (keyboardist and singer): I remember when we first started we would just be like, all the lineups [in Brisbane] would just be like one token electronic act, with like four rock bands. And now that's the opposite.
>
> Col, 23 (keyboardist and guitarist): Now that's the opposite yeah, it's like one rock band, so they can bring amps, and then a bunch of electronic bands. And it's – it probably won't be this way for much longer – but generally a lot more popular.

Comments like these show how a scene can be defined less by fixed tastes or practices than by a narrative in which these and other elements change over time. The Brisbane scenes under consideration are not fully defined by musicological boundaries, nor by fixed casts of participants, while most local venues do not have a sufficient lifespan to define a scene for more than a few years. Consequently, collective memory plays a major part in the continuity of these scenes, by incorporating such changes into a larger story.

An analogous observation can be made about the presentation of individual identity by interview participants. As shown in Chapters 3–5, individuals may construct a coherent identity over time from the consumption of disparate musical genres and sources. The same applies on the production side, as a number of the musicians who were interviewed described serial or simultaneous musical projects with notably varied genres. For example, Karl (30) had recently wound up his long-term work as a hip hop producer and rapper and commenced a new acoustic folk project, while Lily (25) was writing and performing in an electronic hip hop and an acoustic folk group simultaneously. Liz (26) was in two bands that she respectively labelled as synth-pop and powerviolence (a subgenre of hardcore punk). In a number of cases, musicians described their music in hyper-specific terms, with detailed reference to subgenres or even specific influences, as in the following examples:

> Sal, 27 (DJ): I guess probably I would describe it more as alt-hip hop but I also have crossovers with techno, and ghetto house, mainly ghetto tech.
>
> Allie, 27 (guitarist and singer): Well I guess both of my bands are kind of pale attempts to recreate different eras of Magic Dirt's career.[1]

These musicians did not define themselves by one genre, but by uniquely detailed approaches to a range of musical types over time. Nevertheless, they recognised musical categories as significant: for example, Karl said that for the time he was in a hip hop group, his personal listening and gig attendance skewed towards hip hop, reducing his attention to other genres; Lily said she found expression for different aspects of her personality in her folk and hip hop projects and observed different audiences for each, to the extent that some people have been surprised to learn of her involvement in the project that was less known to them; Liz also perceived audience divisions in respect of her two bands and harboured a desire for her synth-pop band to share a bill with a 'quite heavy' band, in response to which she hoped the audience would be 'a bit confused but not too confused'. Thus, although these music scene participants did not view genre as a strict limitation, they nevertheless associated it with significant collective and personal meanings that informed their practices, relationships and identities. Also, despite their misgivings, all interview participants were familiar with and more or less capable of conforming to the convention of situating their consumption and production practices in relation to established categories.

My intention when fieldwork began was to recruit interview participants associated with the dance, hip hop and indie music scenes I had observed in the local context of Brisbane. Due to both the snowballing recruitment process and the self-descriptions of participants, the additional category of rock 'n' roll was added, as described later in the chapter. The participants, their scenes and modes of participation are summarised in Appendix 1. Methods of self-identification varied between the scenes. Those who identified with hip hop or rock 'n' roll were forthcoming in using these terms to describe their tastes, practices and associations. The category of dance music was comprised of more specific and varied self-descriptions, including electronic, as well as subgenre terms referring to various forms of house, techno and beat-based music, although as discussed below there was a shared emphasis on dancing to music. Some participants used the term indie to describe themselves, although in some cases this was presented as inadequate or embarrassing albeit broadly useful; related terms like underground, alternative and experimental'were also used. The interview data showed each of these descriptive categories to refer to a variety of musical styles and production practices, making it difficult to establish purely musicological distinctions between them. However, the patterns that emerged in people's peak music experiences can be grouped meaningfully according to these four categories, as shown below.

Scenes as peak music experiences

As discussed in Chapter 3, particular narrative forms in the remembrance of musical experience identify the storyteller with a particular group, such as fans of a specific artist or genre. In the same way, the qualities and elements emphasised in people's descriptions of their peak music experiences reveal shared priorities within the respective dance, hip hop, indie and rock 'n' roll scenes in Brisbane. These will now be considered in turn.

Dance

The very name of 'dance music' highlights a particular kind of experience. Peak music experiences with this music involve substantial emphasis on the act of dancing, but more specifically, value is placed on dancing that is collective and ecstatic, revealing an ideal of self-transcendence in collective subjectivity. This demonstrates a neo-tribal sociality, consistently with studies of dance music by Bennett (1999a), Malbon (1999) and Riley et al. (2010). However, outside of such moments, they are reflected upon in more rational and projective terms. Scene members often remembered and judged dance music events by reference to dancing and atmosphere, as shown in the following, typical interview excerpt:

> Jane: I remember the first time I saw [live house music act] Holy Balm. That was amazing.
> Col: That's a great one. Tell Ben about that.
> Jane: I just, I remember it was at Black Bear [...] everyone was dancing, it was like heaps of people, it was a really good vibe.

This evaluative criterion is explicit in the following quote from dance music event promoter, John (25), who claimed to prioritise the physical engagement of the audience above the number of paying entrants when he gauged the success of an event:

> Yeah, the successful nights, I always gauge success by response of the crowd. I wasn't really in it for the money at any time. [...] Trippy Turtle saw about 60 to 70 people in. They were crammed to the front! They were up on stage, he came down off the stage and started dancing around, hands in the air, jumping around, and he told me he was like, "Mate, this was a really fun show! This was awesome!" And I was like, "Are you sure? There wasn't a lot of people." He was like, "I don't care, it was awesome, it was so much fun!" So the success that I gauged was how passionate these guys were. How, you know, sort of, how engaged the crowd was. I didn't wanna bring 200 people through the door and have 150 sitting out back in the smokers' [area], which is what happens a lot of the time, I wanna bring a hundred people through the door and put a hundred people on the dancefloor, that's all I gave a shit about.

Speaking about another event that he did not organise, John described aspects of crowd behaviour that, along with dancing, contributed to his ideal experience:

> One of the best nights I've ever had was not my night it was [a performance by music producer] Ten Walls [...] and it was one of the most inviting, incredible, euphoric, community-oriented nights I've ever been

around. People were just smiles all round. You'd bump into someone, they'd turn around and be like, "Yeah bro!" It was just really, really fun.

This quote further illuminates the type of atmosphere that is common to peak music experiences in the dance music scene, described by Jane as a 'really good vibe'. In the ideal atmosphere, individuals lose or transcend individuality by surrendering their bodies to the (dis)ordering effects of music and collective movement, joining a shared emotional state defined by positivity and fellow feeling ('good vibe', 'fun', 'inviting', 'euphoric'). Everyday boundaries are dissolved, including personal space and decorum as well as barriers between performers and audiences.

The dance music performers and DJs who were interviewed prioritised this atmosphere over other artistic concerns. Making people dance was a well-understood part of the DJ's job, guiding their selection and presentation of music. Similarly, live performers designed their 'set' to build an audience's excitement and physical participation. In their descriptions of peak music experiences, collective dancing and the attendant ecstatic atmosphere were also presented as intrinsic rewards for the performers themselves. Sal (27), a dance music DJ, described two of her favourite performances in the following terms:

> I think some party must have ended somewhere and a lot of people came, so it didn't feel like the stereotypical night at the [venue] with like a bunch of hippies all sitting around outside [...] I got up on the bar and was just like dancing, and all of my friends were there, and I was playing all of my favourite music [...] and people were just really responsive [...] it was really crowded and they all wanted to stay and they didn't want me to stop. And that was really cool. [...] And this other time, I thought it was fun playing at the [community radio station fundraiser]. I really got to be more, I guess like artistic, just choose what I thought was good music and mix things that I thought would sound good. But also there was a little bit of limitation where like I did have to think about the crowd a little bit, like, I dunno, you don't wanna be standing there playing and having no one dancing. But that to me is all a part of the skill of deejaying. You can be really self-indulgent if you want to and I totally respect that, but it feels better to have people dance.

Sal's discussion of these peak music experiences as a DJ makes it clear that while she valued opportunities to pursue her personal taste and artistic goals, this was made possible and indeed enjoyable for her by the engagement of the dancing crowd. Sal could be seen to submit to the ecstatic atmosphere through dancing on the bar, but also through the more rational process of song selection, in which her conscious and goal-oriented decisions were guided and limited by the collective subjectivity she experienced. Thus, while participants in an event might share a collective, experiential goal, their modes of participation and therefore their particular experience might differ, depending on their specific roles. The experience of a performer or organiser is further demonstrated in the following quote from Joe (32), who also described rational decision-making in service of a disindividuated, emotionally excessive sociality, for his audience as well as himself:

> There was this night that I used to run [...] when dubstep sort of became a big thing. And I just loved the explosiveness of the music and the way it made people just go wild and things like that. And I know it's terrible music, but I just loved the way it made people feel, or made people react. And those nights where I would be deejaying and I would have a whole room of people jumping up and down and, like I would randomly get people, which was completely against the rules, to come and stand on the DJ decks and dance, and I would buy like six or seven bottles of bubbly [sparkling wine] just to give to people and spray people. Like, just to [see], just how wild it would make people go and their reaction. Things like that was like, amazing. [...] Just being able to get that reaction from them to me, being able to control that many people at once, was, yeah, like, amazing. That was, yeah, that was a great feeling. And *(laughs)* at the time I was super drunk and super wasted and I'm glad a lot of that was caught on footage [...] because I don't remember any of it. But I just remember how high it would make me feel.

Joe's feeling of 'control', juxtaposed with intoxication and feeling 'high', highlights again the unique experience of a performer or organiser in relation to the idealised collective experience that guides an event.

It is apparent that the focus on creating a particular experience in the dance music scene informs attitudes towards music itself. This is apparent in Sal's explanation of song selection as a DJ, as well as Joe's self-deprecating statement that the dubstep music he played was 'terrible' but he 'loved the way it made people feel [and] react', although this was probably exaggerated for conversational purposes and also an assessment made in hindsight, after the dubstep genre had passed its peak and lost some subcultural capital. Col (23) compared post-punk, where the audience's understanding of musical and other references would be significant, to dance music, which he considered 'more accessible' as 'you can just go and have a bloody dance'. This contrasts with Malbon's (1999) finding that despite the utopian claims made about dance music scenes, cultural capital and identity policing could operate to exclude people, or at least to require a process of initiation and learning. Accordingly, caution must be exercised in using peak music experiences, which express individual and collective ideals, to describe fully the lived experience of an actually existing scene. However, as ideals, they are an important aspect of affective scene belonging. The values encapsulated in peak music experiences contribute to both inclusion and exclusion, and they may inspire individuals to persist with or against the challenges of scene initiation and the limiting aspects of ongoing participation.

Hip hop

Studies of hip hop emphasise that the term does not refer solely to music, but to a multi-dimensional cultural system also encompassing dance, visual art and postural/style elements (Tate 2003). These are often understood as the 'four elements' of hip hop, being MCing, DJing, graffiti writing and break-dancing, which originated in urban, largely African American contexts and are articulated trans-locally, including in Australia (Mitchell 2003). Consistently with this extra-musical definition, Brisbane's hip hop scene participants emphasised their musical eclecticism. Musician and record label operator Tim (22) described hip hop as 'naturally the collage art of music'. DJ and rapper Nathan (36) said that hip hop was 'the best part out of all genres. So being hip hop gives me access to all music and I'm not restricted by anything [...] so I can play dubstep or Frank Sinatra or whatever'. Rapper Daz (32) illustrated this sentiment with a simile: 'Hip hop's like pizza man, you know, you can put any different kinda topping on it. [...] Same base, different topping'. This could refer to the layering of diverse sonic elements over characteristic rhythmic patterns or 'beats', but the consistent base could also be seen as a particular set of values, which were claimed by interview participants more explicitly than in any other genre considered in this project, as well as emerging through their descriptions of peak music experiences. The core ideals that emerged in these ways were self-expression and community.

Self-expression was a prominent element of people's peak music experiences as hip hop listeners and performers, highlighting the prioritisation of personality and honesty in the hip hop aesthetic. Fans of rapping tended to remember when they were first impressed by lyrical skill or wordplay, as well as times when they were informed or persuaded by rap lyrics (such as Lily's story in Chapter 4 about quitting her job after hearing 'ReEvaluate' by GDP). Local rappers in particular tended to remember the first time they heard someone rapping in an Australian accent, which was confronting for some but ultimately understood as an authentic self-representation through the musical form. This points to the importance of authenticity in self-expression, consistently with the well-known hip hop principle of 'keeping it real' (Mitchell 2003). A strong illustration of authentic self-expression as part of a peak listening experience is hip hop producer Matt's (31) story (presented in Chapter 4) of hearing a recording of a girl in a youth detention workshop singing about love, which 'felt realer' than his previous experience of 'middle-class people rappin' about hardcore stuff', leading to a re-evaluation of his own artistic practice. From the perspective of a performer, Nathan (as quoted in Chapter 7) said that his greatest moment was rapping in front of thousands of people, who knew the words and rapped along with him. To have one's words echoed by a crowd is a powerful confirmation of being heard and validated as authentic. Accordingly, there is symmetry between the peak music experiences of performers and listeners with respect to the shared ideal of self-expression.

Rappers emphasised the personal nature of their words, explaining that it is not common to 'cover' other people's raps when beginning to perform, in contrast to rock music where this is a normal course. More often, rappers learnt and demonstrated their credentials by freestyling, a practice in which lyrics are composed spontaneously, often in a competitive setting. This process of initiation is demonstrated in the following story told by Cam (40) about the moment in his teens when he was recognised as a rapper:

> One day, I saw these guys, they were all having a little rap battle-off and I went, "This is my time, I've gotta step up". So I did, to the guy that was actually the king rapper of the town [...] and they're looking at me like, "This guy, we've heard about this guy" [...] And he just started going off, in my face, going, "You should stick to this, you should stick to that", all in flow. I'm going, "Oh God", I could feel inside of myself, "This is real. This is real." But then I went, wait a minute, this guy's dissing me, and I've loved this guy forever. He's been a hero of mine. I don't know why we've gotta battle. So when he stopped, he looked at me going, "What are you gonna say to that?" And I said to him, how about we stop fighting and just be friends, blah blah, I don't even know what I said but it was based on the idea of: I don't wanna battle you, I don't wanna take over your job, I just wanna do it, I'd rather work with you, I think you're rad. And that stumped him! He was like, alright! And then from that day he was like, "You're a rapper, you're in, you're serious. I'm gonna make sure everyone knows that."

This quote demonstrates how the skilful yet honest expression of identity and personality is at least an ideal and perhaps even a requirement of hip hop performance. Such expression is presented as fulfilling for the performer, and believable and relatable for the listener. The emphasis on self-expression is related to an interest in empathetic relations between people. Hip hop fan and rapper Daz (32) explained how he and his friends first 'listened' to hip hop as teenagers, rather than simply 'hearing' it, when they found they could relate to the storytelling of influential hip hop artists Tupac Shakur, who performed as 2Pac, and Biggie Smalls, who performed as Notorious B.I.G.:

> We listened to hip hop and we were hearing it, you know, but we weren't listening to it until Tupac and Biggie came out. That's when the five of us boys [...] would just play Tupac and sit in the loungeroom and try and analyse everything he'd say. And that's how we connected with hip hop. That's when we knew right then that we needed to tell our story. [...] I think it was Tupac and Biggie Smalls's storytelling. I think it was

their wordplay, I think it was just, you know that Biggie Smalls track 'Juicy', how it says "I'm outside trying to feed my daughter" [in reference to drug dealing], stuff like that. We could relate to that. We saw that through friends, kids who were having kids in high school, who were struggling. We saw that. Same with Tupac, you know, saying the struggle [*sic*] and saying about "living in the system" and all that stuff.

Thus for Daz, hip hop reflected his experience of 'the struggle of Inala', a suburb in Brisbane's south-west. This shows how the ideal of self-expression is closely related to community identification and representation, which is the other common ideal that emerged in peak music experiences with hip hop.

Daz, an Aboriginal man, said that in his hip hop group, 'nothing beats performing in front of our people on a NAIDOC [National Aboriginal and Islander Day Observance Committee] family day at Musgrave [Park]', a place of significance to Aboriginal people in Brisbane. This highlights the sense of a community affirming itself through musical events. Equally, hip hop performers claimed to take pleasure in representing their communities to others. Cam, an Aboriginal singer and rapper, described a performance by his band at a local festival that celebrated various Pacific cultures. This was especially meaningful for him as an experience of cultural representation and exchange, as described in the following quote:

Three songs in particular, one was 'Point the Bone' which is basically cursing all these people that are thinking selfishly and monetary-wise, they're destroying the world so I point the bone at them. Another song called 'Reggae Bounce', which is based on when I went to New Zealand and feeling a different vibration. So it was like, "This is a song I wrote about being over in *your* world, so thank you for that, here's what I've got". And then another one was like this signature song, which is 'Shake A Leg', based on, "This is what our culture is about", in a modern context, yeah? So doing that, in that performance, and I made sure I spoke to the people and I basically said look, I don't care what my country says or my politicians say about this, but *I* welcome *you* here. You guys are welcome here because I understand, and sing about it, we know that the islands are flooding. So yeah, that's where I believe that music has a stronger word than politics.

Outside of the performer's perspective, the sense of community feeling and collective pride idealised in hip hop experiences is well illustrated in Daz's memory of a local concert by US hip hop group, Bone Thugs-N-Harmony. Daz met the group members before their sold-out concert and presented them with hats emblazoned with the postcode of Inala, 4077:

I got there, I gave 'em the hats, they wore the hats onstage. Representing my 'hood, Inala. So they wore 4077 hats and they were onstage. Just being backstage and watching people from my community in the crowd, seeing their reactions, like, "How the heck did they get them hats?" It was just game, set and match for me. This is what we live for, moments like these.

To represent one's place in the community through words and other symbols, such as the hats in this story, is to 'signify', an important practice in hip hop (Mitchell 2003). In peak music experiences associated with the Brisbane hip hop music scene, the closely related ideals of self-expression and community representation can be discerned. While this is consistent with existing studies of hip hop music culture, a focus on peak music experiences highlights how these ideals are embodied and understood through strongly felt and memorable experiences that inspire initial connections, influence modes of scene participation and motivate ongoing practices.

Indie

Just as the term 'dance music' emphasises a particular activity as a defining aspect of musical genre, the category of 'indie' refers most clearly to a value system. The ideological aspects of indie have been the focus of scholarly commentary, noting that it is 'positioned at the intersection of various aesthetic, social and commercial phenomena' (Hibbett 2005) and encompasses a 'mixed bag of practical, historical and aesthetic ideologies' (Rogers 2008). As the name derived from 'independent' suggests, indie is defined by way of opposition to the economic and aesthetic values of a perceived mainstream, which makes it a stylistically evolving genre. As with punk, the term has nevertheless become associated with specific sonic elements of its original manifestations in the 1980s, such as 'jangly' guitars and overtly basic production values (Bennett 2001; Bannister 2006). However, especially in this century, indie has been defined partly by eclecticism, embracing exotic, often non-Western musics and even commercial pop with 'varying degrees of irony and revision' (Rogers 2008). Accordingly, Hibbett (2005) focuses on indie rock as a field of knowledge which distinguishes itself from mass culture in a similar way to the Bourdieusian formulation of high art. Based on a review of popular music literature, Hibbett concludes that indie 'opens up vast space for the management of power and the manufacturing of identities: purposes far removed from the innocuous pleasures of listening' (ibid.: 57). However, ethnographic studies have concluded this is not the whole story, finding aestheticism and emotion to be central to indie music. Fonarow's (2006: 30, 196) United Kingdom-based study argues that like the Romantic movement, indie 'valorises emotion as the wellspring of meaning', and like Puritanism its obsessive opposition stems from a central focus on 'how an audience can have the purest possible experience of music'. The Brisbane indie music scene is described by Rogers (2008: 645) as 'a small, informal but close-knit network of people motivated first and foremost by the desire for intensified leisure'. Based on research among hobbyist musicians, Rogers finds that the drive for distinction is only an aspect of their more fundamental quest for feelings of meaning and belonging, involving 'pleasurable engagements with music as a creative canon [...] and as a social binding agent' (ibid.: 646). Consistently with this literature, the analysis of peak music experiences among Brisbane indie scene participants reveals common ideals of difference, exploration and intimacy. Further, and significantly in the context of the above debate, this perspective shows these values to be inseparable from the embodied pleasures of engaging with music.

The valourisation of difference, usually in comparison to a perceived mainstream, is most clearly apparent in those peak music experiences involved in the personal histories discussed in Chapters 3 and 4. As shown there, interview participants who identified themselves with indie (albeit often through alternative terms) tended to present narratives in which their taste progressed away from the mainstream and towards increasingly obscure music and artists. These narratives were anchored by peak music experiences that illuminated new directions, which I have called 'gateway experiences'. These experiences highlight the idealisation of difference itself, as demonstrated in the following quote from indie fan and musician Pete (33) about watching Sonic Youth perform at the Livid Festival in 1998:

> [There were] a lot of people there but it was an interesting kind of experience because, you know a third of them were just having their minds blown and I was in that third but another, you know, another third were wishing that they'd play something from *Goo* [1990, Sonic Youth's first major-label album and a commercial high-point], and then another third were just there for a look and were just going, 'What the fuck is going on?', because it was this sort of, amazing, like my feeling from that was just going, 'I have no idea what they're doing'. Like it was just like, just, it was, I'm sure the acid[2] was helping but it just seemed like they were kind of from a place that none of the other bands at that festival were from [...] I think that at a certain point, that difference was what I came to really value as a criteri[on] in music.

This quote illustrates the academic understanding of indie as an oppositional or at least separatist culture, distinguishing itself and participants from mainstream artists, music and audiences. However, this quote also exemplifies the presentation of this affinity for difference as strongly felt, rather than rationally calculated. Pete claimed that he found the Sonic Youth performance amazing because it was bewildering, thus foregoing the opportunity to present his response as evidence of superior taste and knowledge, whether innate or learned. His visceral, non-rational experience of difference continued when the community radio station 4ZZZfm, heard in the cab home, played more of Sonic Youth's music:

> 'Anagrama'? Yeah, those kind of, SYR [record label on which the band self-released a series of experimental works] kind of um, yeah lengthy

noise improvisations, and I was just, still sort of buzzing along [under the influence of LSD], and I got out of the cab and sat in my car, for like an hour, just having this really intimate kind of experience of noise, really, for the first time. Yeah I think that evening was really pivotal in a lot of ways to the way that I, what I became hungry for, and what I enjoyed, and, you know I think that came into – I guess it was like moving away from form and, you know, pop writing and song structure, and getting more into texture.

In this story, Pete presents his interest in non-traditional, non-mainstream music as very much motivated by the pleasures of listening that some regard as innocuously distant from power and identity management (Hibbett 2005: 57). Pete cites this peak music experience as not an outcome but a cause of his taste, which is a common claim among interview participants. In this narrative, people become aware of their taste for musical difference through the strong feelings produced by musical experiences.

The prioritisation of difference is related to the emphasis within indie music culture on exploration and novelty, as people seek to stay ahead of both mainstream tastes and their own previous experience. The peak music experience stories of interview participants show that for them, the search for new music is in part a search for transcendent experience. Sally (30), for example, described a youthful and continuing desire to 'explore music and [...] get to the outer limits of what was out there'. When asked what she liked about hearing something new and different, she replied, 'It's kind of exciting, you know, it's adrenaline or something', drawing attention once again to embodied pleasure. This is illustrated in a peak music experience described by Sally, involving a malfunctioning playback of an already outré piece of music, in a youthful context of friends and recreational drugs:

> I remember one time we were in Byron Bay, it was in 2002, and we went down to Splendour in the Grass [music festival] and um, we were taking ecstasy[3] as well as um, as marijuana *(laughs)* and um, we were hanging in the hotel room and we'd just smoked like, a lot, and we were actually listening to *Bitches Brew* by Miles Davis *(laughs)* funnily enough. And then after about an hour, or maybe more, we realised *(laughs)* the CD had been skipping and it was playing the same one minute, like *(laughs)* it had been, like we were just like... I dunno, you know, we just kinda thought it was an amazing one minute of music!

Through stories like this, participants in the indie music scene display an immediate appreciation for music that some would find difficult. As Hibbett (2005) notes, comfort with high art concepts can be a marker of cultural capital. Importantly, however, the appreciation the participants evince is not rational but associated with direct and embodied pleasure, which is contrary to typical high art discourse. The stories emphasise feelings of surprise, bewilderment, awe and enthusiasm, which are more consistent with Fonarow's (2006) comparison of indie with Romanticism. It is possible that to (claim to) take physical and emotional pleasure in non-mainstream music is itself a method of distinction, as it might show an innate or successfully learnt embodiment of uncommon, good taste. However, this is no reason to assume that the interview participants have fabricated their passionate claims to enjoy such music deeply and to have arranged their lives around that enjoyment. The fundamental point is that both distinction and enjoyment are discursively shaped practices, reflecting the shared aesthetic of a scene. This does not diminish either their experiential reality or social significance, but helps to explain both.

As to collective musical settings, peak music experiences in the indie scene reveal a common preference for live and intimate performances. Once again, the participants tended to present a narrative of personal development, in which early and inspirational experiences in the relative anonymity of music festivals led eventually to current scene experiences in more intimate contexts. As discussed in Chapter 7, the desired intimacy is as much between audience members as between the audience and performers, as explained by Nick (27):

> You could go with one friend to the Hi Fi [a large, purpose-built, licensed venue] and just watch the show and not talk to anyone, or you could go to something at the Waiting Room [a small, unlicensed, venue in a house] and know a whole lot of people and talk to them.

Rogers (2008: 644) notes that this is partly a necessity of music-making within the indie scene, as 'face-to-face informal networking gatekeeps and governs the indie live circuit', or as one of his interviewees says, 'You've got to go to gigs to get gigs'. This intimate community is also an end in itself, as Nick for example claims to enjoy 'meeting the people, going to the gigs and, you know, swappin' stories, swappin' songs'. The intimacy valued in the indie scene also appears as a space in which to experience and express uncommon and personal emotions through musical experience. This is exemplified in Holly's description of a peak music experience involving her attendance at a 'house show' (see Chapter 7), in which she perceived a 'shared vulnerability' in the musical performance and the audience response. This is consistent with Fonarow's (2006: 364) finding that 'an emotional feeling of community and connectedness' between musicians and audiences is central to indie music. This emotional intimacy was an element of peak music experiences for indie performers as well, as Trish (37) explained by reference to a gig that was a turning point for her:

> Any house show I've done has just been very essential I think. Just being involved as an audience member and performer. I remember for my album launch a couple of years ago I played at the Toff in Town, which is

great, it's a bigger venue for me in another city [Melbourne], and it was fine, but then a few months later I went down and played in a tiny book-shop, and they just cleared it out, and again it's about 60 people, and it was just a totally different thing for me, in a positive way. And after that I just thought, "Ah, I don't think I'll play in venues any more! I'm just gonna do these house gigs and shopfront gigs everywhere and just spread the word on the street rather than using PR and just sidestep the machine that is". [...] I think the smaller shows are really, um, perfect on an energy exchange level.

Here, Trish links the indie imperative to 'sidestep the machine' to a desire for a more perfect 'energy exchange', bearing out Fonarow's (2006) compar-ison between indie and religious Puritanism in their search for more direct and meaningful experience, through the removal of unnecessary media-tions. This aesthetic can be seen in relation to gentle, folk-inflected forms of indie performed by Trish, as well as more sonically and physically active forms also associated with this scene.

Analysis of peak music experiences in Brisbane's indie music scene con-firms that, as reported elsewhere, scene participants value difference, explo-ration, live music and intimate community. However, these values are not solely markers of distinction and exclusivity, removed from the pleasures of listening. Instead, this perspective shows that the values and practices that define the Brisbane indie music scene are inseparable from the embodied pleasures of musical practice. Scene members become aware of their affinity for scene values like difference, exploration and intimacy, and thus their af-fective belonging to the scene, through the strong feelings produced by peak music experiences.

Rock 'n' roll

The term rock 'n' roll is typically used in popular music literature to refer to a broad musical style developed from the late 1940s to the early 1960s, typ-ified in its dominant guitar-centred form by Chuck Berry (see for example Bradley 1992). However, the term was used specifically and emphatically by participants in this research to refer to a current, trans-local scene and its local manifestations in Brisbane. This forthright self-description was itself a point of difference from the other scenes, and is probably related to the relative clarity of its stylistic dimensions. Guitarist and singer Tracy (39) referred to 'that sort of debaucherous rock 'n' roll sound, not a care; influ-enced by, you know, the Stooges, the New York CBGBs sound [referring to an iconic venue], Sixties garage [rock], that kinda thing'. When describing her own rock 'n' roll band, she included reference to specific musical ele-ments, the 'blues formula' and 'simple riffs'. The rock 'n' roll scene in Bris-bane was observed to coexist most closely with the punk scene, in terms of venues, events and social groups, and this was also noted by some interview participants. The peak music experiences that people described with respect to this form of rock 'n' roll revealed shared ideals of forthrightness, self-acceptance and communal, physical abandon.

Forthrightness refers here to both honesty and boldness, which emerged from interviews as ideals for both the form and content of rock 'n' roll music. This quality is exemplified in the following peak music experience:

> Alicia (34): The Dead Moon gig at the Gabba [Hotel], a million years ago, was - I didn't even know the band at the time, they're now one of my favourite bands. But they just absolutely mesmerised me. And I haven't really had that before, I didn't know a band and they just, you couldn't move, you sort of feel paralysed. That was special.
>
> Interviewer: What was it about that, do you think?
>
> Alicia: I'd just never seen anything like it. It was just so unashamed and forthright and they don't care how they play, their songs are classics. Dunno, I really couldn't even tell you. You must be hearing that a lot, "I couldn't even tell ya!"

Alicia elaborated on these qualities when considering how her taste in music may have influenced her personal values:

> I can't say how but I definitely came to find in sort of punk and rock 'n' roll some kind of honesty. Like for all the bullshit and bravado some of it will have, that raw, "I'm gonna tell you exactly what's going on", sorta thing. I don't know, I guess just the liberty to express whatever. That's as close as I can come to pinning that down.

As shown in this quote, bravado in rock 'n' roll is coupled with rawness, involving the honest and even vulnerable acceptance of the self, often through hardship. In this regard, the subject matter, performance tropes and musical limitations of rock 'n' roll are complementary. The open expression of vulnerability and struggle was a defining feature of Jim's (44) peak music experience when he saw a favourite local rock 'n' roll band, HITS, for the first time:

> [The singer] was onstage, dressed to the nines in this beautiful burgundy suit that of course is long since trashed and he's probably never been able to wear since. [...] And they had two women in the band, that was really important. The women were playing guitar, both of them, they weren't playing bass, they weren't playing supportive roles, they were actually the ones that were kinda blasting off on either side of the stage. And then you had a male singer [...] who was projecting all of his insecurities and all of his demons from the stage, being backed by a male rhythm section. The men were playing the supportive roles and expressing all of their vulnerability while the women were just kind of –

Elly [another interview participant]: Firing off. *(Laughs)*
J: Just firing off each other.

In this exemplary rock 'n' roll experience, the singer's performance and lyrics represent the honest expression of vulnerability while the 'blasting', 'firing' guitars represent boldness, adding a celebratory edge to the themes of complaint and acceptance. The same combination of qualities can be seen in Allie's statement, as quoted in Chapter 5, that it is 'life affirming' to see a band that is 'just as messed up and fucked up as I am [...] doin' fuckin' great'. The ideal of persistence through hardship is illustrated quite practically in the following memory of rock 'n' roll musician, Rick (49), concerning a gig he attended:

> When I was a teenager and the QUT campus club used to be Wednesday nights, the Celibate Rifles were playing there, they had a fucking car accident on the way up here. There were two cars, one of the cars went off the road, two of the guys were in hospital in a really bad way. So the Celibate Rifles played as a three-piece and they charged three-fifths of the door price to get in. And that stuck in my head as being one of the coolest things that I've ever seen in my life. It was like, fuck, the show must go on.

This story illustrates the tendency to conceive of rock 'n' roll performance as heroic, in terms of its direct self-expression, radical self-acceptance and dogged endurance or even defiant celebration of personal struggle. As Jim's aside about the HITS singer's trashed suit suggests, the suffering that rock 'n' roll performers express and with which listeners empathise is to some extent self-inflicted, and this is also perceived in heroic terms.

Peak music experiences in the live setting reveal a rock 'n' roll ideal of collective, physical exuberance. As in dance music, this is an ecstatic experience of the loss or transcendence of self within a crowd of disindividuated bodies and shared emotions. This is illustrated in the following quote from Tracy (39), as she progressed from describing a specific, memorable performance by her band, to a broader statement about 'amazing gigs':

> Yeah that [gig] was incredible. Just an incredible - most of the amazing gigs we've had have been the smaller shows that are jam-packed, sweaty, rowdy, debaucherous, we're on the floor, we're not on a stage, and the crowd is right in our faces. That's where we thrive. And yeah, those kind of gigs are just really memorable, just because of that interaction between the crowd and us. It's like, it goes back to that feeling I had at my first Livid Festival when I went, oh my god everyone's in this together, like we're one, we're one community. Whenever we play on really big stages and up high, there's always that kind of disconnection a bit. It's becoming better because when we are playing bigger shows

now, we've got more of a following so there is more of that interaction. But the dirty, just party gigs where there's beer flying everywhere and everyone's just in the moment and there's not a care in the world about what's happening outside. It's just that moment.

Alicia described her 'amazing live moments' in similar terms:

> [Some were] just fucking chaos and that got a bit addictive. [...] I just think that boundary between the band and the crowd gets lost. It's very physical as much as it's anything else. Yeah I think it's just that freedom of it all. [...] People don't seem to care if they're being observed anymore, I think. I just have this sort of picture of limbs everywhere and lots of bad singing and lots of smiling and people start huggin' strangers. Yeah that sort of thing!

These quotes illustrate that ideal experiences in rock 'n' roll involve the transcendence of self in a shared subjectivity or 'moment', in which bodies interact freely ('limbs everywhere') and boundaries between audience members and performers are also lost. In these respects, the ideal is similar to that of dance music. However, in contrast with the more positive and escapist emotions of dance music, interview participants tended to describe rock 'n' roll experiences with reference to looseness, messiness and dirtiness. Tracy acknowledged this in the following terms:

> It puts the grit in life, you know. Things that are too sterile or polished don't appeal to me. I wanna hear the humanness in things and I think that's why I love, you know, going to gigs that have that sort of connection and that looseness about it. 'Cause it celebrates imperfection.

Participants also frequently used metaphors of drug use, such as 'shooting up' (i.e. intravenous drugs such as heroin), as well as literal references to alcohol (such as the 'beer flying everywhere' quote above) and other intoxicants. Descriptions of alcohol and drug consumption at gigs were often self-deprecating and celebratory at the same time, reflecting again the simultaneous lamentation of personal shortcomings and celebration of personal endurance. This further illustrates how the various elements of musical experience, including but not limited to the music itself, can be understood as complementary in reinforcing particular ideals.

Conclusion

Within Brisbane's local music scene, there are articulations of trans-local, genre-based scenes, including dance, hip hop, indie and rock 'n' roll. Scene is an appropriate theoretical frame for these loosely bounded, overlapping cultural spaces, within which a range of musical practices coexist and interact (Straw 1991) in local, trans-local and virtual dimensions (Peterson and Bennett 2004). Consistently with Bennett and Rogers's (2016) observations about peripheral cities, musical practice in Brisbane is not neatly divided along stylistic lines and there are porous boundaries between the audiences, physical spaces and performers for given music styles. However, the genres listed above provide a functional basis for affective scenes bound by an ethic of the aesthetic, centred on particular ideals of musical experience. These ideals are revealed in the analysis and comparison of scene participants' peak music experiences.

The findings in this chapter are based on a total of 44 in-depth interviews across the four categories (see Appendix 1), resulting in a quantitatively limited sample of each scene. Nevertheless, this was sufficient to identify shared ideals and ideal experiences within each music scene, demonstrating the potential of peak music experiences as an approach to scene studies. The findings are consistent with ethnographic research literature concerning the defining values of these music cultures. However, the lens of peak music experiences provides a new perspective on how these values are understood, articulated and reproduced by music scene participants. In particular, this provides a new way of understanding affective scene belonging and contributes to the developing understanding of collective memory as a central force in music scenes. The scenes are held together by an ethic of the aesthetic (Maffesoli 1991) which, beyond notions of good taste and specific objects of appreciation, involves preferred kinds of musical experience as well as shared ways of remembering and describing such experience. A particular combination of experiential priorities can be seen to distinguish each scene, and these are exemplified in peak music experiences. The peak music experiences of participants in all four scenes celebrate live and collective settings for music, building on the observations made about popular music more generally in Chapter 7. However, the character of the collective subjectivity produced in such settings, and the means by which individuals may participate in it, differs between the scenes as revealed by their respective peak music experiences.

In both dance music and rock 'n' roll, the loss or transcendence of self is achieved and expressed through energetic, physical participation in collective activity. By contrast, the indie collectivity is joined and experienced by way of emotional intimacy and immersion in musical texture, while in hip hop the individual serves and represents the community through overt identification with recognised symbols including words, movements and musical elements. Meanwhile, the equally physical ecstasies of dance and rock 'n' roll are distinguished by their separate emotional focus, which in dance is a euphoric escape from everyday reality while rock 'n' roll values a heroic recasting of the everyday. While the latter value is shared in broad terms by hip hop, the difference is that the honest, grounded self-expression of rock 'n' roll is self-deprecating and even destructive, while in hip hop it is self-promoting and improving. These various experiential concerns can be correlated with musical priorities: both dance and indie emphasise sensory immersion, although in dance music this serves the imperative to dance while in indie it serves more internal, emotional activity; rock 'n' roll's directness and self-acceptance align with basic instrumentation, formal economy and performative 'looseness', while its forthrightness and decadent hedonism are expressed in volume and distortion; hip hop's collage method (captured in the pizza analogy) permits individual self-expression on a communal base, as well as privileging storytelling through rapping. The experiential ideals of the scenes are also reflected in their physical settings, or hard infrastructure; for example, while rock 'n' roll prioritises an 'honest' rawness in its musical style, indie prioritises the same value in its settings and logistics, which tend towards spartan in service of the desired emotional intimacy. By way of contrast, the ideal venue for dance music serves the scene's euphoric, escapist ends through unworldly lighting and decor.

Accordingly, peak music experiences in these scenes reveal a somewhat homological synchronisation of elements, including musical style, thematic content, physical activity, preferred settings and substance use. However, unlike the concept of homology developed and applied in the context of subcultural theory (Willis 1978; Hebdige 1979; see Chapter 2), these clustered preferences need not be attributed to structural causes, although these may be considered later. Instead, they are elements of a shared aesthetic that resonates in the idealisation of particular kinds of experience. Thus, peak music experiences offer a teleological perspective on music scenes, by epitomising the ends around which various production and consumption activities are oriented. Beyond specific combinations of desired sensations and pleasures, although these are important, peak music experiences represent shared values, conceptions of self and others, and ways of being in the world.

Notes

1 Magic Dirt is the name of an alternative rock band formed in Geelong, Victoria in the 1990s. Over two decades, the band progressed from a 'fuzz'-heavy sound and unconventional song structures to more concise pop-rock songs across a total of eight albums, so that different 'eras' could be identified within their career.
2 A slang term for lysergic acid diethylamide (LSD), a hallucinogenic drug that Pete had taken.
3 Ecstasy refers to MDMA, a psychoactive drug.

9 Themes and conclusions

Peak music experiences and new perspectives

This book has presented a sustained sociological investigation and theorisation of peak music experiences. This has partly been a matter of recognising and critically analysing a significant set of popular narratives and practices. It has been shown that peak music experiences are an important aspect of how many people relate to popular music, as well as a major ingredient in the production of identity and belonging. They are relevant and useful to a range of scholarly perspectives and projects concerning popular music, both as a subject of research in their own right and as a new conceptual tool in sociological study. In this chapter, I will discuss and develop key themes that have been developed over the course of this book. First, I will return to the questions I asked at the outset and consider how peak music experiences offer insights regarding the specific appeal of music and its unique power in relation to individuals and society. I will then draw from the various findings to discuss how peak music experiences play a role in both affective sociality and reflexive individualisation, demonstrating the co-existence and interaction of these ostensibly opposed models of late- or post-modern social being. Third, I will consider how peak music experiences demonstrate the operation of collective memory and sensibility in structuring both narrative and affective aspects of identity and practice, especially in the context of music scenes. I will then outline some implications of this concept for future research. Specifically, I will offer suggestions regarding the extension of the peak music experience concept from music scene research into broader cultural settings; the use of peak music experiences as a lens for considering how structural factors shape people's engagements with music and the implications of the peak music experience perspective for questions of music's value, particularly with respect to cultural policy and technological change.

Music: why, what and how?

At the outset of this book, I asked why people listen to, perform and otherwise interact with music, and further why they place such importance on those activities and invest so much of their time, energy and various resources into music. I suggested that in answering these questions, we might

DOI: 10.4324/9781003093244-9

first ask what music can do and how it does so. The ensuing chapters have shown that a reason why people engage with music and value it so highly is their understanding that it can and has contributed to their life through peak music experiences. In fact, it is common for people to engage reflexively with those fundamental questions and answer them with reference to peak music experiences. For those who devote themselves to musical activity through participation in music scenes, these experiences are an important element of understanding what music does, how it acts and why it is valued.

The important roles that peak music experiences play in identity were considered in Chapters 3–5. People interpret and value music, generally and in terms of specific songs, artists and styles, by way of an ongoing relationship with it, described in Chapter 3 as a history of listening. Peak music experiences anchor and frame these histories of listening. The common narrative forms of first encounters, gateway experiences and conversion experiences present these histories as uniquely personal while situating them in relation to group contexts. These forms highlight the specific appeal of certain music and the cultural values underlying such preferences, but also reproduce more fundamental ideals of music and listening that are shared across popular music genres. In particular, by privileging reactions to music that are surprising, emotional and physical, these narratives promote the notion of music acting directly on listeners who have unmediated responses to it and natural affinities for it. These ideals also permeate the autobiographical narratives discussed in Chapters 4 and 5. There it was shown that participants in Brisbane's local music scenes credit peak music experiences with inspiring and influencing who they are and what they do, musically and otherwise. As embodied experiences and remembered ideals, peak music experiences offer both a reason and a guide for current practice, making them a key source of motivation for specific kinds of ongoing musical activity and scene participation. People invest in music scene activities partly because they remember peak music experiences that revealed and affirmed the subjective value of those activities, and they seek to create similar experiences. In such experiences, they find an intrinsic reward for action and an affirmation of identity, reminding them viscerally of what they hold important and why. Peak music experiences therefore provide substantial answers to the questions of what music can do and, in turn, why people engage with it.

Focusing on singularly memorable and meaningful moments shows the dynamism of both music and the people who interact with it. Instead of musical texts with fixed meanings and people with set dispositions, in singular experiences we can see how both are 'simultaneously recompose[d] … in situ', as Hennion (2001: 3) puts it, over a history of encounters. Hennion (2001: 5) suggests that people now tend to 'sociologise' their music taste by readily citing determinants like class. However, we have seen that peak music experiences are discussed in ways that downplay predictable social and cultural factors, emphasising instead the unpredictable, transcendent power of music and the authentic individuality of the responses it evokes.

Accordingly, like Hennion's strategies for 'desociologising' his interviewees (ibid.), the study of peak music experiences draws the focus of research from assumed determinisms and tastes to dynamic practices and states, in order to see what people do with music and what it does for them. Nevertheless, by recognising peak music experiences as a discursive frame, it is possible to re-sociologise those details – that is, to show how highly personalised musical practices and states, and the ways people talk about them, are situated in socio-cultural contexts. Taking seriously the lived experiences of music lovers means not only paying attention to those experiences, but critically analysing their construction. I will return to this point later in this chapter with reference to collective memory.

Considering music in terms of the experiences it produces highlights the extent to which perceptions of its form, meaning and value are bound up with feelings, in the emotional and physical sense. Indeed, the descriptions of peak music experiences by participants in this study tended to emphasise their affective aspects, with especially strong feelings often appearing as a defining feature. These feelings are essential to the interpretations, judgements and dispositions that people develop through peak music experiences. Repeatedly, participants explained the meaning and value of particular music, and more reflexively their own orientations towards it, by reference to the embodied experiences in which they encountered it. This demonstrates the intentionality (directedness) of emotions and indeed their importance as a means of intending and interpreting the world, as observed in the pragmatic philosophy of Dewey (2004b) and the emotional sociology of Crossley (1998) and Ahmed (2014) outlined in Chapter 2. Consistently with Ahmed's (2014) cultural politics of emotion, people's feelings about musical objects such as songs, artists and styles depend on how they have been affected by those objects. Peak music experiences are, in part, affective encounters that produce especially intense and therefore lasting impressions, which as Ahmed suggests are an apt term for bodily sensations, emotions and evaluative thoughts that are experientially inseparable. These encounters shape the subjective perception and affordances of specific objects, but also (or more accurately) reorient subjects, with consequences that can extend beyond musical practice. In these respects, peak music experiences can be taken as exemplars of the more continuous and subtle processes of affective interaction and world-making in which music is involved.

The theories of emotion cited above refer broadly to interactions between people and their worlds, although they have been applied here to interactions with music. Similarly, Hennion's (2010) pragmatics of taste is conceived in such a way that it also applies to food and sport, for example. As well as applying such general theories to music, I have also sought to gain insight into music's specific power and appeal. In this regard, the analysis of peak music experiences shows that the affective appeal and temporality of music are key to how it acts. The peak music experiences described in this book tend to exceed and sometimes even contradict what might be found by an objective analysis of the musical texts involved, especially in the case of song lyrics, yet it is also clear that *that* music was crucial to the character and consequences of those experiences. The concept of affordances (DeNora 2000) is useful in understanding how music offers possibilities that are generated as well as limited by inherent, personal and social factors. Peak music experiences further underline the highly contextual nature of these affordances and their ultimate manifestation in particular meanings and effects. Considering music in terms of experiences, as opposed to separate texts or objects, reveals the extent and importance of its non-verbal and indeed non-signifying elements. While these aspects were identified in people's descriptions of their peak music experiences, they were also made apparent by a struggle to describe those experiences in words, with frequent resort to exclamations ('whoa'), superlatives ('amazing') and metonymic descriptions of physical reactions ('goosebumps'). This is not to suggest that those experiences escape discoverable structures or meanings. There is a notable difference between the precise ideas people hold about their peak music experiences, on which they purposefully reflect and by which they measure new experiences and organise parts of their lives, and their limited ability to recount and explain those experiences in words. This points to music's capacity to organise and encapsulate aspects of experience in ways that cannot necessarily be translated. Consistently with both Frith (1987) and DeNora (2000), I have linked this to music's direct emotional intensity as well as its relatively open referentiality. As DeNora (2000) argues, music is a temporal medium which structures experience as it unfurls, contributing to the shape and quality of feeling and thus bringing it to the intersubjective plane on which it can be sustained and made known to oneself and others. In this sense, music can provide the emotionally infused, aesthetic unity that according to Dewey (2004b) defines 'an experience', and more specifically what I have called a peak music experience.

Music's capacity to structure feelings in time and then represent them in memory is shown most clearly in Chapters 6 and 7, in analysing the interpersonal and collective ramifications of peak music experiences. Chapter 6 considered how music can colour experiences of particular events and situations, including at an intersubjective level. It has been recognised that music articulates and thereby shapes emotional experience and interpersonal relationships by what it signifies, especially through lyrics (Horton 1957; Frith 1989). Beyond such signification, the analysis presented in Chapter 6 demonstrates that music can create an affective space in which people may experience, express and share particular feelings. This depends on its inherent affordances, such as the tempo and aesthetic features that can structure time and activity, as well as personally and socially ascribed affordances, such as the understanding of what is possible and expected when listening to particular music in particular settings. Examples include a slow rhythm and a pretty melody for dancing, a stirring seasonal hit at Christmas and a shared favourite song on the radio at home. The music lovers who were interviewed described how sharing experiences of music with family, friends and loved ones enabled them to acknowledge, explore, articulate and celebrate aspects of those relationships, in turn creating peak music experiences by which those people and relationships were understood and remembered. There is a reflexive element to these uses of music, so that for example people might plan their attendance at a concert, or give tickets as a gift, with a view to sharing a meaningful experience and thus celebrating or developing aspects of their relationship.

The creation of a shared affective space through music was explored on a larger scale in Chapter 7, as a defining aspect of live music and a reason for its valourisation. This was the setting for the majority of peak music experiences described by research participants. As ideal instances of live music, these experiences reveal the most important factors in the live setting, and the different priorities by which those factors might be evaluated across music scenes (also discussed in Chapter 8 and later in this chapter). Most importantly, these various factors create the conditions for extraordinary experiences and expressions of the self, with an emphasis on affective belonging to both a physical crowd and often a broader, implied collective such as a music scene. The special status of live music across popular music cultures is attributable in large part to its capacity to produce such peak music experiences. These can be seen as peaks among peaks, as they are ideals of live music which is in turn an idealised setting for popular music. Accordingly, they epitomise the importance of peak music experiences in popular music culture and exemplify a central thesis of this book. That is, a major reason why people value music and a factor that guides their engagements with it is that music has a unique capacity to create especially affecting and meaningful experiences that affirm or renew our understandings of ourselves, our relationships to other people and various aspects of the world.

Affective sociality and reflexive individualisation

We have seen that peak music experiences are involved in both disindividuating, affective sociality and reflexive, rational individualism. These are ostensibly opposed meta-narratives of contemporary social life, as outlined in Maffesoli's (1996) theory of neo-tribal post-modernity on one hand and the late modernity theorised by Giddens (1991) and Beck (1992) on the other. The former theory describes a movement away from a society of individuals rationally contracting around political, future-oriented projects, into a disindividuated sociality comprising fluid, affectively driven identifications that find their end in the feeling of being together. The reflexive modernisation thesis associated with Giddens (1991) and Beck (1992) also starts with the decline of stable identity and political engagement, but theorises that this engenders a heightened individualism marked by reflexive choice. This study of peak music experiences shows how both affectively disindividuating and rationally individualising tendencies co-exist and interact in the sensibilities of music scene participants. This contributes to a small body of research that explores both of these social developments in the context of popular music consumption, with ramifications for the broader understanding of culture and society (Malbon 1999; Bennett 2009; Riley et al. 2010; Green 2018).

As noted earlier in this chapter, the most prominent and common feature of peak music experiences is an intensity of feeling, which is often privileged over rational judgement when people describe them. Physical and emotional responses are said to exceed prior expectations and precede reflective understanding. Similarly, chance and fate are emphasised over deliberate planning in the creation of these encounters. It is common to grant agency to music over listeners, such as when people claim that music 'hit me' or 'changed my life'. These aspects of peak music experiences, as discussed at length in Chapter 4 in particular, downplay the individual choice that is a hallmark of reflexive modernity and instead highlight the non-conscious attraction and repulsion of affect that characterises neo-tribalism, which Maffesoli (1996: 90, 147) describes as 'animalistic' and 'stochastic'. Another celebrated aspect of many peak music experiences is the ecstatic loss or transcendence of the individual self, in the sensory effects of music, in flow states and in harmony with a crowd or environment (see Chapters 5 and 7). As discussed above, live music is especially valued as an opportunity to experience the loss of individual identity, within a collective subjectivity and through the performance of contextual personae. In these settings, belonging is less a matter of rational contracts about future-oriented projects, than emotional affinities with a hedonistic focus on the present. These are neo-tribal forms of sociality, favouring temporary identifications over fixed identity, collective over individual subjectivity, emotional over rational pacts and the tangible present over an abstract future.

However, while peak music experiences are by definition transient and transcendent, they can have enduring significance for everyday identity and collective solidarity. Although they are often irrational and to some extent ineffable, they are rationalised and narrated as part of the 'reflexive project of the self' (Giddens 1991). A central theme of this book has been the use of peak music experiences as a resource for constructing coherent self-narratives. They exemplify and explain biographical facts and developments, in accordance with Denzin's (1989) theory of epiphanies. Chapters 3 and 4 considered how immediate, ecstatic responses to music can retrospectively become inspirations and influences for planned courses of conduct and projective identities, such as being a musician or a fan. By emphasising the power of music over more mundane social and cultural determinants of taste and identity, peak music experiences may contribute to a modernist rhetoric of individual self-construction. Chapter 5 examined the paradox that peak music experiences characterised by a loss of self-awareness and everyday time can become conscious motivations for ongoing, everyday practice within a music scene, as remembered ideals and future goals.

In these ways, the temporary transcendence of the self in intense musical experiences contributes to the long-term construction of the self. As stories and as embodied events, peak music experiences can disrupt or transcend but also affirm identity. For example, a temporary persona that is performed in the ecstatic atmosphere of a gig or club can become characteristic through weekly repetition, perhaps being regarded as a deeper, truer self than that which is performed in the workplace or home (see for example the stories of Jim and Holly in Chapter 7, 'In the moment'). Friends and family might experience and express uncommon emotions in a musical setting, but these extraordinary moments might inform and represent lasting aspects of their relationships (see Chapter 6). Peak music experiences can affirm a collective identity beyond those who are physically proximate, for example by celebrating the values of a music scene or more traditional forms of community (see Chapters 7 and 8 and the following section of this chapter). In all of these ways, peak music experiences are involved in both the transcendence and construction of social selves.

To an extent, a dialectical relationship between affective sociality and reflexive individualism was recognised at the practical level by the participants in this study. They presented their music tastes and scene identities as ongoing constructions that were deliberate, yet shaped by chance encounters and unwilled affinities. They acknowledged that music motivated actions and attractions partly by its emotional force, blurring any strict division between feelings and projects. While the self-narratives that incorporate peak music experiences are reflexively individualistic in the sense that they project coherent identities over time, they subjugate rational agency to the power of music and the mystified attraction and repulsion of affect. In explaining their motivations for musical practice, interviewees tended to de-emphasise social and financial rewards in favour of the intrinsic rewards epitomised in peak music experiences (see Chapter 5). Here, reflexive self-construction involves a rational project that is directed towards an affective present. This is consistent with Maffesoli's (1996: 17) notion of neo-tribal sociality being exhausted in its own creation, albeit repetitively, through ritual. Further, people's narratives of peak music experiences show a clear understanding that despite their conscious strategies to produce them, music's effects are ultimately unpredictable. These music scene participants find rational meaning, individual purpose and social identity in feelings they claim neither to control nor to understand fully.

Collective memory and the scene aesthetic

Over the course of this book, I have sought to maintain a focus on how the highly subjective peak music experiences that people have, and the deeply personal stories into which they are woven, are collective productions. They follow shared forms and reflect contemporary cultural values associated with popular music, as well as specific music scenes. In turn, peak music experiences and the ways they are spoken about contribute to collective identities, so that music scenes can be understood as partly organised around ideal experiences and ways of experiencing. These findings map a new perspective on the operation of collective memory in music scenes, which is a crucial but under-explored aspect of participation and belonging in these cultural spaces (Bennett and Rogers 2016).

The very concept of peak music experiences is a cultural frame that organises elements of lived experience into a recognisable and communicable form. A fundamental finding is that research participants from Brisbane's local music scenes had a notion of what I have called peak music experiences, and often made reference to them as a means of discussing music and themselves. This is consistent with and probably informed by the frequent representation of peak music experiences in popular music media, as discussed in Chapter 1. However, outside of formal fieldwork I have found that the concept is not as prominent or even readily recognisable for all people (which suggests further research questions as discussed later). In any case, it is apparent that having a concept of peak music experiences, and talking about them in particular ways comprise cultural knowledge and practice. In Chapter 3, I proposed that understandings of peak music experiences are promoted through narratives that are common across popular music genres and scenes. The tropes of first encounters, gateway experiences and conversion experiences construct shared ideals of how music acts, what kinds of musical experience are most valuable and how people may relate authentically to music. They depict music affecting people in immediate but enduring, highly personal ways that challenge and exceed expectations associated with its well-known mass commercial contexts as well as social determinants. They prioritise experiences with music by the emotional response they evoke and the profoundness of their impact on the listener's subsequent understanding of music and themselves. The circulation of these narratives creates expectations through which people perceive, interpret and present their experiences. Having such peak music experiences is therefore an affirmation of identity, for example as a fan or musician, while narrating them is a performance of that identity according to specific cultural notions of authenticity. This connects peak music experiences to cultural memory, which is a source of both formative and normative impulses for collective identity and provides a group with self-awareness (Assman and Czaplicka 1995). Peak music experiences shape and are shaped by cultural memory at the level of popular music fandom generally, as well as more specific groups such as scenes.

The common frame of peak music experiences makes apparent the common and divergent priorities of participants in different music scenes. As discussed in Chapter 8, Brisbane's local dance, hip hop, indie and rock 'n' roll scenes have fluid and overlapping boundaries in terms of members, venues and even musical elements. However, the peak music experiences of participants reveal clusters of priorities that show these scenes to be organised around ideals of musical experience. Broadly, peak music experiences in the dance scene emphasise shared euphoria and self-transcendence through collective physical activity; those in hip hop celebrate self-expression and the representation of community; the indie scene privileges experiences of difference and exploration as well as emotional intimacy; and the rock 'n' roll scene favours experiences involving forthrightness, self-acceptance and communal, physical abandon. Thus, peak music experiences, as exemplars for ways of experiencing music and forms for remembering and discussing it, contribute to an ethic of the aesthetic (Maffesoli 1991) within music scenes. This shows common ground between neo-tribal theory and scene theory, especially the concept of affective scenes (Bennett 2013). These forms of collective identity are bound and structured by shared ways of experiencing music. Further, peak music experiences demonstrate how scene values and practices are bound up with the embodied, emotional and sensory experience of scene participants. The narratives of peak music experiences contribute discursive shape to the affective aesthetics that unite each of Brisbane's music scenes, as well as providing individuals with narrative maps for rationalising these affinities in the project of constructing identities. Accordingly, peak music experiences help to structure both the affective and rational parameters of scene belonging.

I stipulated in Chapter 1 my intention to follow Scott's (1992: 38) dictum that experience is 'not the origin of our explanation, but that which we want to explain'. Through the ensuing analysis of peak music experiences, I have sought to explain how ways of experiencing, and therefore experiences and the subjects they constitute are discursively shaped. This brings a new perspective to the understanding of how music plays a role in sociality. It does so not only as an object that is invested with shared significance, but also as a driver of experiences that are known and understood through shared frames. In this way, the study of peak music experiences complements existing approaches to understanding popular music-based sociality and especially music scenes.

Broader implications and further research

Scenes and everyday listening

I have argued that peak music experiences must be understood within social contexts, and I have applied this perspective within the specific contexts of local music scenes. The same perspective might be applied to other kinds of music scene, noting the local, trans-local, virtual and affective levels that have been identified (Peterson and Bennett 2004; Bennett 2013) and the centrality of collective memory in music scenes (Bennett and Rogers 2016). While Chapter 8 showed how the concept of an affective scene is important to understanding physically interactive, local scene activity, that concept was developed with reference to people who do not interact at this face-to-face level, namely ageing music fans whose physical participation has declined (Bennett 2013). Accordingly, attention to peak music experiences would be useful in considering affective scenes to the extent they are distinct from the local activity on which this book has focused. As shared frames for experience and its narration, peak music experiences should be expected to play a significant role in these other forms of scene belonging.

The concept of peak music experiences might also be usefully applied in research that is concerned with music in 'everyday life', beyond the most overt forms of fandom and scene participation (for example, DeNora 2000). It seems likely that peak music experiences would be less apparent and important among people for whom popular music fandom and participation are less central to identity, and who are less exposed to the circulation of peak music experience narratives. However, as observed in Chapter 1 with reference to advertising and non-specialist media discussions of music, peak music experience narratives circulate in broader popular culture and especially in the commercialisation of popular music in everyday contexts. A clearer picture of the inside(s) and outside(s) of the peak music experiences framework would enhance understanding of the common and differing ways in which people relate to music.

Structure and experience

In this book, social categories such as class, gender and ethnicity have emerged occasionally as factors that contribute to the character of peak music experiences and can also be reflexively understood and navigated through such experiences. Sustained and systematic attention to the role of these factors in peak music experiences would provide a new perspective on the social structuring of musical practice and reception. The development of a cultural sociology of popular music has tended to challenge theoretical approaches that too readily assume musical meaning and taste to be structurally pre-determined (Bennett 2008). It remains necessary to develop more nuanced understandings of how socio-economic positions and cultural experiences interact. For example, this book has made substantial use of the observation that music is a temporal medium, and it is uncontroversial that people's understanding and experience of time is informed by their position within economic systems. If, as Marx (1946: 244) observed, it is no mystery that '[m]oments are the elements of profit' in a capitalist system of production, this might be expected to colour those subjective moments we call peak music experiences. This book has also focused extensively on the role of the body in the reception of music and the construction of meaning. If people's experience of their bodies is shaped by social constructions of gender, race and ability, then we can expect these to have a significant bearing on embodied musical experiences. Peak music experiences can therefore act as a lens that offers nuanced insight into the interaction between social structure, cultural identity and lived experience.

Valuing music

Peak music experiences provide an important perspective on how music is valued, as discussed in detail in the first half of this chapter. This perspective can therefore have implications for research in the area of cultural policy, in which the question of how cultural practices and objects are valued is crucial. Paying attention to peak music experiences highlights the substantial role played by music in identity and community, beyond the important aspects associated with work and economics. To take a prominent example, live music has become a significant policy concern for various levels of government in Australia and elsewhere, but as noted in Chapter 7 the research that informs such policy has been dominated by economic considerations while the social value of live music remains under-examined (Behr et al. 2012; Frith 2012). In the same chapter, I showed that peak music experiences are a way of understanding the particular social value of live music and identifying the factors involved in creating that value. This brings a cultural sociology perspective to the expanding body of research on live music as an 'experience economy' (Pearce 2013).

Another area in which the value of music is at issue is technological change. The digitalisation of music, involving dematerialisation and radically increased ease of access, for example through relatively inexpensive online streaming services (the 'celestial jukebox': Burkart and McCourt 2004), has fuelled concerns about the general devaluation of music (for example, Havighurst 2015). Among other things, it is suggested that because less investment is required to listen to a vast and expanding selection of music in a range of contexts, the resulting experience might become less meaningful. This is a contemporary iteration of Walter Benjamin's (1968) theory of the withering of artistic 'aura' in the age of mechanical reproduction (see also Green 2017). However, research about the uses of music in everyday life (such as DeNora 2000) including through personal listening technologies (Beer 2007; Bull 2007) reveals ways that increased possibilities for individualised musical experiences contribute to music's value as a resource for self-construction. Auslander (2002a: 83–84) de-emphasises material factors by suggesting that the self-conscious discourses of authenticity in popular music recreate the conditions that governed the perception of works of art and imbued them with aura prior to mass reproduction. I have shown that peak music experiences are linked to these discourses of authenticity. The peak music experiences presented throughout this book show music having profound effects in a variety of situations, including at live performances, with objectified recordings, on radio and television and through personal music players, involving both planning and chance. However, these experiences also reveal the specific role played by particular media technologies, including the physical formats of recordings, the particular function of television and radio in many late 20th century childhoods, the anticipation involved in purchasing an album on a shop assistant's recommendation, and the practical and symbolic effects of the technology used in live performance. In this way, peak music experiences show what changes and what is retained across various music media and technological developments. I have considered in detail how peak music experiences are a way of seeing change over time for individuals; by extension, this perspective could be fruitfully applied to larger-scale change over generations.

Conclusion

Hennion (2007) posits that there is no music without the gradual collective production of listening, or a specific 'ear', from general frames of attention to personal habits. This book has shown that in the present historical moment, at least in the context of local scenes oriented around the performance of popular music, people's relationships to music are partly defined by what I have called peak music experiences. They are a way of understanding the inspirations, influences and motivations of people who participate in music scenes and they help to define those scenes and what it means to belong to them. The analysis of peak music experiences also provides broader insight into how music is significant to individual and collective identity. This perspective contributes to the understanding of contemporary social life, including the interaction of affective sociality with reflexive individualism and the operation of collective memory in relation to lived experience. For researchers and music scene participants, peak music experiences are a way of understanding what music can do, how it does so and why it is valued.

Appendix 1

Interview participants

Table A.1 Interview participants

Participants	44
Female	20
Male	24
Dance scene	8
Hip hop scene	10
Indie scene	19
Rock 'n' roll scene	7
Age 20s	14
Age 30s	19
Age 40s	9
Age 50s	2

Note: Each interview participant has been identified with one scene, despite some instances of secondary interests and activities (see Chapter 8).

Table A.2 Scene activities

Performing musician	30
Performing rapper	8
Performing DJ	8
Fan who does not make music	6
Performing dancer	3
Event/venue organiser	11
Recording/production	5
Video producer	2
Music writer/journalist	3
Music radio host	7
Record label/distribution	4
Music retail worker	1
Music teacher (instrument or business)	3
Technical production (lights/sound)	3

Note: Some participants reported more than one activity. The categories are intended to provide a general overview of the range of activities represented in the sample.

References

Adorno T (1941) The radio symphony: An experiment in theory. In: Lazarsfeld PF and Stanton F (eds) *Radio Research.* New York: Duell, Sloan & Pearce, 110–139.

Adorno T (1976) *Introduction to the Sociology of Music* (translated by Ashton, EB). New York: Seabury.

Adorno T (1990 [1941]) On popular music. In: Frith S and Goodwin A (eds) *On Record: Rock, Pop and the Written Word.* New York: Pantheon Books, 301–314.

Advisory Editors (2005) Can we get rid of the 'popular' in popular music? A virtual symposium with contributions from the International Advisory Editors of Popular Music. *Popular Music* 24(1): 133–145.

Ahmed S (2004) Collective feelings: Or, the impressions left by others. *Theory, Culture & Society* 21(2): 25–42.

Ahmed S (2014) *The Cultural Politics of Emotion* (second edition). Edinburgh: Edinburgh University Press.

Albertine V (2015) *Clothes Music Boys* (first paperback edition). London: Faber and Faber.

Assmann J and Czaplicka J (1995) Collective memory and cultural identity. *New German Critique* 65: 125–133.

Auslander P (2002a) *Liveness: Performance in a Mediatized Culture.* London: Routledge.

Auslander P (2002b) LIVE FROM CYBERSPACE or, I was sitting at my computer this guy appeared he thought I was a bot. *PAJ: A Journal of Performance and Art* 24(1): 16–21.

Auslander P (2006) *Performing Glam Rock: Gender and Theatricality in Popular Music.* Ann Arbor: University of Michigan Press.

Bailey S (2005) *Media Audiences and Identity: Self-Construction in the Fan Experience.* New York: Palgrave Macmillan.

Banks M (2012) MacIntyre, Bourdieu and the practice of jazz. *Popular Music* 31(1): 69–86.

Bannister M (2006) *White Boys, White Noise: Masculinities and 1980s Indie Guitar Rock.* London: Ashgate.

Barthes R (1989 [1977]) The grain of the voice. In: Frith S and Goodwin A (eds) *On Record: Rock, Pop and the Written Word.* London: Routledge, 293–300.

Beck U (1992) *Risk Society: Towards A New Modernity.* London: Sage.

Becker H (1953) Becoming a marihuana user. *The American Journal of Sociology* 59(3): 235–242.

Becker J (2004) *Deep Listeners: Music, Emotion and Trancing*. Indianapolis: Indiana University Press.

Beer D (2007) Tune out: Music, soundscapes and the urban mise-en-scene. *Information, Communication and Society* 10(6): 846–866.

Behr A, Brennan M and Cloonan M (2016) Cultural value and cultural policy: Some evidence from the world of live music. *International Journal of Cultural Policy* 22(3): 403–418.

Benjamin W (1968 [1935]) The work of art in the age of mechanical reproduction (translated by Zohn H). In: Arendt H (ed) *Illuminations*. New York: Schocken Books, 1–26.

Bennett A (1997) 'Going down the pub!': The pub rock scene as a resource for the consumption of popular music. *Popular Music* 16(1): 97–108.

Bennett A (1999a) Subcultures or neo-tribes? Rethinking the relationship between youth, style and musical taste. *Sociology* 33(3): 599–617.

Bennett A (1999b) Hip hop am Main: The localization of rap music and hip hop culture. *Media, Culture & Society* 21(1): 77–91.

Bennett A (1999c) Rappin on the Tyne: White hip hop culture in Northeast England – an ethnographic study. *The Sociological Review* 47(1): 1–24.

Bennett A (2001) Plug in and play! UK indie guitar culture. In: Bennett A and Dawe K (eds), *Guitar Cultures*. Oxford: Berg, 45–62.

Bennett A (2005) *Culture and Everyday Life*. London: SAGE.

Bennett A (2008) Towards a cultural sociology of popular music. *Journal of Sociology* 44(4): 419–432.

Bennett A (2011) The post-subcultural turn: Some reflections 10 years on. *Journal of Youth Studies* 14(5): 493–506.

Bennett A (2013) *Music, Style and Aging: Growing Old Disgracefully?* Philadelphia, PA: Temple University Press.

Bennett A and Rogers I (2016) *Popular Music Scenes and Cultural Memory*. London: Palgrave Macmillan.

Bennett A and Rogers I (2018) The making and remaking of Brisbane and Hobart: Music scenes in Australia's second-tier cities. In: Brunt S and Stahl G (eds) *Made in Australia and Aotearoa/New Zealand*. New York: Routledge, pp.111–120.

Bennett A and Waksman S (2015) Introduction. In: Bennett A and Waksman S (eds) *The Sage Handbook of Popular Music*. London: SAGE, 1–10.

Benzecry CE (2011) *The Opera Fanatic: Ethnography of an Obsession*. Chicago, IL: University of Chicago Press.

Benzon W (2001) *Beethoven's Anvil: Music in Mind and Culture*. New York: Basic Books.

Black CL, Jr (1986 [1979]) My World with Louis Armstrong. *The Yale Law Journal* 95: 1595–1600.

Blum AF and McHugh P (1971) The social ascription of motives. *American Sociological Review* 36(1): 98–109.

Bourdieu P (1983) The field of cultural production, or: The economic world reversed. *Poetics* 12(4–5): 311–356.

Bradley D (1992) *Understanding Rock and Roll: Popular Music in Britain, 1955–1964*. Buckingham: Open University Press.

Bridges J and Denisoff RS (1986) Changing courtship patterns in the popular song: Horton and Carey revisited. *Popular Music and Society* 10(3): 29–45.

Bull M (2007) *Sound Moves: iPod Culture and Urban Experience*. London: Routledge.

Burkart P and McCourt T (2004) Infrastructure for the celestial jukebox. *Popular Music* 23(3): 349–362.

Campaign Brief (2012) Coca-Cola launches new component of its 'Share a Coke and a Song' campaign and TV commercial during the AFL grand final this weekend. *Campaign Brief*, 2 October. Available at: http://www.campaignbrief.com/2012/10/coca-cola-launches-new-compone.html (accessed 20 August 2017).

Campbell S (2013) Australian independent music and the experience economy. In: Tschmuck P, Pearce P and Campbell S (eds) *Music Business and the Experience Economy: The Australasian Case.* London: Springer, 41–57.

Carey J (1969) Changing courtship patterns in the popular song. *American Journal of Sociology* 74(6): 720–731.

Cavicchi D (1998) *Tramps Like Us: Music & Meaning among Springsteen Fans.* New York: Oxford University Press.

Chaney D (1994) *The Cultural Turn: Scene-Setting Essays on Contemporary Cultural History.* London: Routledge.

Cohen P (2005) Subcultural conflict and working-class community. In: Gelder K (ed) *The Subcultures Reader* (second edition). Abingdon and New York: Routledge, 86–93.

Cohen S (1991) *Rock Culture in Liverpool.* Oxford: Clarendon Press.

Cohen S (2012) Live music and urban landscape: Mapping the beat in Liverpool. *Social Semiotics* 22(5), 587–603.

Coon C (2012) Joe Strummer: 'I shudder to think what would have happened if I hadn't gone to boarding school'. *The Guardian*, 21 December. Available at: https://www.theguardian.com/music/2012/dec/21/rocks-backpages-clash-joe-strummer (accessed 22 August 2017).

Cope J (1995) *Krautrocksampler: One Head's Guide to the Great Kosmische Music – 1968 Onwards.* Yatesbury: Head Heritage.

Crossley N (1998) Emotion and communicative action: Habermas, linguistic philosophy and existentialism. In: Bendelow G and Williams S (eds) *Emotions in Social Life: Critical Themes and Contemporary Issues.* London and New York: Routledge, 16–38.

Crossley N and Bottero W (2015) Music worlds and internal goods: The role of convention. *Cultural Sociology* 9(1): 38–55.

Csikszentmihalyi M (1975) *Beyond Boredom and Anxiety.* San Francisco, CA: Jossey-Bass.

d'Escrivàn, J. (2006) To sing the body electric: Instruments and effort in the performance of electronic music. *Contemporary Music Review* 25(1–2), 183–191.

Dennis LJ and Powers JF (1974) Dewey, Maslow and consummatory experience. *Journal of Aesthetic Education* 8(4): 51–63.

DeNora T (2000) *Music in Everyday Life.* Cambridge: Cambridge University Press.

DeNora T (2003) *After Adorno: Rethinking Music Sociology.* Cambridge and New York: Cambridge University Press.

DeNora T (2004) Historical perspectives in music sociology. *Poetics* 32(3): 211–221.

Denzin N (1970) Problems in analyzing elements of mass culture: Notes on the popular song and other artistic productions. *American Journal of Sociology* 75(6): 1035–1038.

Denzin N (1989) *Interpretive Biography.* London: SAGE.

Denzin N (1992) *Symbolic Interactionism and Cultural Studies: The Politics of Interpretation.* Cambridge: Blackwell.

Denzin N (2001) *Interpretive Interactionism*. London: SAGE.

Dewey J (2004a [1929]) From *Experience and Nature* (1929). In: Capps D and Capps JM (eds) *James and Dewey on Belief and Experience*. Champaign: University of Illinois Press, 251–267.

Dewey J (2004b [1934]) From *Art as Experience* (1934). In: Capps D and Capps JM (eds) *James and Dewey on Belief and Experience*. Champaign: University of Illinois Press, 268–284.

Dhaenens F and Burgess J (2019) 'Press play for pride': The cultural logics of LGBTQ-themed playlists on Spotify. *New Media & Society* 21(6): 1192–1211.

Dowd T (2007) The sociology of music. In: Bryant CD and Peck DL (eds) *21st Century Sociology: A Reference Handbook (Volume 2)*, Thousand Oaks, CA: SAGE, 249–260.

Drozdowski T (2014) It might get loud: The 10 loudest rock bands of all time. *Gibson.com* 18 February. Available at http://www.gibson.com/News-Lifestyle/Features/en-us/10-Loudest-Rock-Bands.aspx (accessed 23 August 2017).

Duffett M (2003) Imagined Memories Webcasting as a 'live' technology and the case of Little Big Gig. *Information, Communication & Society* 6(3), 307–325.

Duffett M (2013) *Understanding Fandom: An Introduction to the Study of Media Fan Culture*. New York: Bloomsbury.

Dylan B (2004) *Chronicles Volume One*. New York: Simon & Schuster.

Epstein JS, Pratto DJ and Skipper JK (1990) Teenagers behavioral problems and preferences for metal and rap music: A case study of a southern middle school. *Deviant Behavior* 11: 381–394

Eyerman R and Jamison A (1998) *Music and Social Movements: Mobilizing Traditions in the Twentieth Century*. Cambridge: Cambridge University Press.

Feldman C (2009) *'We are the Mods': A Transnational History of a Youth Subculture*. New York: Peter Lang.

Finnegan R (2007 [1989]) *The Hidden Musicians: Music-making in an English Town* (revised edition). Middletown, CT: Wesleyan University Press.

Fleicher R and Snickars P (2017) Discovering Spotify – a thematic introduction. *Culture Unbound: Journal of Current Cultural Research* 9: 130–145.

Fonarow W (2006) *Empire of Dirt: The Aesthetics and Rituals of British Indie Music*. Middletown, CT: Wesleyan University Press.

Forbes K (2012) Glasgow as a live-music city: an analysis of the "legendary" Apollo venue and its audience. *Social Semiotics* 22(5): 605–621.

Fornäs J, Lindberg U and Sernhede O (1995) *In Garageland: Rock, Youth and Modernity* (translated by Teeland J). London: Routledge.

Forster R (2016) *Grant & I: Inside and Outside the Go-Betweens*. Melbourne: Penguin Books Australia.

Frears S (dir) (2000) *High Fidelity* (film). Burbank: Buena Vista Pictures.

Frith S (1986) Art versus technology: The strange case of popular music. *Media, Culture & Society* 8(3): 263–279.

Frith S (1987) Towards an aesthetic of popular music. In: Leppert R and McClary S (eds) *Music and Society: The Politics of Composition, Performance and Reception*. Cambridge: Cambridge University Press, 257–273.

Frith S (1988) *Music for Pleasure*. London: Polity.

Frith S (1989) Why do songs have words? *Contemporary Music Review* 5(1): 77–96.

Frith S (1992) The cultural study of popular music. In: Grossberg L, Nelson C and Treichler P (eds) *Cultural Studies*. New York: Routledge, 174–186.

Frith S (1998) *Performing Rites: On the Value of Popular Music* (first paperback edition). Cambridge, MA: Harvard University Press.

Frith S (2007a) Why music matters: Inaugural lecture given at the University of Edinburgh, 6 March 2007. *Critical Quarterly* 50(1–2): 165–179.

Frith S (2007b) Live music matters. *Scottish Music Review* 1(1), 1–17.

Frith S (2012) Editorial. *Social Semiotics 22*(5), 517–522.

Fritsch M and Strötgen S (2012) Relatively live: How to identify live music performances. *Music and the Moving Image 5*(1): 47–66.

Gabrielsson A (2011) *Strong Experiences with Music: Music Is Much More Than Just Music* (translated by Bradbury R). Oxford: Oxford University Press.

Giddens A (1991) *Modernity and Self-Identity: Self and Society in the Late Modern Age.* Cambridge: Polity Press.

Gilbert J and Pearson E (1999) *Discographies: Dance, Music, Culture and the Politics of Sound.* London: Routledge.

Gilbert J (2010) Music is power. *Art press 2* 15: 106. Available at: https://jeremygilbertwriting.wordpress.com/2010/11/03/music-is-power/ (accessed 22 August 2017).

Gilbert J and Pearson E (2002) *Discographies: Dance, Music, Culture and the Politics of Sound.* London: Routledge.

Gooley D (2004) *The Virtuoso Liszt.* Cambridge: Cambridge University Press.

Grácio R (2016) Daughters of rock and moms who rock: Rock music as a medium for family relationships in Portugal. *Revista Crítica de Ciências Sociais* 109: 83–104.

Gracyk T (2001) *I Wanna Be Me: Rock Music and the Politics of Identity.* Philadelphia, PA: Temple University Press.

Green B (2016) 'I always remember that moment': Peak music experiences as epiphanies. *Sociology* 50(2): 333–348.

Green B (2017) Having the sceptre: Wu-Tang Clan and the aura of music in the age of digital reproduction. *Popular Music* 3(36): 427–440.

Green B (2018) Reconciling neo-tribes and reflexive individualisation: The transcendence and construction of self through peak music experiences'. In: Hardy A, Bennett A and Robards B (eds) *Neo-tribes - Consumption, Leisure, Tourism.* Melbourne: Palgrave, 169–184.

Grossberg L (1994) Is anybody listening? Does anybody care? On 'the state of rock'. In: Rose T and Ross A (eds) *Microphone Fiends (Youth Music & Youth Culture).* New York: Routledge, 41–58.

Hakanen E (1998) Counting down to number one: The evolution of the meaning of popular music charts. *Popular Music* 17(1): 95–111.

Halbwachs M (1992) *On Collective Memory* (edited by Coser L). Chicago, IL: University of Chicago Press.

Hann M (2016) Bruce Springsteen: 'You can change a life in three minutes with the right song'. *The Guardian*, 30 October. Available at: https://www.theguardian.com/music/2016/oct/30/bruce-springsteen-interview-born-to-run-change-someones-life-right-song-donald-trump (accessed 20 August 2017).

Havighurst C (2015) The devaluation of music: It's worse than you think. *Medium* 11 October. https://medium.com/cuepoint/the-devaluation-of-music-it-s-worse-than-you-think-f4cf5f26a888 (accessed 19 October 2015).

Hebdige D (1979) *Subculture: The Meaning of Style.* London and New York: Methuen.

Hennion A (2001) Music lovers: Taste as performance. *Theory, Culture & Society* 18(5): 1–22.

Hennion A (2007) Those things that hold us together: Taste and sociology. *Cultural Sociology* 1(1): 97–114.

Hennion A (2010) Loving music: From a sociology of mediation to a pragmatics of taste. *Comunicar* 17(34): 25–33.

Hennion A (2015) Enquêter sur nos attachements. Comment hériter de William James? *SociologieS* [online]. Available at: http://sociologies.revues.org/4953 (accessed 20 August 2017).

Hennion A (2017) Attachments, you say? … How a concept collectively emerges in one research group. *Journal of Cultural Economy* 10(1): 112–121.

Henriques J (2010) The vibrations of affect and their propagation on a night out on Kingston's dancehall scene. *Body & Society* 16(1): 57–89.

Hesmondhalgh D (2013) *Why Music Matters*. Chichester: Wiley Blackwell.

Hibbett R (2005) What is indie rock? *Popular Music and Society* 28(1): 55–77.

Hornby N (1995) *High Fidelity* (novel). London: Victor Gollancz Ltd.

Horton D (1957) The dialogue of courtship in popular song. *American Journal of Sociology* 62(6): 569–578.

Jones S (1988) *Black Culture, White Youth: The Reggae Tradition from JA to UK*. London: Macmillan Education.

Kahn-Harris K (2004) Unspectacular subculture? Transgression and mundanity in the global extreme metal scene. In: Bennett A and Kahn-Harris K (eds) *After Subculture: Critical Studies in Contemporary Youth Culture*. London: Palgrave, 107–118.

Krause AE, Maurer S and Davidson JW (2020) Characteristics of self-reported favorite musical experiences. *Music & Science* 3: 1–17.

Kreps D (2016) Bruce Springsteen reveals eight 'desert island' songs. *Rolling Stone* 18 December. Available at: http://www.rollingstone.com/music/news/bruce-springsteen-reveals-eight-desert-island-songs-w456636 (accessed 20 August 2017).

Laing D (1985) *One Chord Wonders: Power and Meaning in Punk Rock*. Milton Keynes: Open University Press.

Leadbeater C and Miller P (2004) *The Pro-Am Revolution: How Enthusiasts are Changing Our Society and Economy*. London: Demos.

Lest J (2008) Gateway Band. *Urban Dictionary*, 19 July. Available at: http://www.urbandictionary.com/define.php?term=Gateway%20Band (accessed 21 August 2017).

Lewisohn M (2013) *Tune In: The Beatles – All These Years Volume 1*. New York: Crown Archetype.

Leys R (2011) The turn to affect: A critique. *Critical Inquiry* 37(3): 434–472.

Lowe A (2015) Pandora unveils first local integrated campaign. *AdNews*, 9 November. Available at: http://www.adnews.com.au/news/pandora-unveils-first-local-integrated-campaign (accessed 20 August 2017).

MacDonald D (1953) A theory of mass culture. *Diogenes* 1(3): 1–17.

MacDonald I (2005) *Revolution in the Head: The Beatles' Records and the Sixties*. Chicago, IL: Chicago Review Press.

Maffesoli M (1991) The ethic of aesthetics. *Theory, Culture and Society*, 8(1): 7–20.

Maffesoli M (1996) *The Time of the Tribes: The Decline of Individualism in Mass Society* (translated by Smith D). London: Sage.

Malbon B (1999) *Clubbing: Dancing, Ecstasy and Vitality*. London: Routledge.

Marcus G (2005) *Like a Rolling Stone: Bob Dylan at the Crossroads*. London: Faber and Faber.

Marx K (1946 [1867]) *Capital: Volume One* (translated from the fourth German edition by Paul E & C). London: Everyman's Library.

Maslow A (1962) *Toward a Psychology of Being.* Princeton, NJ: Van Nostrand.

Maslow A (1993) *The Farther Reaches of Human Nature.* New York: Penguin.

McRobbie A (1980) Settling accounts with subcultures: A feminist critique. Reproduced in Frith S and Goodwin A (eds) *On Record: Rock Pop and the Written Word.* London: Routledge, 66–80.

Minichiello V, Aroni R and Hays T (2008) *In-Depth Interviewing.* Sydney: Pearson Education Australia.

Mitchell T (2003) Australian hip-hop as a subculture. *Youth Studies Australia* 22(2): 40–47.

Moore, A (2002) Authenticity as authentication. *Popular Music* 21(2): 209–233.

MS (2012) Gonna do it anyway, even if it doesn't pay. *The Economist*, 16 February. Available at: https://www.economist.com/democracy-in-america/2012/02/16/gonna-do-it-anyway-even-if-it-doesnt-pay (accessed 28 February 2021).

Nowak R and Bennett A (2014) Analysing everyday sound environments: The space, time and corporality of musical listening. *Cultural Sociology* 8(4): 426–442.

Ou S (director) (2015) *Stranded* (documentary film). ABC Television broadcast, 15 September.

Panzarella R (1980) The phenomenology of aesthetic peak experiences. *Journal of Humanistic Psychology* 20(1): 69–85.

Pearce P (2013) From discord to harmony: Connecting Australian music and business through the experience economy. In: Tschmuck P, Pearce P and Campbell S (eds) *Music Business and the Experience Economy: The Australasian Case.* London: Springer, 1–9.

Peatman JG (1942) Radio and popular music. In: Lazersfeld PF and Stanton F (eds) *Radio Research.* New York: Duell, Sloan & Pearce, 335–396.

Peterson RA and Bennett A (2004) Introducing the scenes perspective. In: Peterson RA and Bennett A (eds) *Music Scenes: Local, Trans-Local and Virtual.* Nashville: University of Vanderbilt Press.

Pini M (2001) *Club Cultures and Female Subjectivity: The Move from Home to House.* Hampshire and New York: Palgrave.

Plato (1966) *Republic* (translated by Richards IA). Cambridge: Cambridge University Press.

Pollner M and Stein S (1996) Narrative mapping of social worlds: the voice of experience in alcoholics anonymous. *Symbolic Interaction* 19(3): 203–223.

Prior N (2011) Critique and Renewal in the Sociology of Music: Bourdieu and Beyond. *Cultural Sociology* 5(1): 121–138.

Reynolds R and Press J (1995) *The Sex Revolts: Gender, Rebellion, and Rock 'n' Roll.* Cambridge, MA: Harvard University Press.

Riley S, Morey Y and Griffin C (2010) The 'pleasure citizen': Analyzing partying as a form of social and political participation. *Young* 18(1): 33–54.

Riley T (2011) *Lennon: The Man, the Myth, the Music – The Definitive Life.* New York: Hyperion.

Rimmer M (2012) Beyond omnivores and univores: The promise of a concept of musical habitus. *Cultural Sociology* 6(3): 299–318.

Rogers I (2008) 'You've got to go to gigs to get gigs': Indie musicians, eclecticism and the Brisbane scene. *Continuum: Journal of Media & Cultural Studies* 22(5): 639–649.

Rolling Stone (2010) 100 greatest singers of all time. *Rolling Stone* 2 December. Available at: http://www.rollingstone.com/music/lists/100-greatest-singers-of-all-time-19691231/smokey-robinson-20101202 (accessed 21 August 2017).

Ross A (2009) *The Rest is Noise: Listening to the Twentieth Century.* London: Harper Perennial.

Sabine W (1923) *Collected Papers on Acoustics.* Cambridge, MA: Harvard University Press.

Sarantakos S (2005) *Social Research* (third edition). Houndmills: Palgrave Macmillan.

Sayer A (2010) Bourdieu, ethics and practice. In Silva E and Warde A (eds) *Cultural Analysis and Bourdieu's Legacy.* London: Routledge, pp. 87–101.

Schmutz V (2005) Retrospective cultural consecration in popular music: Rolling Stone's greatest albums of all time. *American Behavioral Scientist* 48(11): 1510–1523.

Schutz A (1951) Making music together: A study in social relationship. *Social Research* 18(1): 76–97.

Shuker R (2001) *Understanding Popular Music (Second Edition).* London: Routledge.

Scott J (1992) Experience. In: Butler J and Scott J (eds) *Feminists Theorize the Political.* New York: Routledge.

Shank B (1994) *Dissonant Identities: The Rock 'n' Roll Scene in Austin, Texas.* Hanover: University Press of New England.

Shuker R (2004) Beyond the 'High Fidelity' stereotype: Defining the (contemporary) record collector. *Popular Music* 23(3): 311–330.

Small C (1987) *Music of the Common Tongue.* London: John Calder.

Small C (1998) *Musicking: The Meanings of Performing and Listening.* Middletown, CT: Wesleyan University Press.

Smith N (2012) Parenthood and the transfer of capital in the Northern Soul scene. In: Bennett A and Hodkinson P (eds) *Ageing and Youth Culture: Music, Style and Identity.* London: Bloomsbury Academic, 159172.

Stack S and Gundlach J (1992) The effect of country music on suicide. *Social Forces,* 71(1): 211–218.

Stafford A (2004) *Pig City: From the Saints to Savage Garden.* Brisbane: University of Queensland Press.

Stahl G (2004) 'It's like Canada reduced': Setting the scene in Montreal. In: Bennett A and Kahn-Harris K (eds), *After Subculture: Critical Studies in Contemporary Youth Culture.* Basingstoke: Palgrave Macmillan, 51–64.

Stratton J (1983) What is 'popular music'? *The Sociological Review* 31(2): 293–309.

Straw W (1991) Systems of articulation, logics of change: Scenes and communities in popular music. Cultural Studies 5(3): 361–375.

Street J (2012) *Music & Politics.* Cambridge: Polity Press.

Strong C (2010) The Triple J Hottest 100 of all time 2009 and the dominance of the rock canon. *Meanjin* 69(2): 122–127.

Strong C (2011) *Grunge: Music and Memory.* London: Ashgate.

Tate G (2003) In praise of shadow boxers: The crises of originality and authority in African American visual art vs the Wu-Tang Clan. *Souls* 5(1): 128–136.

Thornton S (1995) *Club Cultures: Music, Media and Subcultural Capital.* Hanover: Wesleyan University Press.

Threadgold S (2018) *Youth, Class and Everyday Struggles.* New York: Routledge.

Tsitsos W (2012) Slamdancing, ageing and belonging. In: Hodkinson P and Bennett A (eds) *Ageing and Youth Cultures*. London: Berg, 66–78.

Urry J (1990) *The Tourist Gaze: Leisure and Travel in Contemporary Societies*. London: Sage Publications Ltd.

Van Dijck J (2006) Record and hold: Popular music between personal and collective memory. *Critical Studies in Media Communication* 23(5): 357–374.

Varriale S (2016) Beyond distinction: Theorising cultural evaluation as a social encounter. *Cultural Sociology* 10(2): 160–177.

Vroomen L (2004) Kate Bush: teen pop and older female fans. In: Bennett A and Peterson RA (eds), *Music Scenes: Local, Trans-Local and Virtual*. Nashville: University of Vanderbilt Press, 238–254.

Walters J (Producer) (1987) *Peeling Back the Years – Part 1* (BBC radio broadcast). Available at: http://www.bbc.co.uk/6music/events/peel/peeling.shtml (accessed 21 August 2017).

Ward L and Throop R (1989) The Dewey-Mead Analysis of Emotions. *Social Science Journal* 26(4): 465–479.

Wiener J (1984) *John Lennon in His Time*. Champaign: University of Illinois Press.

Williams P (2004) *Bob Dylan: Performing Artist, 1960–1973* (second edition). London: Omnibus Press.

Willis P (1978) *Profane Culture*. London: Routledge and Kegan Paul.

Wilson R (Director) and Faulkner L (Producer) (1988) *Brisbane Bands* (documentary film). Available at https://vimeo.com/135619660 (accessed 20 August 2017).

Winchester D and Green KD (2019) Talking your self into it: How and when accounts shape motivation for action. *Sociological Theory* 37(3): 257–281.

Wood C (2012) Everything is free now: Artists do more than amuse and we've got ourselves a creativity glut to contend with. *Alternatives Journal* 38(3): 48.

Woodward I (2001) Domestic objects and the taste epiphany: A resource for consumption methodology. *Journal of Material Culture* 6(2): 115–136.

Young N (2012) *Waging Heavy Peace*. London: Penguin Viking.

Index

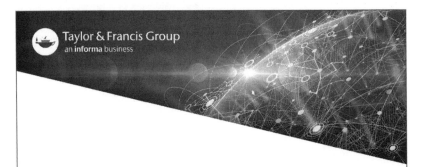